Theatre of Chaos

In this unique and invigorating study, chaos theory and quantum mechanics are employed as the basis for a clearer understanding of the often confusing contemporary theatre world. Examining numerous antecedents to contemporary thought on chaos and the cultural roots of the notion of chaos, William Demastes suggests links to playwrights ranging from Shakespeare and Ibsen to Tom Stoppard, Sam Shepard, and Tony Kushner. The author investigates parallel developments across the arts and sciences: connections between the dramatic naturalism of the late nineteenth century and Newtonian thought, for example, and theatre of the absurd and chaos theory.

After centuries of isolation and increased specialization, Demastes contends, it may once again be time to consider the "arts" and "sciences" together and to acknowledge their interrelations. These intersections confirm that "orderly disorder" is displacing a far more rigid and less viable system of knowing our world, and ushering in a rich, varied, and forward-looking theory of existence for contemporary society.

THEATRE OF CHAOS

Beyond Absurdism, into Orderly Disorder

William W. Demastes

CAMBRIDGE
UNIVERSITY PRESS

PUBLISHED BY THE PRESS SYNDICATE OF THE UNIVERSITY OF CAMBRIDGE
The Pitt Building, Trumpington Street, Cambridge, United Kingdom

CAMBRIDGE UNIVERSITY PRESS
The Edinburgh Building, Cambridge CB2 2RU, UK
40 West 20th Street, New York NY 10011–4211, USA
477 Williamstown Road, Port Melbourne, VIC 3207, Australia
Ruiz de Alarcón 13, 28014 Madrid, Spain
Dock House, The Waterfront, Cape Town 8001, South Africa

http://www.cambridge.org

First published 1998
First paperback edition 2005

Typeset in Melior and Antique Olive

A catalogue record for this book is available from the British Library

Library of Congress Cataloguing-in-Publication Data

Demastes, William W.
    Theatre of chaos : beyond absurdism, into orderly disorder /
William W. Demastes.
        p. cm.
    Includes bibliographical references and index.
    ISBN 0 521 58245 8 hardback
    1. English drama – History and criticism – Theory, etc. 2. American
drama – History and criticism – Theory, etc. 3. Absurd (Philosophy)
in literature. 4. Order (Philosophy) in literature. 5. Literature
and science. 6. Quantum chaos. I. Title.
PR625.D46 1997
822.009′384–dc21   97-11055
                                                           CIP

ISBN 0 521 58245 8 hardback
ISBN 0 521 61986 6 paperback

A. A violent order is disorder; and
B. A great disorder is an order.
These two things are one.
  Wallace Stevens, "Connoisseur of
    Chaos"

For what is the heart but a sort of – A
sort of – *instrument* – that translates
noise into *music,* chaos into
order. . . .
  Tennessee Williams, *Camino Real*

A door like this has cracked open
five or six times since we got up on
our hind legs. It's the best possible
time to be alive, when almost
everything you thought you knew is
wrong.
  Tom Stoppard, *Arcadia*

It's the end of the world as we know
    it, and I feel fine.
  R.E.M.

Contents

ACKNOWLEDGMENTS

PORTIONS OF THIS BOOK have been published in the following works, reprinted by permission of the editors:

"The Hurlyburly Lies of the Causalist Mind: Chaos and the Realism of Rabe and Shepard" (with Michael Vanden Heuvel), in William W. Demastes, ed., *Realism and the American Dramatic Tradition* (Tuscaloosa: University of Alabama Press, 1996), pp. 255–74.

"Jessie and Thelma Revisited: Marsha Norman's Conceptual Challenge in *'night, Mother,*" *Modern Drama* 36.1 (March 1993), pp. 109–19.

"Of Sciences and the Arts: From Influence to Interplay Between Natural Philosophy and Drama," *Studies in the Literary Imagination* 24.2 (Fall 1991), pp. 75–89.

"Re-Inspecting the Crack in the Chimney: Chaos Theory from Ibsen to Stoppard," *New Theatre Quarterly* (August 1994), pp. 242–54.

Many of the ideas and approaches in this book were strengthened through the generous influence of participants at numerous venues where I first presented these ideas, specifically the 1991 ATHE Conference in Seattle; the 1993 Comparative Drama Conference in Gainesville, FL; the 1994 SCMLA Conference in New Orleans; and specially arranged lectures at University College, Galway, Ireland, in March 1994, at Middle Tennessee State University in October 1994, at Catholic University in May 1995, and at Louisiana State University's Philological Club gatherings in

1993 and 1994. I wish to thank Christopher J. Wheatley (at Catholic University and UCG), Kevin Donovan (at MTSU), and Reggie Young (at LSU), who demonstrated confidence in my work by arranging these special talks. Those forums were indispensable in helping me to formulate my arguments.

Also indispensable were my talks/debates/arguments/feuds with friend and colleague Michael Vanden Heuvel and with friend and brother Jim Demastes, the "scientist" in our family. Speaking of family, this work would have been impossible without the support of my wife, Jean, and daughter, Erin, a perfect fusion of orderly disorder in my life. To them this book is dedicated.

PREFACE

Awash in Chaos

"T HE WHOLE WORLD'S in a state o' chassis," bemoans Captain Boyle in Sean O'Casey's 1924 classic *Juno and the Paycock*. Boyle's 1922 Dublin was in fact a world of chaos and turbulence, but Boyle, his sidekick Joxer, and all of Dublin (except perhaps Juno) seem bound by a mindset that sees only the tragedy in this disorderly "state o' chassis," failing to envision that rising disorder paves the way for opportunities of change, relocation, and improvement. Disorderly "chassis" provides an opportunity O'Casey seems to have wanted his fellow countrymen to realize and grasp.

Even today, chaos is terrifying for those longing for the ordered, "simple" life of stability and constancy, especially given the prevailing cultural assumption that chaos is the absence of order, order's polar opposite. However, if one looks at order and disorder/chaos not so much as either/or propositions but as places on an order-to-disorder (and disorder-to-order) continuum, then the almost irrational fear of disorder/chaos becomes a surmountable cultural phobia. It is not necessarily a case of black or white wherein one has either order or disorder in one's life. Rather, one can look at existence as resting upon a sliding scale of varying degrees of order and disorder, where one extreme of complete order is little more than unendurable static tedium and the other extreme of complete disorder is nothing but random frenzy, equally unendurable. The vast middle ground between the two extremes is where life occurs and what makes life worth living.

This adjustment to an appreciation of orderly disorder entails a terminological adjustment as well. Captain Boyle uses "chaos" as our culture generally uses it, as equivalent to and synonymous with disorder and randomness. This use, however, is a relatively recent one in the course of human events, centuries old, perhaps, but not at all millennia old or objectively irreducible. History shows us that chaos need not necessarily be synonymous with randomness and disorder, and the term need not have the negative connotation we currently attribute to it. In many premodern cultures, chaos was often seen as the soup of energy out of which change, creativity, and hope have sprung. While most of us would agree that a world of inexplicable randomness would be unendurable, a world of chaos need not be dreaded, provided, of course, that we re-vision chaos and look upon it as it was once perceived.

In fact, after centuries of seeing chaos as the exact opposite of order, contemporary Western civilization is once again beginning to adjust its vision to see chaos as a place of opportunity, a site of interactive disorder generating new orders and of order transforming to regenerative disorder. Chaos is increasingly being seen – again – as a dynamic blending of disorder *and* order, not as the entropic, final result of *de*generation but as embodying the loop and cycle of constant generation, degeneration, and regeneration. To the static "being" of order and the eruptive "nonbeing" of randomness has been included a vast middle realm, the "becoming" of chaos.

For most of us, however, all of this very likely seems little more than the rantings of lunatics, lovers, and poets, heartened by the touching but impractical thought that much madness is divinest sense. We have heard this all before but have yet to fathom its fundamental reality. Significantly, the twentieth century has spawned yet another group of men and women that perhaps should be added to the list of lunatics, lovers, and poets. That least likely of groups is scientists, especially a growing band of thinkers known as chaoticians who are now challenging the static Newtonianism that seems always to have existed and that has so thoroughly demonized the notion of chaos.

With the advent of thermodynamic studies, quantum physics, and ultimately chaos theory, scientists have mounted a challenge to the static visions of existence we have so long *desired* to verify and validate. These new scientists are demonstrating – rationally and empirically – that our desire for stability is tantamount to a rejection of natural dynamics themselves and amounts to little more than a desire for death, the consummate stability. Life, these scientists argue, is a soup of vitality demanding change and functioning in rich patterns of nonlinear creativity. Theirs is a neo-Romantic vision that challenges the "Newtonian" world governed by a strictly linear causality, which asserts a world of invariance and which ultimately results in a vision of an unchanging "Eden" where every day is like the next and where individuation is ultimately impossible.

Echoing a distant premodern vision, nonlinearity, these new scientists argue, is what best describes our world. Between the extremes of order and disorder lies a vast middle realm that embraces a certain stability as it also promotes change. The stability we experience is a temporary matter, not a culmination but part of a process of ascent and decline as time progresses. Because this stability is temporary and nonlinear, it is not as invariable as order's linearity, but neither is it random as pure disorder is. We have orderly disorder. This is what the new scientists call "chaos": nature's pursuit of patterns of order amid a constant sea/constancy of change and reorder.

This vision of chaos is not fundamentally a new one; what is new is that our new twentieth-century prophets – those men and women whom we today trust rationally and empirically to describe truth and reality and whom we call scientists – are validating for us (at least for those requiring such validation) the visions of lunatics, lovers, and poets. They are recovering ideas from the marginalized realms of culture and placing them once again on center stage. This time, however, the ideas are supported not by magic and mystery but by the very sciences that once relegated them to the margins. Validation, clarification, and demarginalization are these scientists' contributions, for what their work in the latter half of the twentieth century has given us is an opportunity to "test," understand, and more clearly articulate these visions, not via a return to premodern mystery but through a full engagement of postmodern machinery. Catching up to the arts and formally validating their suggestions as the sciences now appear to be doing, the results could very well lead to an interdisciplinary reintegration of the arts and sciences through a large feedback loop wherein one discipline helps to crystallize the musings of the other, and vice versa.

This book looks at numerous antecedents to contemporary thought on chaos, at the cultural roots of the notion of chaos, and at the new sciences themselves (including thermodynamic studies, quantum physics, and chaotics). It then focuses the resulting observations on several selected events in contemporary Western theatre. The aim is to demonstrate a crucial twentieth-century interconnectedness of thought between the various disciplines that help to promote critically essential and vitally new cultural visions of existence.

While the recent "new" sciences have moved along a path of nonlinearity, so have the arts, each in ways initially conceived of as unique and distinct. A close look reveals that parallel concepts found in the arts and sciences suggest a meeting of minds that must be more than coincidental. Admittedly, quantum physicists like Werner Heisenberg use theatrical metaphors to describe their work. And playwrights like Tom Stoppard occasionally actually discuss chaos theory in their plays. But the actual depth of the interconnections is rarely acknowledged, perhaps because it is so rarely directly evident. However, while the various connections may not be direct, parallel developments suggest implicit, culturally prevalent synaptic cross-wirings utilizing a network of cultural connectors that dart bits of information from one discipline to the other and guarantee that the "separate" paths will eventually merge and then continue on parallel trajectories. Put another way, there appear to be nonlinear influences interaffecting the arts and sciences themselves, assuring an orderly, almost parallel progress even amid seeming disorder. While this study does have opportunity to observe direct links, often the connections are far more tenuous. While Stoppard will provide two crucial opportunities to see self-conscious interaction at work, the efforts of other playwrights are less directly connected to the science movement.

It is on these independently derived points of coincidence that perhaps even greater value should be placed, for while emulation has its unquestioned virtues, elucidation and validation through an apparently entirely separate creative process seem even more significant, if for no other reason than the apparently mystifying parallelism. With the new science articulations, however, such mystification begins to reveal rational, defensible foundations. The "mystery" of parallel thought that this study documents can in part be explained by the coincidences of that thought springing from mutually experienced single cultural influences and focusing on a single subject – "nature." Given that both artists and scientists strive to understand nature, and given that points of curiosity and matrices of approach are culturally influenced, it only makes sense that they will at least occasionally hit upon parallel conclusions.

With these parallels in mind, this study will also confront the related point that the work of the scientist and that of the artist are not as distinct as they are fabled to be. Because of recent breakthroughs in thinking about the scientific process, even traditional scientists are beginning to accept the proposition that culturally predicated influences affect their work and that inspiration has its place in the lab. Likewise, the contemporary notion of the artist as an isolated, self-inspired, almost renegade thinker requires adjustment. Artists, too, are culturally influenced. In essence, after centuries of isolation and increased specialization, it may once again be time to consider the "arts" and "sciences" as allied enterprises and to acknowledge interrelationships between them similar to the accepted blendings of the arts and humanities in the "natural philosophy" that preceded the triumph of eighteenth-century Newtonianism.

Traditional Newtonianism – in fact and in inclination – is the thing chaotics challenges, both in the new sciences and in the arts. In the sciences, Newtonian thought has been the modern cornerstone, rigorous in its causal assumptions, asserting a strict, inescapable linear interaction between events and objects, arguing for a precise and inescapable universal order. But as scientific developments cracked away at Newtonian order and confidence, a growing concern arose that order and meaning could only be replaced by disorder, meaninglessness, absurdism. Chaotics swings the pendulum back to an acceptable middle ground in that it denies the extreme "meaningful" order of linearly comprehensible Newtonianism but it also rejects the extreme visions of an embracing random, incomprehensible disorder.

So, too, with the recent history of the theatre. Dramatic naturalism of the late nineteenth century created a theatrical dynasty of technique and philosophy based on a strict Newtonian causal order that could be seen as the culmination of Aristotelian thought itself. When that tight, ordered vision began to show its cracks, the theatre of the absurd produced an evolved vision of the universe as being "governed" by total randomness, which at its best equated such randomness with the existentialist concept of freedom unfettered by objective truths. While theatre of chaos agrees with the absurd and denies the linear order of naturalism, it also in part sides with naturalism by challenging the randomness of the absurd. Like the chaotics of science, it espouses a vision of dynamic interaction leading to orderly disorder.

One may sense that theatre of chaos is not any more new than chaotics in general is new. To a large degree this point is true, as evidence of a chaotics theatre surfaces among the Greeks and Elizabethans as well as among other pre-twentieth-century theatre venues. What we have come upon in the twentieth century, however, is a precise means to articulate a vision that has been aging and ripening for centuries, awaiting the right cultural moment to be brought out of the cellars. Like chaotics, which derives from a long history of scientific thought, theatre of chaos, though technically postabsurdist and postnaturalist, is really more a theatre path – one of many the theatre has taken – that one can follow back to Thespis himself, who rose out of the security of the Chorus into the great unknown of individuation, bored with ordered security and risking disorder to investigate the possibility of new orders.

It is my hope that this book will succeed as a "prolegomenon" to future speculations on the nature of chaos, science, and the arts. I should emphasize that chaotics is not a conception that needs to be limited to twentieth-century studies. Although I focus on a very limited group of twentieth-century playwrights, I hope it becomes increasingly apparent that chaos theory extends well beyond my subjects and indeed well beyond theatre, into other arts disciplines as well, elucidating that which has often been thought but perhaps never so well expressed.

Finally, and most significantly, these ventures into chaotics should lead to even larger feedback loops, incorporating more than just science and the arts and expanding to include individual and cultural patterns of understanding and behavior as well. Instead of bemoaning a "world o' chassis," perhaps we can evolve attitudes that embrace orderly disorder as inevitable states of nature that we must learn culturally to emulate. Rather than longing for returns to idyllic orders that very likely never existed, we can adjust to embrace dynamically variable orders. Instead of isolating ourselves in insular, static orders, perhaps we can grow to learn the universality of a new sort of ordering system and thereby eliminate constricting nationalism, racism, sexism. Perhaps we can all learn to be more like lunatics, lovers, and poets – and scientists – and perhaps the world will be a better place for it.

The New Science Metaphor and Modern Drama

A Brief History of Western Thought

> The first power to come into being was Chaos.
>
> . . . .
>
> And out of Chaos black Night and Erebos came into being,
> and out of Night then came the brightness of Aither and Day,
> whom she conceived by lying in love and mingling with
> Erebos
>
> Hesiod's *Theogony*[1]

WORLDS REASONABLY CERTAIN of ontological, epistemological, and cosmological frames produce art that reflects that certainty with a benignity and confidence that assures its public of ultimate order even in the face of apparent disorder. Classical Greece, medieval Europe, Elizabethan England, and Enlightenment Europe are regularly held up to us as paradigms. Try as we might, however, the twentieth century has failed to secure such frames of confidence.

This desire to find meaning and order in the universe has typically taken two forms throughout history. The earliest frames of order were of the sort that acknowledged a necessary interplay between order and disorder, an interplay occupying the realm of chaos. In such frames, there was no desire for the destruction of or control over chaos; rather, chaos was perceived as an essential and integral contributor to life and creative processes. The great systems of the East held to such a belief and were frequently – though incompletely – incorporated into Western thought through the

1

works of such poet-thinkers as Hesiod (c. 700 B.C.) and through such cult groups as the worshippers of Dionysus.

The second great system – more recent and therefore often considered more progressive or advanced – held that order was to be desired over its mortal foe chaos, that chaos was a force of destruction and decay, or, in moral terms, was a product of the triumph of disorderly evil over orderly goodness. The consequent human goal was to create a world that struggled against chaos and strove to establish order through complete understanding and ultimate control of life's "irregularities." The unpredictability of even a benign, seemingly harmless chaos was undesirable because it precluded human dominion. In the classical Greek world, this overall hunger for dominion culminated in the work of Aristotle – though it didn't exist without challenge – and was revitalized in the early modern Western world through the rediscovery of Aristotle and in the works of such minds as Descartes and Galileo. With very few exceptions, the modern world has continued to see chaos as undesirable, dangerous, deadly, evil. The triumph of order has been established as the goal of modern human thought and has increasingly been seen as an attainable goal.

Generally speaking, the centuries-old Aristotelian empirical process remains today the primary basis of the most commonly subscribed conclusions concerning reality. The world is "out there," the human senses are available for observation of that material, and the mind can be developed to draw objective conclusions about that world. The process itself has rarely been called into question, but particular Aristotelian conclusions often have been. What stands tall is the cornerstone of Aristotelian thinking: the concept of causality. It is a concept that presumes that all natural events have predictable outcomes because of various interactive qualities inherent in the natural world. The ancients called this causality *foederi fati,* the laws of fate. The modern world would come to call it scientific law. The visions are the same, stemming from a growing confidence that humanity has the tools ultimately to understand and then triumph over nature. Simply put, if we could understand nature's laws, we could control them and manipulate nature for our own ends. And if an explicable natural causality in fact rules existence, then our powers of mind and observation should concentrate on fully understanding that causality.

In the classical world of the ancients, one philosopher of particular note challenged that ontological belief in a strictly explicable causality, attempting to return to the world view of his mystic predecessors but working for less mystical explanations in his pursuit of that return. Lucretius (95–55 B.C.) confronted the Aristotelian models of a world governed by *foederi fati* models. For Aristotelians, "unexpected" events were quite simply events whose causes we had not yet uncovered. Lucretius, however, saw a terrible flaw in such an orderly model. Agreeing with an Aristotelian urge for empirical study, Lucretius used an Aristotelian methodology of reasoned observation to challenge Aristotelian conclusions by observing that if such *foederi fati* conclusions were true, history (natural and human) would merely record an eternal repetition of the same. The world would be void of any potential for genuine newness, void of any significant creative potential, since a spark of creativity could not exist, only a finite combination of recurring, already existent options. Without the unexpected, genuine change and development would be impossible. If Aristotelians accepted such stasis, an observant Lucretius did not. So into the Aristotelian model of finite, ordered, and orderly matter, Lucretius inserted what he called the "clinamen," a force unencumbered by explicable laws of necessity that disrupts orderliness and introduces unanticipated (and unanticipatable) opportunities for diversity. Stable patterns are disrupted, forcing a subsequent reorganization that results in a novelty or diversity that is nature itself. Lucretius observes:

> [I]f all movement is always interconnected, the new arising from the old in a determinate order – if the atoms never swerve so as to originate some new movement that will snap the bonds of fate, the everlasting sequence of cause and effect – what is the source of the free will possessed by living things throughout the earth?[2]

For Lucretius, mechanical laws of fate necessarily interact with urges liberated from those laws to create a dynamic flow that challenges the static linear equilibrium of Aristotelian philosophy. Lucretius speaks of human free will, but he also posits a natural free will that produces natural diversity as human will has produced human diversity. Sparks of genuine change occur within patterns of general stability.

With this fundamental Lucretian shift of focus, as Michel Serres observes, "The creative science of change and of circumstance is substituted for the physics of the fall, of repetition, and of rigorous trains of events."[3] Though anticipating many of the empirical breakthroughs of the nineteenth and twentieth centuries, Lucretian philosophy has gone unheeded for essentially two millennia, Aristotelianism remaining the dominant mode and form of thought. N. Katherine Hayles tantalizingly observes, "Had Lucretius's vision of the clinamen prevailed, the world might be dedicated to chaos rather than order."[4]

But before Lucretian philosophy could be culturally reclaimed in the modern age even only as a tentative option, another mechanical confirmation of Aristotelian causality would be introduced, reinforcing in painstaking detail the general Aristotelian paradigm and the traditional rationalist-causalist's increasing belief that order would finally triumph over disorder/chaos. Isaac Newton (1642–1727) gave the Western world exactly what it wanted: a clear, linear blueprint of natural behavior. He was for centuries to follow, as Ilya Prigogine and Isabelle Stengers observe, "the 'new Moses' who had been shown the 'tables of the law.'"[5] The epitaph Alexander Pope proposed for him speaks in similar terms: "Nature and Nature's laws lay hid in night: / God said, let Newton Be! and all was light."

Except for the magnitude of Newton's influence upon Western thought, one could almost call his a cult following. Social sciences, ethics, philosophy all joined in to create systems modeled on the Newtonian vision of order. Elevated nearly to godlike status, Newton introduced a system that explained all physical behavior, from the microscopic to the macroscopic. Seen as ushering in a new golden age of classical science, Newtonianism[6] itself, say Prigogine and Stengers, "was now applied to everything that dealt with a system of laws, with equilibrium, or even to all situations in which natural order on one side and moral, social, and political order on the other could be expressed in terms of an all-embracing harmony" (*Order Out of Chaos*, p. 29). Like Aristotle's world, Newton's world was a smoothly operating mechanical world, a world of pulleys and simple machines, of bodies subject to the exchange of energy and interaction with gravitational forces. Newton's world placed an emphasis on static behavior energized by linear motion striving itself to return to stasis/equilibrium, only to be re-energized by future causal influences. Newton clearly described for us a world focused on the physics of solid bodies, and his followers extended and applied Newton's principles to virtually all natural behavior. As John Briggs and F. David Peat point out, the result was a belief that

> [c]haos was merely complexity so great that in practice scientists couldn't track it, but they were sure that in principle they might one day be able to do so. When that day came there would be no chaos, so to speak, only Newton's laws. It was a spellbinding idea.[7]

In most circumstances the spirit of Newtonianism reigns supreme even today.

However, even as Newtonianism was solidifying its hold on cultural thought, a relatively minor "Lucretian" counterstrain was making itself heard, namely the Romantic revolution of the late eighteenth century, which disassociated itself from scientific stasis/balance/order and asserted a superrationalist organic universe where inescapable causality and tight equilibrium are not necessarily desired conditions. Opposed to a mechanical vision of the universe, Goethe, Wordsworth, Blake, Byron, Shelley, and others engaged the world, creating subjectivist perspectives and inspired, creative interaction. It was a clinamen-like engagement rather than distanced, Aristotelian-based "objective" observation of strict causality. What they saw was that *change,* disorder, and disequilibrium could be viewed as positive rather than negative features of nature. They saw a universal vitality much as Lucretius saw it, as providing vital life-fostering opportunity rather than ordaining destructive disruption and imbalance. Like Lucretius – though like Lucretius, they did not know it – they were advocating nonlinearity.

But while Romantic organicism perhaps captured the intellectual imagination of a notable few, the Victorian juggernaut of scientific and human progress drowned out the essence of Romanticism, adopting at most superficial rather than fundamental Romantic tenets and arguing that Newtonianism still reigned, at least until the scientific process could prove otherwise. Visions of organic vitality, along with Romantic processes of engagement/ interaction, would, like Lucretius's philosophy, need to wait for yet another scientific revolution in order to receive confirmation of its perspectives.

Newtonianism took on different particular permutations

throughout the mid- to late nineteenth century with the widespread introduction of steam power into the civilized world's industrial production processes. Though the Newtonian urge for causal comprehension (Newtonianism) persisted, Newton's actual laws were being challenged, as were their optimistic premises, for there evolved an increasing need to account for entropy within the thermodynamic systems that were powering industrial machines. Entropy describes a system of universal decay and predicts eventual cosmic death, whereas Newton's laws presumed a perpetual dynamic activity that was itself, macroscopically, a static given. Motion perpetually occurred within a static universal frame; energy never "died." The world for Newton would never wind down. But entropic theories argued both against Newtonian equilibrium and stasis – the sources of the Enlightenment world view – as well as against the recently developed Victorian vision of a world engaged in orderly *progress,* a concept that even transcended original Newtonian confidence. But both Newtonian balance and equilibrium and the nineteenth-century subscriptions to *advancement* came to be questioned by the entropic model. Unfortunately, this new problem did not immediately effect a fundamental evaluation of human knowledge and its basic assumptions. Rather, thermodynamic entropy confirmed for the Victorians that forces of chaos, identified as part of the entropic scheme, would require redoubled resistance if humanity were eventually to prevail. Humanity would need to struggle against this perceived insidious force of nature, and with an understanding of the natural mechanisms at hand, human success at "improving" nature seemed almost a Newtonian certainty. Humanity was practically destined to prevail.

This redoubled resistance, however, could not ultimately overcome the critical flaw of Newtonianism, despite decades of self-willed effort at numerous levels, social as well as natural. Newtonianism is a linear science, expressing complex ideas in reductive (a "good" term for science), simple terms. Basically, minor causes result in minor effects, major causes in major effects, and so forth. Such a system could not cope with the fact of entropy because there can be no cause "major" enough to reverse entropy. In fact, this general linear thinking process cornered many Victorians into numerous entropically self-destructive actions (most notably World War I). We can temporarily resist the consequences of linear thought, but without a fundamental attitudinal change of mind, the end is inevitable, and it was not the end the Victorians predicted.

This is where chaos theory and its ally – theatre of chaos – come to the rescue, encouraging different frames of thought and explaining the cosmos, though in ways formerly deemed to be incomplete. Among the many explanations is how order derives from disorder, how life derives from decay/entropy. Nonlinearity is the key, of course, because Newtonianism's measure-for-measure logic cannot account for a more-from-less or something-out-of-nothing (even if it is merely an appearance of something-out-of-nothing) world view. Entropy can be circumvented at numerous junctures along its development, and so can any number of other dilemmas which confounded the traditional Newtonians and disheartened the late Victorians, modernists, and even many postmodernists.

Moving beyond a disheartening Victorian legacy, existent still nearly a hundred years after the collapse of Victorian culture, is the goal of chaos theory and of the theatre of chaos.

Preliminary Thoughts on Contemporary Science

James Gleick's book *Chaos: Making a New Science*[8] argues that "chaos theory" is a recent, 1970s phenomenon, suggesting that questions of orderly disorder, nonlinearity, chaos, and so forth, only recently received the attention of scientists, philosophers, and other visionary minds. What seems abundantly clear is that since Lucretius – and even earlier – subjects relating to chaos theory have been of interest, from simple speculation to full-fledged experimentation. Gleick does make a strong case in seeing the latter part of the twentieth century as sufficiently technologically equipped to pursue chaotics-based questions with a thoroughness previously impossible. However, most science historians today identify Henri Poincaré in the late nineteenth century as the father of modern chaos theory, noting the unfortunate fact that his breakthroughs took a back seat to quantum physics in the early twentieth century and additionally needed to wait for the necessary technology to help advance them to scientific center stage. The computer is the new tool of the chaotician, what Poincaré needed (though some science historians are correct to note that the computer was not critically essential), as revolutionary a tool as the telescope and microscope were in their times.

While credit should be given to Poincaré and other early pioneers, it is probably fair to identify chaos theory as a science formally activated in the 1970s, especially if we consider an important point that Gleick and numerous others have failed fully to make. The point is simple: our contemporary culture has become obsessed with issues of unpredictability and uncertainty at numerous levels – economic, social, political, spiritual. The postmodern world of the late twentieth century is a world of even greater turmoil than the nineteenth-century or early twentieth-century worlds, so its *choice* to recognize and concentrate on such phenomena should be conceived of as something of an appropriate choice. Seeing chaos not as the death of order but rather as the pool of reorganization has become a cultural desire. Cultural desire has in many ways forced science to look at its subject (nature) in ways that can help us to understand our seemingly new surroundings and to move beyond the despairing conclusions our current knowledge has forced upon us.[9]

While necessarily relying on the sciences, we must also be aware that a too heavy reliance is ill-advised. Significantly, scientists argue that "chaos theory" is too inexact a term to describe this new science, to which N. Katherine Hayles, in her study of chaos theory and literature, observes:

> First, a disclaimer: "chaos theory" and the "science of chaos" are not phrases usually employed by researchers who work in these fields. They prefer to designate their area as nonlinear dynamics, dynamical systems theory, or, more modestly yet, dynamical systems methods. To them, using "chaos theory" or the "science of chaos" signals that one is a dilettante rather than an expert. (*Chaos Bound*, p. 8)

Hayles's disclaimer is significant because it ackowledges many scientists' continued desire for an "objectivist's" control over their material; "chaos" is a term entirely too pregnant with "unscientific" connotations to be itself adequately controlled, and so scientists avoid the term – ironically because of its *unfortunate* richness and complexity.

This richness and complexity, however, is precisely what should summon our attention. Hayles makes the following observation as to why she chooses to keep "chaos" as a central term in her literary study: "part of my project is to explore what happens when a word such as 'chaos,' invested with a rich tradition of mythic and literary significance, is appropriated by the sciences and given a more specialized meaning" (*Chaos Bound*, p. 8). Utilizing the term "chaos" allows Hayles to study the interaction among several disciplines – not the least of which are the sciences – in their efforts to come to grips with "orderly disorder." I would add to Hayles's mythic and literary concerns the matter of philosophical significance as well, and would agree with her that "[t]he older resonances do not disappear" (pp. 8–9) despite the efforts of the scientific community to banish "chaos" from its terminology. Indeed, moving away from dominant thought and reconsidering the anti- or nonrational ramblings of a shaman, a Blake, a Wordsworth, or a Whitman, can open up vistas wherein chaos is a positive force. Chaotics – both the scientific and nonscientific brands – takes that position, forcing its way into dominant cultural discourse and demanding a qualitative re-evaluation.

Interestingly, Prigogine and Stengers, the radical advocates of the perspective arguing that order arises from chaos, and David Bohm,[10] whose theories of implicate order support Prigogine, have often been labeled mystics rather than scientists by the scientific community. More sympathetically, however, Renée Weber argues that scientists like Prigogine and Stengers and Bohm, indeed all the great twentieth-century minds from Einstein to Hawking, confirm that "the search for unity in science itself [is] a spiritual path."[11] With Prigogine and Stengers and Bohm, at least, science has begun to confirm the cosmological assertions first recorded in Eastern mythology, deriving scientific evidence that chaos is the soup of creation from whence order arises. They are using science, in essence, to unearth answers to questions our culture requires for its health and possibly even its continued existence.

Stephen H. Kellert, among others, has addressed the issue of cultural and scientific interactions in his work *In the Wake of Chaos*.[12] Kellert suggests that a key to past cultural dismissals of chaotics is "the social interest in the exploitation of nature, an interest that contributed to the institutionalized disregard of physical systems not readily amenable to analysis and manipulation" (p. 120). The study of disorder was, as Prigogine and Stengers observe, "repressed in the cultural and ideological context of those times" (*Order Out of Chaos,* p. 20). Without clearly *quantitative* forms of linear-based, precise prediction – rather than the chaotician's *qualitative* "patterning" of events – science fails to provide knowledge that could allow "man a degree of control over his surroundings."[13] More insidiously, perhaps, this scientific inclination toward control supported and was supported by what Karen Warren calls a "logic of domination,"[14] wherein control of nature justified control of other elements – like women and minorities – within social strata.

Perhaps in part because of a growing acceptance of social diversity, the Newtonianist preference for control within the sciences has come under scrutiny in the last few decades. But this shift entails the need for both epistemological, ontological, and cosmological re-evaluation as well. Since chaos theory undermines the assumption of predictability and of any attendant control, this limitation on results challenges our cosmological faith in determinism itself. The challenge that chaos theory faces, as Kellert sees it, is to convince others "to welcome this openness and not see it as a cause for regret" (*In the Wake of Chaos,* p. 48).

While one cannot help but acknowledge that chaos theory has become "dreadfully fashionable,"[15] we must also be forewarned that, as Kellert argues, in many ways "chaos theory is not as interesting as it sounds" (*In the Wake of Chaos,* p. ix). Chaos theory does not precisely undermine or overturn Newtonian laws; it quite simply redirects our viewing of them and of nature so as to appreciate the chaos that was heretofore ignored. It reveals the limitations of Newtonian laws and goals, and it allows us to see the macroworld from a different perspective. We are, as Robert Shaw observed, now at a point where we must confess: "You don't see something until you have the right metaphor to let you perceive it."[16] This is where I see Kellert understating the point. Chaos theory may in fact *not* be a "new" science in ways that will become apparent later in this study. But chaos as a paradigm *is* revolutionary because it asks us to see the world from a different metaphorical stance. It is the metaphor that hits the mark in ways others to varying degrees have not. In fact, often chaos is quite literal and not metaphorical at all. That is how precise it can be.

What there is of "revolution" in this art and this science lies primarily in our willingness to adjust what and how we choose to see.[17] As scientists have now accepted new metaphors as models for perception, so too, it seems, should our culture in general adjust. Or perhaps it is exactly culture's own as yet foggy inclination for an adjustment that has encouraged science to take the steps it has. Whatever the case, it appears that science and art have reached a point where they are once more sharing the same metaphors and mutually contributing to complementary visions.

Where Science and Theatre Converge: A Sample and a Summary

This book in part works to see how recent scientific and technological conclusions have been anticipated by and later incorporated into our dominant cultural discourses. Noting the success of this general cultural–scientific interaction in turn allows us to concentrate on recent manifestations of that interaction in theatre – that most "cultural" of art forms. What we will see are not isolated, incomprehensible adventures into the abstractions of the impossible or improbable, as many confused audiences and critics may have deduced in the past, but foreordinations of a burgeoning new vision of reality, confirmed by the "scientific" forces of "truth" and in turn generating their own insights, which further encourage continued investigation among contemporary sciences themselves. This interaction undermines the notion that science has a singular hold on truth, confirming the validity of aesthetic and philosophical forays into chaos that both preceded and followed actual developments in chaos science.

While the theatre is full of examples of avant-garde theorizing, the success of that theorizing can only be announced when something more than a coterie audience accepts it. As such, this study will focus on mainstream events that demonstrate the evolutionary nature of the thing here called theatre of chaos. While much of this theatre has at times confused audiences, to a greater degree it has moved in ways nonetheless familiar, perhaps even occasionally appearing reactionary. What the theatre has done, however, is create a more clear and precise alternative picture of reality and art, not a picture incommensurate with its predecessors but rather one engaged in a sort of dialogue with them. This theatre has neither retreated to a reactionary position nor moved to an untenably extreme position, but rather has created a picture suitable to its culture's needs and growing sophistication, albeit quietly and without the benefit of revolutionary flourishes and announcements.

The interaction between the new sciences and new art is rich, full of resonance, breaking the arts–sciences dichotomy culturally inscribed for so many generations in the Western world. Aristotle, that unique man of science *and* aesthetics, can be set before us as a generic model, a spirited blend of human curiosity discouraged in this age of fragmented specialization wherein one world/enterprise/specialist cannot speak to the other. The potential for a reintegrated existence is within reach, once again, in the soup of a life-generating chaos from which science and art find their contemporary inspiration.

Though the scientific and aesthetic urges found their first unified voice in Aristotle, the disciplinary cross-fertilization we see in his work is by no means unique. One must be reminded that all literary artists and commentators tend to reflect the understanding of the natural world that prevails during their times. This suggestion ties appropriately into mathematician Ralph Abraham's observations, speaking specifically of chaos theory, that "[c]omplex dynamical systems theory [today] provides a new modeling strategy for social systems" and that "[d]ynamical models may be used as navigational aids for cooperation or conflict resolution in situations where goodwill prevails yet does not suffice."[18] Nonscientific enterprises such as art (or politics or psychology) may be well served by the models provided by science. Without such models or "navigational tools," artistic imagination could drift off track into the realm of fantasy or of the fantastically improbable. If Sophocles and Shakespeare can be said to have profited from models of their own contemporary scientific thinking, so too can it be argued that modernist and postmodernist artists have profited or can profit. Zola is a good modernist case in point.

Derived from Auguste Comte's positivist philosophy (*Système de philosophie positive* [1824]) and digested by the physiologist Claude Bernard (*Introduction à l'étude de la médecine expérimentale* [1865]) and literary and social historian Hippolyte Taine (*Histoire de la littérature anglaise* [1864]), Zola's naturalism borrowed from science the concept of the scientific method of observation and experimentation. Conclusions derived from such observation were fundamentally of a linearly determinist nature (the result of Bernard's observations) and, in the human sciences, were influenced by initial conditions of race, milieu, and moment (Taine's conclusions). Science had provided a modified reincarnation of the classical Aristotelian concept of *foederi fati* for Zola and the naturalists to utilize. To those concepts Zola added the nineteenth-century thermodynamic concept of universal entropy to his philosophy, creating a "scientific," deterministic explanation of a universal downward spiral toward tragedy. Ibsen's *Ghosts* and Strindberg's *Miss Julie* are the dramatic masterpieces of this naturalist epistemology, ontology, and cosmology.

Despite their unsavory negativism, Zola's ideas nonetheless still find a place in contemporary thought. But perhaps more significant is Zola's general procedure, what Martin Esslin calls the naturalist *impulse,* "a spirit of free enquiry, totally unprejudiced, unburdened by preconceived ideas."[19] This latter-day Newtonian-Aristotelian "objective" scientific *process* in art is Zola's naturalist legacy, a movement toward empirical verification, consciously adopted today by playwrights and critics alike, including expressionists and absurdists as well as the more traditional realists.

There is an important irony to Zola's theatre practices. Hungry for objective results, even Zola eventually realized the subjective nature of the choices he made. He discovered, as others would, that the scientific process was not what it was billed to be. In fact, the classical assumption that scientists could be godlike, objective eyes, observing reality undisturbed, would be incontrovertibly undermined by quantum physics only a few decades after Zola's work in the theatre. Scientists were forced to re-evaluate and confront the possibility that the scientific process in general was little more than an activity wherein one form of subjectivity ("rational" inquiry) was, through an exercise in mass delusion, elevated to the level of objectivity. The fact is, choices are made that "direct" results. And choices of what to study are themselves inherently prejudicial.

The result of downgrading science from a godlike, objective enterprise is not that science becomes fruitless; rather it is that we must understand the full consequences and limitations of what we claim to have learned when we do "scientific" inquiry. Such inquiry appears still to be our best means of understanding the world, but we must now realize that when we engage in such enterprises, we are *interacting* and not merely observing from a distance. This revelation alone has several positive consequences, echoing the assertions of the late eighteenth-century Romantics. For one, it breaks down the rationalist assumption that humanity is "outside" of or above/beyond nature. The revelation (belatedly) forces us to accept our integrated status with nature. It also forces the confession that right-brain activity and left-brain activity are not separate, distinct, and irreconcilable activities. This confession leads to the realization that art and science themselves are more closely entwined than many of us previously wanted to admit. Zola realized this, yet critics, both defenders and opponents of naturalism, have often missed the point.

Because of its ostensible advocacy of scientific processes, naturalism has suffered ongoing misconceptions of its "scientific" nature and has perversely been associated with efforts at "heartless" objectification of reality. Naturalism's presumed legacy has been to establish a belief in the ability to present objective reality on the stage, while the very process – proceeding from Zola himself – has confirmed the subjective nature of this objective-seeming enterprise. As Esslin oberves, Zola's

> recognition of the subjective nature of all perception marks the really decisive breach with any theory of art which believed in the possibility of embodying absolutes, *absolute verities,* in great enduring works. As such, Naturalists were the first conscious *existentialists* in the realm of aesthetics. ("Naturalism in Context," p. 71)

Popular theatre history, of course, does not acknowledge this fact, perhaps because popular culture was not – and perhaps may still not be – prepared to accept such subjectivity in the human pursuit of "truth." Zola's aesthetics indirectly but accurately paralleled the redefinition of science that would soon follow, while popular history saw (and still sees) Zola's aesthetics as inscribed by the standardly accepted but soon to be outmoded definition of scientific inquiry. Once the changed definition is accepted, perhaps Zola's aesthetics will also be granted re-evaluation.

In this matter science and art can help each other and in the process can help a culture badly in need of embracing a new paradigm of existence in the face of the fact that the old paradigms are crumbling. Rationalist, linear credos need re-evaluation. Recent inquiry has uncovered counterintuitive reality in the subatomic world of quantum mechanics, leading to a loosening of the soil in which macroscopic discoveries are derived. Chaos theory reopens means of comprehension only hinted at by marginalized philosophers like Lucretius. But the cultural need is now here, and re-evaluations are at least cautiously encouraged.

The process of creating new paradigms involves science and art working interactively. This is a key subject of this book, to observe instances of interaction, mutual reification, and reinforcement between science – now seen not as timeless, universal, and objective but as culturally specific and subjective – and theatre. While the various enterprises grouped under the rubric "chaos theory" are central to this discussion, related antecedent and contemporaneous developments will also be included in an effort to suggest a new aesthetic, one already pursued by visionary artists but perhaps heretofore imprecisely articulated and evaluated.

The consequences of this study are manifold in the field of theatre studies, but perhaps most affected are the two modern philosophical and aesthetic extremes of naturalism and absurdism. The late twentieth century has created an arena wherein their contrary natures converge, the realm of chaos theory. There are actually two crucial points of convergence. Naturalism and absurdism both recognize the gloomy consequences of the entropic model, though invariably with signals that artists in both camps wished reality to be otherwise than it is. Chaos theory – and chaos theatre – also acknowledge the fact of entropy but add to the naturalist and absurdist realizations a transcendent truth that sees regeneration and reorganization rising out of many entropic events. Chaotics reveals and the chaos theatre argues that entropy is a momentary reality, a transitional phase, rather than an inevitable conclusion. Hope, finally, is not a futile illusion, as naturalism and absurdism both suggest, but is rather the quality to hang on to until the next stages of the chaos model materialize. The second aspect of this convergence involves the apparently irreconcilable discrepancy between the naturalist's faith in logic and orderly universal behavior versus the absurdist's insistence on alogic, irrationality, and disorderly universal behavior. Ironically the chaos paradigm recognizes both positions as "right," but they are relatively right (and wrong) under contrary circumstances, along a long spectrum whose extremes are order and disorder but whose extensive middle ground engages degrees of both. Order (naturalism) dominates at one extreme, disorder (absurdism) at the other. But in the main, most existence engages a combination of both. And in that large expanse the one is in fact responsible for generating the other. The revelation of chaos theory is that neither position holds final sway over existence but consistently interacts and alternates to create the richness, variety, and spontaneity that is life itself. Postnaturalism and postabsurdism have found their ways to the fertile hybrid high ground of theatre of chaos.

Chapter 1 of this book concentrates on quantum physics, the predecessor of chaos theory that rocked the foundation of scientific certainty in the field of particle science. Tom Stoppard's play *Hapgood* takes full advantage of the quantum paradigm to construct a human model of understanding, a direct debt to science itself. From *Hapgood's* direct use of the paradigm one can extend the science–art connection to various other works of the theatre – I suggest *Death of a Salesman* – which produces a potentially rich new spin on the Western dramatic canon, past and present.

Chapter 2 moves directly into chaos theory, explaining the breakthroughs of this new mode of perception and understanding as it directly relates to our macro-universe – the world in which we live rather than the world occupied by subatomic "particles." The breakthroughs in chaos science quite literally apply to *our* world, undiluted by a need for metaphor, though seeing its metaphoric value as at times appropriate. The section suggests that a theatre of chaos marks a continuation – perhaps a terminus – between the dynamic debate between the determinist philosophy/art of naturalism and the indeterminate philosophy/art of the theatre of the absurd. In fact, it is fair to suggest that theatre of chaos sprung out of this dialectic with an integrationist force that replaces both visions, because to a great degree it reconciles the differences by recognizing the validity of both as it also insists on the exclusion of neither. Again, Stoppard paves the way with his *Arcadia,* a play modeled on chaotics.

Chapter 3 observes that, though many contemporary American dramatists – specifically Sam Shepard and David Rabe – do not literally demonstrate an actual debt to chaos science, chaos theory does provide a critical perspective from which to understand their work, a signal that chaos has entered our cultural consciousness from avenues other than the scientific laboratory. Simultaneously the lab and the stage have evolved similar conclusions about existence, in much the same way that the confederacy of absurdists nearly a half century earlier independently gleaned their visions not from philosophy or science but from experience itself. At once farsighted and perhaps visionary, these writers are also products of their times and speak with urgency of the need to re-vision existence, a re-vision seen clearly in the chaos science paradigm. Marsha Norman likewise falls into this camp of visionaries, putting the additional spin on the point by presenting her conclusions from the perspective of a woman challenging a dominant linearity that is the hallmark of our patriarchally controlled society.

Looking backward and forward, Chapter 4 suggests a connection between chaos theory and the reflections of such cultural theorists as Jan Kott, whose model in the 1960s for reassessing Shakespeare, when moved even further into the present and utilizing a chaos model, demonstrates the fertile potential of reflecting upon the past not simply from an absurdist perspective (Kott's own 1960s perspective) but from a chaotics perspective. If, as Jan Kott demonstrates, absurdism can be found in Shakespeare, so can we make a similar reflection that chaotics likewise exists in works of the past, Shakespeare certainly included.

In the same section, it is suggested that concepts like the plague and cruelty – numerous revolutionary pronouncements antecedent to chaotics – are rich forerunners to the theatre of chaos, both enriching our understanding of a theatre of chaos and receiving enriching evaluations themselves from the perspective of chaos. As a unifying, harmonizing vision of many of these nexuses, Tony Kushner's *Angels in America* serves quite well, also quite significantly serving as a work that demonstrates the future potential of a chaos vision and a chaos theatre to serve that vision. Perhaps our Newtonianism can accept Lucretius and in some ways return us to a qualitative, integrating vision of humanity's relationship with nature, and of nature's need for chaos, which is ultimately required for human health and sanity.

1

Quantum Physics as Metaphor
Elliptical Beginnings of the New Paradigm

THE HISTORY OF SCIENCE records three revolutionary breakthroughs in the twentieth century: theories of relativity, quantum mechanics, and chaos theory. Despite their revolutionary effect on our understanding of reality, theories of space-time (relativity) and nonlinear dynamics (chaos theory) remain fundamentally rationalist in nature. They are significant adjustments to rather than deviations from a long history of rationalist enterprises. Relativity applies almost exclusively to the astrophysical macro-universe and provides insights only metaphorically or anecdotally applicable to our directly experienced, earthbound world. Chaos theory, on the other hand, directly interacts with the universe immediately experienced by humanity and so actually has literal (as well as metaphoric) value, directly applicable to that middle realm between the atom and the white dwarf. Its fundamentally rationalist bases are therefore all the more important since the rationality it confirms confirms in the process a rationality in our existence. Yet the conclusions derived from its brand of rationality often appear anti- or, at best, nonrational because it introduces nonlinearity into our heretofore accepted belief in rational enterprises as linear.

Like relativity, quantum mechanics can at best be utilized in metaphorical ways to explain our own visible existence, since its object of study is the subatomic micro-universe. But unlike either relativity or chaos theory, quantum physics/mechanics fully disrupts rational expectations and demands from us a willingness to accept significant counterintuitive conclusions. It radically undermines rationalism in a way that can be said to prepare us for the "new" rationalism of its chaos theory successor.

The point here is that chaos theory connects us to our historical, rationalist longings but surges ahead in an altered rationalist state. As such, chaos theory is a true and direct subject of study, immediately relevant to human activity. Relativity rationally expands our understanding of celestial objects and so only glancingly touches our actual existence. As a result, this study will not pursue relativity. But while quantum mechanics also only glancingly touches our actual existence, the direct value of quantum mechanics is that it serves as a sort of bomb blast upon our unquestioned presumptions of the total, complete accuracy of traditional rationalist enterprises. It has softened the earth for the assault of the chaos theoreticians, revolutionary in their own right though perhaps more comfortingly conservative given their confirmation of rationalism, albeit an adjusted rationalism. While classical rationalism confirmed a linear reality now called into question, chaos theory thrusts upon us a nonlinear reality, the significance of which cannot be overstated. And quantum mechanics of the early twentieth century paved the way for such a re-vision.

The assault on traditional rationalism that quantum mechanics initiated may be unique in the scientific world, but it is not unique to human thought. Like chaos theory itself, quantum mechanics finds antecedents in numerous earlier philosophical and literary discourses. A brief digression is here necessary.

Philosophical Antecedents to Quantum Mechanical Conclusions

As noted earlier, the triumph of Aristotelian thought over alternatives like Lucretian philosophy resulted in a cultural attitude based on linear rationalism confirmed by empirical inquiry. The truth stood rock solid; objectivity derived by a process of linear logic was a given. Centuries of either empirical-rational or rational-exclusive inquiry merely presumed as a given the thesis that knowledge of the world could be linearly and objectively derived. And in the Western world the great ages of faith and confidence were founded upon this epistemological premise.

However, even as Western science reached its zenith along this empirical-rational trajectory in the eighteenth century, its epistemological premises were challenged by such philosophers as John Locke (1632–1704) and David Hume (1711–76). Though the dominant modes of thought remained essentially undaunted by these assaults, perhaps the most thorough early manifestation of doubt – a significant seed of doubt – was planted by the German philosopher Immanuel Kant (1724–1804) when he drew the distinction between what he termed "phenomena" and "noumena," a distinction somewhat reminiscent of early Eastern philosophy/theology (of which our more familiar Platonism could be considered a rationalist derivative). That which we perceive are "phenomena," a characterization of the real world as received by the senses and transmitted to cognizant regions of our brains to be organized in accordance with pre-established spatiotemporal mental categories. It is not the "real" world itself, but it is as much of the real world as we as humans, using the receptive media we have, will ever know. As a result, these phenomena are standardly what we daily call "reality." "Noumena," on the other hand, constitute what Kant identifies as the actually real world. However, we can only *assume* this world exists in some unknown "pure" state, since we can never directly "know" it, since our data-collecting sources – the senses – receive only what they have been programmed to receive, and since our mental faculties further manipulate the data to conform to some preconceived vision of reality/order.

Though at first glance Kant's articulation appears to be merely a restatement of Platonic philosophy – particularly Platonic ontology – its consequences are much more devastating epistemologically. Plato questioned the validity of the senses and turned inward to the mind to guarantee objective conclusions. In essence, Plato challenged Aristotelian empiricism (though that challenge met with mixed results since, of course, science is still empirical in its approach). Kant, on the other hand, questions the objectifiability of *all* knowledge of the world around us as well as within us; our senses are suspect, as Plato argued, but so is our mind. Kant's dilemma is a receptor dilemma; what humans know is a result of *active* manipulative reception and interpretation rather than a passive absorption/reception standardly assumed to be the operating mode of the human faculties. The senses and the mind conspire together to mold our visions of external reality. Because humans manipulate the world, re-forming it to conform to preconceived assumptions, we never really know our world as it is, only as our faculties allow us to know it, only as we *choose* it to be. The world we know is in actuality the result of a highly sophisticated, truly subjective engagement of our existence. The rigorous philosophical treatises of Kant anticipate the conclusions drawn by such literary successors as Goethe, Wordsworth, Blake, and Byron. These Romantics were essentially Kantians in their belief that humans enfold themselves into the world, creating subjective realities in the process.

This subjective engagement starkly contrasts the epistemological faith of the ancient Western philosophers (Plato as well as Aristotle) in the objective capacities of the human mind. They believed that the mind saw and faithfully comprehended what actually existed, whether it be the shadow of the real or the real itself. And so for them epistemology did not interfere with ontology (though Plato's and Aristotle's ontologies differed), since what we knew was in fact what there was "out there" to know.

On the other hand, Kant's ontology argued for two worlds: the unknowable (and even unimaginable) noumenal "real" world and the known phenomenal "physical" world. Meanwhile, the Romantics took a different approach to Kant's philosophy as well as to Aristotle's and Plato's. Aristotle basically argued that we know noumena and that this knowledge was uncorrupted by either sensory or mental manipulation. Plato argued that our senses actually only know a second level of reality – not precisely phenomena, however – and we know the first level of reality – something like noumena – through pure reason. The Romantics for the most part rejected both Aristotle and Plato, agreeing with Kant on the matter of corrupted knowledge, but they saw the corruption positively, as a glorious interaction between self and other/nature. Furthermore, they eliminated the noumenal–phenomenal dichotomy, asserting that what Kant called phenomena – this polluted reality – was actually reality itself, enfolding the self with the physical otherness formerly known as "nature" to produce "Nature." Moving to this practical, empirical, phenomenal plane, the Romantics saw epistemology and ontology as very nearly interchangeable terms. That which we perceive to exist – phenomena – is in fact all we need to presume exists, and without an active enfolded perception, this nature is something less than reality.

The problem here, of course, is that every individual creates his or her own reality. Solipsism seems to be the necessary consequent of this theory. Bishop George Berkeley (1685–1753), working on this dilemma several years before the Romantic revolution, derived an intriguing solution to this problem that would soon confront Romantic philosophy. He assumed a skeptical posture and essentially rejected any notion of noumena by concluding, like the Romantics to follow, that existence does not exist unless it is actually perceived. And like the Romantics to follow, he asserted that phenomena – though he wouldn't use that term – constitute our plane of reality. Then, to give existence objective credibility, he inserted a god into his ontology, whose omniscient eye perpetually perceived reality and therefore created stability in this perceiver-created world. Not to put too fine a point on this philosophical material, the following limericks nicely summarize Berkeley's philosophy, the first by Ronald Knox, the second an anonymous reply:

> There once was a man who said "God
> Must think it exceedingly odd
> If he finds that this tree
> Continues to be
> When there's no one about in the Quad."

> Dear sir, Your astonishment's odd;
> I am always about in the Quad.
> And that's why the tree
> Will continue to be,
> Since observed by Yours faithfully, God.[1]

The whimsy of the limericks notwithstanding, the point is significant: humans are simply lesser, more limited, manifestations of this eye/god. The world – or parts of it – does not cease to exist when mortal perception ceases to perceive it since an omnipresent perceiver exists to fill any perceiver void. And since, according to Berkeley, perception precedes essence, the real was *necessarily* what was perceived. Combining ontology and epistemology, Berkeley in his own inimitable fashion had secured for humanity a comfortable, objective relationship with its surrounding cosmos. His human/eye is as much a revolutionary concept as his eye/god is essentially traditional, conventional in its desire for objectivity.

Themselves planted in one of the last great ages of faith, these eighteenth-century philosophers articulated both a growing skepticism toward the possibility of objective certainty and an attendant desire to secure a new certainty, ironically, even as Newtonianism was reaching its high-water mark. Both Kant and Berkeley rather grimly announce the loss of that certainty while Berkeley nevertheless strives to reclaim a new type of certainty. The Romantics, on the other hand, embrace a subjectivity seemingly undisturbed by the loss of objective certainty.

The importance of these philosophers and their Romantic literary counterparts may not be fully recognized today, however, since their impact was not immediately felt, having been overwhelmed by the empirical, mathematical wizardry of Isaac Newton whose explanation of the material world would fully confirm a belief in the objective reality of existence and trigger an age of confidence in perception not seriously called into doubt for at least another century. Newton's precise practicality secured a certainty for the world that seemingly undermined any sense of need to venture into a world of noumena or skepticism. What we saw could be explained by laws that we could understand. If any potentially disconcerting dualist dilemmas arose, they were handled with an objective, rationalist's faith in actual order and harmony and were dealt with accordingly.

Theatrical Parallels

In the world of theatre history, it is interesting to note as well that though the eighteenth century (and nineteenth century) produced significant and important drama, little of it had to do with anything more than "social" philosophy. Such visions deliberately and confidently chose an ontology of facts focused on social activity using a methodology parallel to the scientific, Newtonian model. The artist-thinkers of the time seemingly found no real need – thanks at least in part to Newton – to question how we knew nor to extend questions beyond the accepted, given "reality."

Theatrical antecedents to this confidence are evident in the early modern world when one considers the confidence in the human potential first established by Shakespeare and his Elizabethan contemporaries. But Shakespeare also introduced lingering reservations about humanity's full potential. *Hamlet* is, of course, a crucial touchstone. The play presents Hamlet's existential meanderings, including musings on epistemology, ontology, and teleology. Though Hamlet observes, "There are more things in heaven and earth, Horatio, / Than are dreamt of in your philosophy" ("philosophy" being a term here where we would today read "natural philosophy" or "science"), he nonetheless pursues a course of action that struggles to remain fundamentally empirical and unswervingly objective. That his methods fail to rid Denmark of its scourge seems to be Shakespeare's warning against too great a faith in linearly rationalist thought and its objective potential. After all, it is only after Hamlet gives up the hunt for proof of Claudius's guilt, gives in to "providence," that Denmark is righted. Something other than reason saves Denmark from utter destruction. But this is a warning Shakespeare gives to a world that essentially disregards the message.

The complexities inherent in *Hamlet,* however, are less evident in much of the remainder of Shakespeare's canon. At very least, subsequent generations tended to rework his texts into linear offerings confirming a confidence in a new age of human empowerment. It is this direction that the theatre world more inclined toward, in conformity with the movement toward perfected order we would see culminate in the eighteenth century. A logic of inevitable and linear order is consistently maintained.

The "lesser," carnage-ridden products of the Jacobean and Stuart stages give us more frequent (and far more tantalizingly macabre) outbursts of chaos, but even they ultimately return us to tranquillity's base, perhaps still troubled but finally confident in the reassertion of a vision of a divinely rational order, neatly packaged and finally rationally comprehensible.

Irrefutable empirical evidence of Shakespeare's day insisted that maggots spontaneously generate under the sun's warmth, ironically confirming for us today that what we see – what we think we know – is not always what is. Often it simply is what we want to see. And clearly one of the great human desires is to see order in our existences, often sacrificing truth for coherence. So perhaps what we argue *is* is only what we wish reality to be. That is Kant's point exactly. We selectively accumulate data and manipulate it to conform to prefabricated mental constructs reflecting a human desire built into our very methods of comprehension. Perception is *never* objective, though matter may be singularly perceived in a similar fashion by the great mass of humanity. If that is objectivity, then clearly it is a relative objectivity and hence not objective at all except in an anthropocentric sense. This, too, is very likely the basis for Shakespeare's own halting thoughts on the matter of a rising humanism, a humanism that by the eighteenth century incontrovertibly becomes the measure of all things.

As indicated above, most of these troubling existential concerns would not again become central to the mass of Western civilization for several centuries, thanks to the triumph of thought that led to Newtonian physics, which confirmed that empiricism and the eye/god capacities of humanity could basically reveal "essence" itself, unassisted by outside sources. At very least, what we didn't know, we didn't need to know.

And so the eighteenth century created art that presented ideal society as conforming to and reflecting the smooth machinations of the Newtonian universe. Comedy and melodrama (tragedy rarely cluttered the stage) presented only momentary derailments of the orderly machine of society, soon to be placed back on track. "Decorum" prevailed as a universal necessity.

As the nineteenth century unfolded, dreams of a harmonious order began to dissipate under the weight of increasing entropic realities. Facing such uncertainty, the theatre redoubled its efforts to assert the possibility of rationalist utopias. The playwright-artist remained the eye/god whose clear insights into objective potentialities of orderly social existence directed him to preach how a currently imperfect social world could be improved if only it would follow the prescriptions of this eye/playwright. And this eye/playwright is given "scientific" certification by the prophet Zola, who claims to introduce the scientific model into his naturalist philosophy of art (and existence), but who in many ways can at best be credited with having standardized a practice utilized centuries before him. And we have social activists like Ibsen and Shaw experimenting with that philosophy. And we have the "neutral" reporter's eye of Chekhov, documenting decay but leaving conclusions to be drawn by the eye/audience. In every case, these theatre giants do little and their dramatic imitators do less to question the possibility of failed foundations, attacking instead rationalist misdirection caused by human shortcoming. Little if anything was posited relating to the fundamental reasons why human goals were not being achieved, except maybe that we weren't trying hard enough. Little thought was given either to the relative uselessness of the tools we relied upon or to the possibility that our fundamental ambitions lacked legitimate foundations of support.

This brand of late nineteenth- and early twentieth-century revolt against human shortcomings, as Robert Brustein reports in *The Theatre of Revolt*,[2] becomes the informing element of the new age. It quickly evolved that problems became easier to document than solutions, since any possible solutions would themselves become sources of assault, reductive, incomplete, and unsatisfactory as they were destined to be. There were occasions of halting intimations that all was not right with the Newtonian paradigm – that mending it would not do – but the hints were only whispered, not trumpeted, if for no other reason than that no viable alternatives were ready at hand. The modernist revolt of the late nineteenth and early twentieth centuries, finally, was a limited strain of revolt, lacking real direction. It still was not a revolt against any grand structure. Into an essentially benign Newtonian frame artists inserted a more malign entropic vision against which humanity would need to struggle, but the overriding order remained uncontested and as precise as any Newtonian law in physics could be. An existing objective frame still held to the "truth" that rational order itself predominated – that a teleology still predominated existence – and therefore the vision of the structure of life remained essentially the same. A process of displacement may have occurred in the modern world in which the informing particulars have been replaced, but the dominant, objective structure remained intact, and the question of how to "fix" Newtonianism rather than the question of what should replace Newtonianism was the central concern.

The Quantum Leap

Quantum mechanics offers perhaps the first consistent challenge to the dominant, objective structures unquestioningly held to be self-evident for centuries, providing, in part, scientific verification of Kant's philosophy. Whether speaking of an Aristotelian natural philosophy, Newtonian physics, or entropic naturalism, all prior frames of thought assumed scientific objectivity and ultimately asserted confidence in a pervading sense of rational, logical, linear order and purpose. In its analysis of the subatomic universe — the foundation of all reality as we presume to know it — quantum physics challenges both our sense of objective possibility in attaining commonsense, logical conclusions and our confidence that we can fully know the universe around us. Both our epistemological and our ontological securities are challenged.

Two examples of quantum theory's unraveling of prior assumptions should help reveal the challenges this new science places on prior conceptions of reality.[3] Consider the following experiments and attendant results.

A short-barrelled shotgun is aimed at an impervious screen with two slits; the screen is placed between the gun and a detector-wall (see Figure 1).

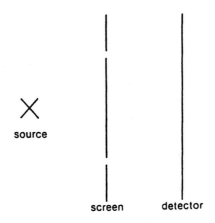

Figure 1. Source/screen/detector.

When the gun is fired, the likely spread (considering ricochets, etc.) of the cartridge's pellets passing through one of the slits and hitting the wall is as depicted graphically in Figure 2.

Figure 2. Single bell curve.

Similarly, it follows that the likely spread of the pellets passing through either slit and hitting the wall would be as depicted in Figure 3.

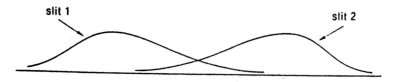

Figure 3. Double bell curve.

Most pellets would strike directly behind one or the other slit, with a trailing off of strikes as one moves further away from the slits, as indicated by the double bell curve.

If, however, one replaces the shotgun with a sound source such as a speaker from a sound system, the experiment will reveal results of wave behavior. A different detector-wall will be set up to measure the frequency of the signal received along points on the wall. Because the oscillating nature of the sound wave will produce a degree of *interference,* the measurement will not be regular but will nonetheless show predictable results of wave activity, given a classical perspective on signal frequency behavior (see Figure 4).

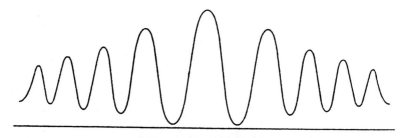

Figure 4. Oscillation graph.

These wave and particle demonstrations reveal traditional expectations of physical behavior. But now we move to the quantum world. Replacing pellets and sound with electrons, the results of the two-slit experiment are quite different and run contrary to any logical, rational expectations whatsoever. Turning the detector-wall into a Geiger counter to report results, the counter is designed to click as electrons strike the wall, which would indicate that the electrons are acting as particles. The clicking sound does in fact occur in such an experiment, but *simultaneously* the detector also reveals that the "particle" accumulation creates not the expected bell curve results but oscillating interference patterns exactly like the above wave results. The electrons, illogically (in the classical sense), are acting as both waves and particles simultaneously. This result is itself highly counterintuitive: How can something be both wave and particle simultaneously?

Yet another problem arises when we work to determine which slot each of the electrons passed through. If we attempt to direct the path of the electrons by leaving only one slit open, the one-slit pattern for electrons will result in a curve similar to the particle-shotgun demonstration. Wave behavior has disappeared altogether, and the electron appears to behave in a traditional manner solely as a particle. Inexplicably, only when both slits are open do we produce *simultaneous* wave and particle results from the electron source. When we limit the electron's potential behavior by choosing to see what it's doing, then it simply behaves as a particle. There is only one, again highly illogical, conclusion that can be drawn about the two-slit experiment: the quantum mechanical conclusion is that for the wave pattern to be made, each individual electron particle must somehow actually pass through *both* slits simultaneously, behaving in essence as waves at the same time they are recorded as behaving like particles. This counterintuitive, illogical, nonrational (irrational?) conclusion is exactly the conclusion that quantum mechanics draws.

Classical logic insists that an object can only be "here" *or* "there," never "here" *and* "there," and the object of study must be either particle *or* wave. But quantum physics challenges that logic with empirical evidence. Quantum "particles" (actually an inappropriate term) can be both here and there – passing through two slits simultaneously – and be both wave and particle. It is actually a matter of regulating quantum behavior that determines whether electrons are particles or particle-waves. Electrons actually change behavior depending on the controls or restrictions placed upon them. If we watch/know/control their trajectory (as in the one-slit test), they behave discretely only as particles; if we eliminate controls (as in the two-slit test) – leaving them unwatched and free to behave as they choose – they behave in counterintuitive, particle-wave ways.

Consider a second demonstration of electron behavior, one that draws equally counterintuitive, illogical conclusions. Marbles of exact size and weight are placed in a machine that discharges them with equal force. The first marble discharged has just enough energy to ascend halfway a small hill set before it; predictably, it stops as its energy is expended and rolls back down to the bottom of the hill. Classical physics assumes, logically, that every subsequent marble of the same exact size and weight will behave exactly the same way when propelled by an equivalent amount of energy. Whatever set of objects is used, predictability of the whole set can be assumed based on the behavior of one precisely studied sample.

However, if these marbles were electrons similarly charged with equal and equally insufficient energy to overcome an obstacle (similar to the above hill), there would remain numerous unpredictable instances when an electron would go against expectations and somehow "tunnel" to the other side. The smooth, predictable release that is seen in the marble example is now replaced by unpredictable, concentrated bursts, according to quantum physics, forcing physicists to admit that determining the behavior of subatomic matter with any degree of certainty (as the classicists once assumed) is an impossibility. Science, now hostage to unpredictability, can only determine the *probability* of behavior, what is likely but never certain to occur.

Unlike classical physics/science, quantum mechanics is a science of probability, not actuality. The world it explores involves a high degree of uncertainty. Such science has clearly lost the precision that Newtonian physics claimed to achieve. In the world of quantum matter, nothing is certain. And virtually *all* of the explanations that this new science presents violate our commonsense logic, our sense of an objectively verifiable, rational, linearly unfolding universe so cleanly articulated by Newtonian physics, the culmination of objectivity and rationalism itself.

Add to this troubling new challenge to classical thought yet another disturbing fact. Efforts to study directly observable quantum phenomena are themselves problematic since observing such "quanta" inevitably entails disturbing subatomic objects of observation by the very means of observation used. Observation alters results, as evidenced in the first particle-wave electron example. In order to locate a particle – as the one-slit experiment allows us to do – its path must be artificially limited to a single trajectory, thereby altering its actual infinite-trajectory behavior. On the other hand, when we loosen our control over the particle – as occurs in the two-slit experiment – quantum material reveals itself to have either no trajectory or every trajectory.

The problem exists in even larger order when considering the whole application of quantum mechanics. When photons (a light source), even x-rays (standard types of observation/recording media, much smaller even than photons) are used to "see" the quantum material under study, these means of detecting quantum activity are powerful enough to alter the behavior of quanta. "Seeing" the object necessitates "bumping" the object, altering its otherwise unobserved behavior. Essentially, we can never "know" a particle's true behavior since the very act of observation alters the results of that observation.

Kant's vision of inevitable human pollution of raw sensory data is verified in this branch of scientific pursuit, in ways that suggest how the human apparatus may actually alter *all* phenomena. Quantum physics concretely verifies the thesis that human reception imposes modification onto reality, in this case an imposition on the subatomic world. But if modification exists on this level, we must at least reopen the question of modification in a more general sense as well, transcending the subatomic world and considering other levels of reality.

So the traditional goal of determining the actual cause-and-effect trajectories of subatomic matter is impossible since quanta apparently have no trajectory. And because "trajectory" cannot even be determined for such observation means as photons and x-rays (themselves being subatomic), scientists cannot determine their effects on the subject and therefore cannot adjust the data received to account for their effects. When adjustments *are* attempted, the environment becomes so artificial (manipulated) that any conclusions about subatomic reality have become subject to almost infinite qualifications and interferences by the observer and his or her choices.

As a result, scientists have accepted a *principle of complementarity,* whereby it is agreed that we will live with the options of knowing either a particle's momentum *or* a particle's position, but because of implicit impossibilities in measurement, we cannot know both simultaneously. We cannot simultaneously see a particle and know how it got there without creating artificial restrictions. In general terms, the result of this dilemma is that conclusions are always highly dependent on choices made by the experimenter and are actually influenced by the mere presence of the experimenter. The very goal of classical physics – the study of position and motion – becomes unattainable. The very "reality principle" that is the foundation of scientific enterprise – that there is a world outside us which is objectively comprehensible – comes under question. As Polkinghorne observes, "Clearly quantum mechanics, with its irreducible degree of disturbance in making a measurement and the consequent uncertainty principle limiting knowledge, has not eased this problem" (*The Quantum World*, p. 72). If objectivity were ever a possibility in an Aristotelian or Newtonian universe, it is certainly an impossibility in a quantum universe. The eye-god objectivity of classical thought is here replaced by the meddling interference of the investigator. In fact, even if eye/god objectivity were possible (eliminating interference), the nature of this subatomic universe is such that the comforting goals of establishing a deterministic scientific view of the universe are no longer possible except in the abstracted realm of probability; future actuality cannot be determined even if it *were* possible to view reality objectively.

Accepting the fact that the above summary of quantum mechanics is vastly simplified and overgeneralized, one very clear philosophical consequence of this new science can nonetheless be made. Quantum mechanics seems to endorse the philosophical positions of Kant's manipulative human faculties and Berkeley's subjective eye/human (that is, Berkeley's vision minus his insertion of the omniscient eye/god). What we know is predicated at least as much on how we see as on what there is. The phenomena that quantum mechanics reveal to us are clearly that – phenomena, not noumena. Subjective choices are made, presumably conforming to some private desire to see a thing as we choose to see it. We make choices concerning apparatus and limit events as a matter of necessity.

This is the position of the celebrated Copenhagen school of quantum theory, that there is no separation between the observer and that which is observed. We are, as pioneer quantum physicist Niels Bohr succinctly stated, inseparably and simultaneously actors as well as onlookers in this universe. If this position in fact is what quantum mechanics verifies, then quantum mechanics actually reveals to us less about the "real" than it does about the limitations of human inquiry. And, furthermore, quantum mechanics seemingly denies teleology, since even minute determinations of cause and effect are impossible. If quantum science's conclusions are accurate, then in Einstein's own despairing terms (Einstein being of a classical inclination despite his vast contributions to postclassical science), the world is chaos and God is merely shooting craps.

The results of this new science argue for the creation of a sophisticated, latter-day process of epistemology (some would call it "gaming") as much as it unearths a revolutionarily new ontology. How we know and what there is are both called into question. A new logic needs to evolve that can embrace counterintuitive conclusions and that can accept a noncausal, unpredictable universe. Can one separate the two paths of study, or the two objects of study? Presumably one cannot.

Finding a Nexus: Quantum Physics and Contemporary Theatre

If the scientific processes and empirical results of quantum mechanics cannot be determined to be "objective," and if what we know is itself called into question, then finally what is the difference between this new science and the arts? Historically the sciences and the arts were two enterprises with the single goal of understanding existence. The essential distinction was that one enterprise insisted that its practitioners strictly adhere to principles of objectivity while the other accepted the subjective engagement of its creator with the work. While Zola worked to unite the two disciplines by making art more like science, with quantum physics an opposite movement has perhaps inadvertently occurred, for if this science can no longer claim strict objectivity, then indeed science itself has become an "art," since it aims to articulate what ultimately amounts to a personal expression or interpretation of existence and belief systems. Ironically, this turn toward subjectivity is actually what Zola's aesthetic philosophy anticipated, popular understandings of Zola notwithstanding (see the Introduction).

Perhaps this "growing together" explains why science (the hard as well as applied and social sciences) in the twentieth century relies more and more on theatrical metaphors to explain itself. Consider the following from Polkinghorne: "What we have succeeded in doing so far is to set the scene for the quantum mechanical play. . . . All the scenery of states of motion is in place and the caste of observable quantities assembled" (*The Quantum World*, p. 29). The extended theatrical metaphor speaks to the very point here that doing science is like creating drama, the scientist being the controller of events much as the playwright and director control the theatre. Furthermore, Polkinghorne's outline reads very much like the "scientific" process that Zola articulates as central to the creation of naturalist drama: selecting agents, ascribing certain inherent qualities to them, and then setting the scene in motion. Later, explaining two contrasting approaches to quantum mechanics, Polkinghorne adds: "In a bizarre extension of our theatrical metaphor, Schrodinger moved the scenery with the actors standing still, whilst Heisenberg left the scenery untouched and let the actors move around" (*The Quantum World* p. 29). This account is admittedly intended for a lay audience, and Polkinghorne even admits the incompleteness of the metaphor. However, as one may recall, Niels Bohr himself, so influential in the development of quantum theory, made the same connection when he asserted, "We are both onlookers and actors in the great drama of existence."

As noted earlier, Martin Esslin, in "Naturalism in Context," observes that though the naturalist scientific doctrine articulated by Zola in the nineteenth century may no longer find strict formal proponents in twentieth-century drama and literature, theatre of all forms nonetheless acknowledges the legacy of Zola and naturalism in that "an experimental exploration of reality in its widest possible sense"[4] is the ultimate goal of theatre. Esslin adds that although naturalism did not strictly remain the dominant mode of expression on the Western stage in the twentieth century (at least not in Europe), "the Expressionism of the 1920's, Brecht's epic theatre of the Thirties and Forties, the Theatre of the Absurd of the Fifties and Sixties were still essentially continuations of and reactions *against* Naturalism" (p. 67). Theatre has accepted and essentially self-consciously absorbed the precepts of scientific inquiry – empiricism and rational process – adopting a naturalist-scientific "spirit of free enquiry, totally unprejudiced, unburdened by preconceived ideas" (p. 70). While we can still see free inquiry at work, we now see, ironically, that neither science nor art escapes prejudice or preconception. Esslin is right, but in ways he did not fully recognize.

The strength of Esslin's argument lies in the fact that Esslin sees an entangling of the scientific and artistic processes. Which discipline influences which now appears to be a central question. Or is it? One should recall that quantum physics developed during the first quarter of the twentieth century, fully blossoming around 1925. The roots of the absurd, surrealism – which assaulted rationalist and determinist foundations – similarly developed prior to and during this period. Could it be that science and art contemporaneously developed similar theories of existence, not necessarily one dependent on the other but both dependent on the current cultural and intellectual spirit? And could it be that once developed, they each reciprocally confirmed and then fed off the other? Could this not lead to a conclusion about a Western cultural Zeitgeist, a suggestion that questions of indeterminacy culturally arose *prior* to scientific and artistic formulations but were a catalyst for both? Were scientists *looking* for indeterminacy (consciously or unconsciously), given the fact that, as David E. R. George points out, "Scientists too are trapped in history and in culture and can do no more than operate on its assumptions"?[5] After all, questions of indeterminacy and uncertainty certainly arose in the arts well before the 1925 formulations of quantum mechanics. Hindsight provides a vision of history that suggests inevitability, but from a local perspective we see that choosing to privilege one vision over another is just that: a *choice.*

The above points lead to one certain conclusion: it is now virtually impossible to determine whether science informs our cultural perceptions of existence or whether current cultural perceptions inform science. Whatever the answer here, it is clear that elements in theatre – particularly performance theory – serve extremely well as metaphors for the current exercises in quantum science and vice versa. George observes three "forces" in theatre as pointing to the forces that are central to the quantum world: "the Spectator, Space/Time, and the Actor" ("Quantum Theatre – Potential Theatre," p. 173). In performance art, the spectator has been invited into the event in the same manner that the scientist has become involved in his or her experimentation. Performance's manipulation of space-time as "playful distortions or futile attempts at reproductions" (p. 173) echoes science's concessions of manipulation or distortion of reality. At least one theatre practitioner in fact comes to mind as one reads the passage by Polkinghorne, here again quoted: "In a bizarre extension of our theatre metaphor, Schrödinger moved the scenery with the actors standing still, while Heisenberg left the scenery untouched and let the actors move around" (*The Quantum World,* p. 29). Robert Wilson's epic productions abound in Schrödingerian episodes of moving scenery and Heisenbergian actors disassociated from the milieu, as well as numerous other distortions of traditional theatrical, rational, linear practices.

George adds to his observation a point less relevant to Wilson but clearly relevant to other instances of contemporary performance: "Directorial loss of control over actors in performance is now experienced by scientists over their 'subjects'" ("Quantum Theatre – Potential Theatre," p. 174). In many cases "purer" forms of theatre eliminate directors altogether, creating "happenings" unpolluted by directorial control and the order of repeated or duplicated performances. In other cases director and performer merge, creating an entanglement between director and material – as in the cases of performance artists like Spalding Gray, Laurie Anderson, and Penny Arcade – similar to the observer–observed entanglement espoused by the early Romantics and confirmed by quantum science.

The theatre of the performance artist may have a limited, elitist, coterie audience, and so the conclusions presented by such a theatre may not necessarily reflect a larger, culturally predominant perspective. But in *Actors and Onlookers,* Natalie Crohn Schmitt makes the observation that though such science–art parallels are evident in smaller, coterie-oriented performance collectives like the Wooster Group, "they are not limited to such theatres." She adds:

> Performances based on this aesthetic also attract sizable audiences in regional theaters and at international festivals, and many college productions use some of these aesthetic principles as a matter of course. The students, raised on postmodern elements of "Sesame Street" and rock video, are undaunted.[6]

Schmitt goes so far as to demonstrate elements of this conceptual revolution in, of all things, *A Chorus Line* to verify the pervasiveness of such thought in our culture. Subjectivity of perception and ultimate indeterminacy of action is virtually a given in all strata of postmodern culture.

Consider recent international events documented by the news media. Though telejournalists may attempt to insist on objectivity in their work, the fact remains that when they, as observers, arrive on a scene, actions and events are invariably modified. That many governments today ban news crews from potentially volatile scenes is as much a result of a desire to avoid negative publicity as it is an attempt to avoid having the crews inadvertently create an atmosphere that encourages protest and violence, something that almost inevitably erupts when such an "observer" audience arrives. The spectator/camera/eye modifies behavior by its presence. The mechanisms of observation alter the behavior of the observed, forcing the spectator and event to interact in ways parallel to the interactive desires of postmodern performance artists as well as in ways similar to the quantum physicist and his/her subject of study. In Eastern Europe and other sites of political and economic crises, similar observer/eye engagement succeeded at undermining and supplanting the omniscient Big Brother (the malevolent political equivalent of Berkeley's eye/god) of corrupt regimes, forcing an adjustment and resulting abandonment of tyrannical behavior in all but the most extreme cases (China being, to date, the most notable exception). It is this new awareness of an inextricably interactive agency in observer–observed performance/behavior of all types that has led Herbert Blau to write his encompassing 1990 treatise, *The Audience,*[7] whereby *all* aspects of this performative interaction in our culture (and prior cultures as well) are addressed.

The spirit of drama itself – not just performance – appears more and more allied to the thinking found in quantum mechanics. Moving back several decades to locate the phenomenon known as theatre of the absurd, one can see that the anti- or counter- or non-rationalist logic developed while explaining quantum behavior validates the absurdist foundations presented in those strange absurdist universes. The metaphysics of the absurd (including the multiple perspectives presented by the playwrights included within that loose-knit collective) has paradoxically been "scientifically" verified.

One critical point to bear in mind is that, though Schmitt accurately argues that this new aesthetic has permeated even popular culture, it is not entirely clear to what extent quantum theory (or the absurd) does or should influence daily, mundane existence. Polkinghorne, for example, notes that Heisenberg observed that, philosophically speaking, quantum mechanics "form a world of potentialities or possibilities rather than one of things or facts" (*The Quantum World*, p. 81). When dealing with the workaday macroworld of things and facts, that world of daily existence and perceptions, rationalist intuitive thought – formally encapsulated in Newtonian physics – still serves admirably to explain most existence. And Schmitt observes that oftentimes even admirers of the new theatre aesthetic that parallels quantum advances,

> share not only Aristotle's commonsense idea that reality is a given – that is, that we possess means that are not problematic both for knowing as fact what exists or happens and for representing it in art – but also the view of reality implicit in Aristotle's aesthetic. (*Actors and Onlookers*, p. 2)

A sort of schizophrenia sets in. Even while our intellectual side may acknowledge some principle of uncertainty, our practical side (to set up an unfair dichotomy) operates under Aristotelian-Newtonian principles of certainty. So when Shakespeare creates a master of uncertainty in Hamlet, he still finds a certain necessity in creating the frame of certain resolution, via Fortinbras, for *Hamlet*. And when Tom Stoppard, in *Hapgood*, sets out in the manner of the metaphysical wits (that is, as Dr. Johnson observed, violently yoking together discordant ideas and images) to ally quantum behavior with human behavior (at least in the world of international espionage), the result is that we enjoy the quantum "gamesmanship" of the play but perhaps resist any urge to accept the full thematic implications of the quantum model when applied to general human behavior. There is a "naturalist" goal of consistency and stability, even a naturalist faith, in the characters that Stoppard creates in his world of *Hapgood*. There are still strong traces of Newtonian determinacy and Aristotelian aesthetics. Only at the boundaries, or perhaps critical intersections, of our culture does indeterminacy find dominion.

This leads us to two points. First, whatever our degree of accepting quantum indeterminacy, virtually all of us behave in our daily existences in a manner more closely reflected in the naturalist brand of art and thought. We implicitly accept the world as governed by causal relations and determined behavior. Otherwise, expectation would be impossible and randomness would prevail within our societies. From this observation on behavior comes the second point. Perhaps because of a reluctant though growing awareness of the inescapable fact that indeterminacy abounds in our culture, that the boundaries and intersections are becoming more prevalent – despite our urge to cling to causal and determinist frames – we have truly become aware of the nature of play, that is, that the rules we live by are like arbitrarily concocted rules to a game set up by its participants. Determinacy is not necessarily some objectively real informing element (as the Aristotelians and Newtonians "scientifically" insist) but is rather a mutually accepted, epistemologically constructed manipulation of behavior. To play in the game of "sane" existence, one must behave according to the rules, more or less, and those rules today engage causal/determinist precepts, though chaos theory, as we shall see, modifies those precepts to accommodate an indeterminacy we increasingly are realizing cannot be overcome, much less overlooked.

The New Science Metaphor

Aristotle the scientist saw order in his universe and described what he saw. Observing that art should imitate nature, he likewise described – in the *Poetics* – the order he saw in drama. Centuries later, we still generally accept both Aristotle's scientific and aesthetic descriptions, turning them into prescriptions about reality and art. The new science, however, calls Aristotle's sightings into doubt on both fronts. What remains is a belief that art should imitate nature, but which view of nature should we follow?

Our modern-postmodern culture is no longer dominated by a pervading frame of thought; or more precisely, a culture like ours is coming to be dominated by a frame of thought that needfully accepts multiple frames of thought in order to explain reality in its totality. This fact does not merely accept the point that other modes of expression may somehow be allowed to exist while one mode nonetheless remains true, a point that many critics still adhere to. Rather, there should be a change in perspective that concedes that our new, postmodern world of actors and onlookers brings with it a realization of human manipulative capacities that open legitimate separate perspectives on observed reality. Currently, however, resistance to new world visions remains, in favor of the objectivist illusion of a single truth/reality, resulting in little more than a humoring tolerance disguising an actual intolerant posture. Schmitt observes the existence of intolerance among the theatre community, even among such respected scholars as, for example, Ronald Hayman, who

> presumes that whereas traditional Aristotelian theater shows us reality, contemporary theater, "anti-theatre," is "hostile to reality, though the anti-world it creates can never provide a viable alternative to reality." In Hayman's view, contemporary theater is "negative, destructive, . . . reductionist and abstractionist." (*Actors and Onlookers*, p. 2)

Hayman, of course, is not alone in his defense of the "true" thought of the "true" theatre against the charlatanism of contemporary upstarts. Like the others, however, Hayman fails to realize or simply rejects the position that contemporary thought puts forward, namely that a theatre that monolithically accepts the Aristotelian-Newtonian-naturalist metaphor is itself reductionist and abstractionist, denying the fundamental interactive agency of the human eye/god in its association with the world and accepting a rationalist, objective frame of understanding when such a frame is undermined by the very scientific process it claims to trust. Defenders of the Aristotelian theatre, such as Hayman, reject the frame of thought that accepts multiple frames. So while the new science frame of thought should accept Aristotelianism as legitimately true for certain conditions within the overall frame of truths-finding, it necessarily must reject any Aristotelian claim of singular primacy. While the Aristotelian theatre could be accepted by the new frame of thought as providing *one* vision of reality operating under certain limiting conditions, its vision must first be stripped of its insistence that it is *the* vision of reality, a significant concession indeed, though not an impossible one, since, as we've seen, even Zola seems ultimately to make such a concession.

It appears that because the epistemological and ontological frame verified by the new science admits an overriding human subjectivity and thereby encourages proliferation of human per-

spectives on truth, we need more than ever to establish and outline their particular foundations, to articulate the premises of each
work of art more clearly than at any time previous. Perhaps, as
Schmitt notes in "Theorizing About Performance,"[8] this need to
articulate premises is itself reason why the art world has become
so involved in theory. In a world where premises can no longer be
universally acknowledged or generically conceded (where even
taste is no longer a cultural constant), foundations need clarification through actual articulation rather than by implication (i.e., by
"seeing" a work and deducing premises), almost at times on a consistently individual basis. As Schmitt notes, "Moving towards no
end, all particles transmutable into other particles, the world does
not express meaning and has no essence. In theatre this idea is no
longer cause for despair" ("Theorizing About Performance," p.
234). We now see that even when we work within a frame that can
fruitfully utilize an Aristotelian vision and creatively *create* an
informing fiction, we more than ever need to articulate what our
choices have been, since they are no longer merely accepted
"givens" universally applicable or universally conceded.

We need to articulate our premises and clarify the fictions we
begin from in our efforts to "play" at ordering our existences. Epistemology and ontology, as Berkeley and Kant argued centuries
ago, have become entangled. There is no objectively observable
"out there"; or if there is, then there is no way, objectively speaking, to know it. In the twentieth century this observation has
become a liberating pronouncement and perhaps ironically has
brought us one step closer to "truth"-as-truth(s)-itself/themselves.

Quantum mechanics clearly opened the door. While Stoppard
ingeniously introduces a quantum metaphor to the stage in his
play *Hapgood,* we should nevertheless bear in mind the less specific but perhaps more important legacy of quantum mechanics,
that it opened the way for fundamental re-evaluations of cultural
assumptions on many fronts, not the least of which led to chaos
theory itself.

Stoppard's "Hapgood": Double
Agency and Quantum Personalities

With *Hapgood* (1988), Tom Stoppard clearly and consciously
entered the realm of contemporary science, using quantum

physics as a metaphor for human behavior. Given that quantum mechanics applies strictly to the behavior of subatomic particles, Stoppard's application of the quantum paradigm is only metaphorical, while chaos theory is more literally applied in his 1993 play *Arcadia*. This limitation notwithstanding, quantum mechanics is aptly utilized in *Hapgood* by an artist who has been interested in the sciences throughout his playwriting career. While *Hapgood* is Stoppard's first actual application of contemporary science, Clive James makes the accurate assessment that "the appropriate analogies" throughout Stoppard's career "lie just as much in modern physics as in modern philosophy."[9] For example, Stoppard credits James D. Watson's *The Double Helix: A Personal Account of the Discovery of DNA*[10] with providing him with a model that explains his own writing process.[11] Indeed, much of his earlier work plays with structures first posited by the scientific community, the double helix certainly included.

With the creation of *Hapgood*, however, there is a direct "new science" influence. Katherine E. Kelly observes that significant portions of dialogue by Kerner, *Hapgood's* resident quantum physicist, derive directly "from *The Feynman Lectures on Physics*, especially those in chapter 37, 'Quantum Behavior.'"[12] And for *Arcadia*, Stoppard acknowledges a debt to James Gleick's *Chaos: Making a New Science*.[13] Perhaps the fact that Stoppard has a son who studies physics, with whom he discusses the sciences, helps explain his increasingly specific interest in the sciences.[14] At any rate, *Hapgood* is Stoppard's first play overtly utilizing science, going much further than his use of science in earlier works.

Hapgood is a spy thriller that operates at several science-informed levels. First, as Kelly has observed, the play follows the pattern of a scientific experiment, reminiscent of Zola's scientific approach to the theatre: "Act 1 leads to a hypothesis; act 2 carries out the experiment. The denouement leaves to us the interpretation of the results" (*Tom Stoppard*, p. 155). The hypothesis to be tested involves the nature of human behavior, whether it involves an "agent" (a term in both espionage and science) whose actions are singular and unified or one whose actions indeterminately "leap" in ways simulating quantum behavior.

The play opens with a "radio play" that initially presents an illusion of objective certainty. We hear factual reports of agent movements, which upon the actual opening of the play become hopelessly muddled. Agents enter and exit changing-room stalls, depositing and exchanging briefcases in a sort of shell game that is virtually impossible to follow. After what amounts to a blown assignment by the British and American forces, the British leader, Hapgood, and her crew conclude that the *only* solution to this shell game had to be that there were two identical Russian agents posing as a single agent. We later discover that two sets of twins – not just one set – were at work.

Kerner, the double agent and physicist who is the center of attention in this espionage matter, reveals that the shell game presented in this first scene amounted to a reproduction of a centuries-old puzzle involving the bridges of Königsberg (interestingly, the home of Immanuel Kant): "An ancient amusement of the people of Königsberg was to try to cross all seven bridges without crossing any of them twice."[15] What finally was concluded was "It can't be done, you need two walkers" (p. 46); the shell game that opened the play "was the bridges of Königsberg, only simpler" (p. 46). This anecdotal event of logical deduction literally sets the stage for more sophisticated applications of scientific/mathematical deductions, but the play's opening actions provide the first intimations of the necessity of accepting simultaneously existent presences in order to provide explanations of actions within the play.

These actions at first are quite simple, involving the mysteries of the cat-and-mouse espionage world. It is at this stage that we are introduced to quantum mechanics. As Kerner notes,

> The particle world is the dream world of the intelligence officer. An electron can be here or there at the same moment. You can choose; it can go from here to there without going in between; it can pass through two doors at the same time, or from one door to another by a path which is there for all to see until someone looks, and then the act of looking has made it take a different path. . . . It defeats surveillance because when you know what it's doing you can't be certain where it is, and when you know where it is you can't be certain what it's doing. (*Hapgood*, p. 48)

Confusing at first, this quantumlike espionage plot re-enacts and reveals material crucial for Stoppard's final points, for the double-double agents' shell game works like Stoppard's coin-tossing opening in his 1966 *Rosencrantz and Guildenstern Are Dead:* in both cases they are crucial starting points explaining and explained by the play. In the case of *Hapgood,* the literal twin trick becomes more complexly a "twinning" trick where one "agent" becomes two and where observer becomes observer and observed, an entwining of twinning first glimpsed at the play's opening but developed beyond mere anecdote as the play progresses.

What these grown adults – the entire cast – are acting out on the stage is what Kerner "teaches" us about quantum machanics – the material Stoppard borrowed from Feynman's lectures. The thing that quantum mechanics challenges – the notion of an objective, rationalist grounding of reality – is the thing the chief British officer, Blair, needs so desperately to understand in order to recover stolen, nationally sensitive property. It is, however, the thing Blair refuses to grasp. Significantly, it is likely also the thing Stoppard's audiences resist grasping as well.

Kerner observes, "A double agent is more like a trick of light" (p. 10), an observation from which he moves to explain the basic tenet of quantum mechanics, summarized by "the case of the experiment with the two holes."[16] (This experiment was presented and explained earlier in this chapter.) A wave pattern occurs until we watch the experiment, in which instant the particle pattern occurs. As Kerner observes, "Every time we don't look we get wave pattern. Every time we look to see how we get wave pattern, we get particle pattern. The act of observing determines the reality" (p. 12). The telling application to the world of espionage is, "You get what you interrogate for" (p. 12). Kerner proves this point when he observes that the Russians see him in one light while the British see him in another.

At this point we have moved from the literal matter of doubling – as displayed in the opening scenes – to the more sophisticated matter of double agency, that one person/agent can be seen simultaneously two different ways, as quantum material can be simultaneously both particle and wave. A matter of observer prejudice determines how X is (are?) seen. Kerner is a perfect subject for scrutiny under these conditions. He is both physicist and secret agent, by birth German and Russian (having been born in the German city of Königsberg which was annexed as Russian after World War II and renamed Kaliningrad), by current affiliation both Russian and British (working for both governments), by inclination an artist though by training a scientist, fluent in both Russian and English, lover and employee of Hapgood (the father of her son). The job

for Blair and Hapgood is to determine which of each of the oppositions Kerner actually is. That he is both defeats Blair and Hapgood
before they even begin. There is no either/or to be deduced, but a
both/and to be accepted and cultivated.

Trained to exercise rational, objectivist deduction, Blair and
Hapgood refuse to accept simultaneous conjunctions of any of
these qualities. They have, quite simply, become perfected per-
sonifications of the culturally inscribed processes of logical, linear
deduction. Hapgood demonstrates her singular rational grasp of
reality through "the grid," a standard tool of logic which she uses
in her work and which she demonstrates by helping her son at
school find a missing key. Her mind is so well organized that she
can play chess from memory. Even more rigorously logical than
Hapgood (though far less imaginative), Blair is entirely dedicated
to the "technical," at the expense of any distraction that may be
considered "personal." The logic of excluded middle – either/or –
formally rules both of their lives. Again Kerner to Blair:

> You have been too long in the spy business, you think everybody
> has no secret or one big secret, they are what they seem or they are
> the opposite. . . . If only you could figure it out like looking into me
> to find my root. . . . We're all doubles. Even you. . . . [w]e're not so
> one-or-the-other. (p. 72)

Through the course of the play, despite their initial sets of similarities, it does eventually evolve that Blair and Hapgood are fundamentally different. Hapgood's iconoclasm surfaces on occasion,
revealing breaks from linear and rational professionalism that
Blair will never allow himself to pursue. Blair remains a rationalist constant, while Hapgood shows signs of openness to Kerner's
quantum conversion. While Kerner is a center of attention for a
great deal of the play, the potential for Hapgood's conversion to
Kerner's perspective circles onto center stage during the latter part
of the play.

Stoppard's process of focusing on Hapgood's conversion goes
through some initial phases first. The actual twinness of the two
Russians in the opening scene first directs us toward the idea of
doubling, setting the scene for the other set of twins, the Ridleys,
which provides an appropriate conceptual transition. The two
Ridleys succeed at carrying out the Ridley counterespionage plans
in Athens, Paris, and now in London. And the motive for the one

Ridley engaging in counterintelligence leads us into Hapgood's dilemma. The play's Ridley (rather than his unstaged twin) has grown to see the whole espionage enterprise as a useless game, a conclusion that allows his personal side to invade the technical or professional side. He reveals two sides, but he begins to confuse the two. Concerning the plans that are so vital to the British and Russians and which may cost Hapgood her son's life if they are not handed over to the Russians, Ridley suggests:

> Why don't we just give it to them [the Russians]? What does it matter? . . . [A] kid like that, he should be in bed anyway, we can all get some sleep.
>
> Look, what are we talking about? Are we talking about a list of agents in place? Are we talking about blowing the work names? The batting order in Half Moon Street? Any of those and all right, the boy maybe has to take his chances. But what has Kerner got? (*Derisively*) The solution to the anti-particle trap. Since when was the anti-particle trap a problem? (p. 59)

Ridley allows his personal to invade his technical side, in ways superficially similar to Kerner's quantumlike double agency. After all, Kerner appears to have helped the Russians after they discovered that Joe was Kerner's (and Hapgood's) son; Kerner is comfortably willing to sacrifice British security for the sake of Joe. But while Ridley agrees to do the same, he is finally unable to integrate this otherwise schizophrenic behavior in the same ways that Kerner is. He is literally two Ridleys, not two together, but two separate beings.

Kerner understands the nature and consequences of doubling – as evidenced by his quantum metaphor anecdote – and he operates accordingly by enfolding his two halves into a seamless whole. Ridley does not understand, and he muddles his affairs as a result by remaining in the realm of "either/or" (either an agent for Russia or for Britain) rather than the quantum both/and (agent for both Russia and Britain), the realm Kerner engages.

Ridley reveals another level of muddle when he speaks of Hapgood:

> She should have given him [her son Joe] a daddy instead of getting a buzz out of running joes to please an old bastard [Blair] who doesn't want her and never will. . . . I'll get her kid back for her but it's only personal. If she sets me up I'll kill her. (pp. 81, 82)

On this level, too, Ridley basically still sees only an either/or option (either an agent or a friend) and is unable to operate *both* as a government/technical agent *and* as a personal agent. While Hapgood seems comfortable running both j/Joes, Ridley cannot occupy two worlds simultaneously.

Ridley's muddle about the nature of the world(s) he's entered leads to his death while Kerner's clarity about the same leads to his ability to manipulate reality around him, especially those "agents" (again, in both senses of the word) operating from the perspective of the old, linear regime. The knowledge Kerner has leads to his being able to survive within the entanglement of the old order and perhaps even to thrive in the coming new order.

The problem for Hapgood is that she needs to learn from Kerner; what is fortunate is that unlike Ridley she has the opportunity, and unlike Ridley or Blair, she demonstrates the inclination. She shows signs of hungering for such knowledge, the symptoms being her iconoclastic, currently schizophrenic behavior. She sends postcards to her son Joe from foreign undercover assignments, uses secret technology to communicate with a chess opponent in Canada, uses the red phone – a direct line to Downing Street – to call her son. She cherishes the use of the nickname "mother" in her job and equally cherishes sharing business secrets with her son.

But actual, clinical schizophrenia is not what Stoppard calls for, though Stoppard does build on Hapgood's schizophrenic existence by having her actually play her own double in the sting operation that catches Ridley(s). Here Stoppard engages yet another level of human behavior. The Hapgood alter ego is a scattered, profane opposite of the agent Hapgood, a part of agent Hapgood's self she seems thus far to have successfully subdued. Performing as her own alter ego, Hapgood actually analyzes herself before Ridley while under cover:

> Well, she [the real Hapgood] was the scholarship girl and I was the delinquent. Having the kid was good for her, she always thought the delinquents had the bastards and the scholarship girls had the wedding. It shook up her view of the world, slightly. (p. 77)

Playing the opposite role so well could be anticipated by the presentation of the various cracks in Hapgood's more formal personality. And it very tellingly reveals that Hapgood has subdued a very vital "other" within her being, in conformity with cultural expectations of consistent rational behavior (where even delinquency is a sort of consistency and conformity).

What Stoppard appears to suggest is that cultural expectations should change to allow for the more natural full integration of apparently (rationally) irreconcilable behaviors within each self. Schizophrenia alone is of course not the answer. Though there may be a kinship between the two perspectives, schizophrenia is a splitting of personality, while a quantum personality is – counterintuitively – a harmonious coexistence of the seemingly incompatible, the same pattern of behavior(s) as presented in the quantum model. One must recall that schizophrenia is based in part on a rationalist denial of the possibility of contradictory simultaneity. Rationally and empirically speaking, multiple personalities (a documentable illness) and a quantum personality (Stoppard's suggested solution to "illness") may appear to be the same. But making the distinction between the rational perception and the antirational reality of quantum behavior is crucial. Kerner understands and in the process not only masterfully manipulates the intelligence world but life in general as well.

Where Ridley was inclined but failed both to understand and thereby to master this new knowledge, Hapgood is in the position to do both. She has learned that the personal and technical in their broadest reaches constitute the whole of her existence. Following the numerous disruptions of her life in the play, it can be ventured that Hapgood will return to her career a more sophisticated "mother," working quantumlike to be both here and there at numerous levels of reality in a manner she had not previously fully understood. Or it could be ventured that Hapgood realizes that a world run by Blairs is a world worth retiring from. Regardless of her professional decision, now knowing the necessity of such a counterrational coexistence, perhaps she can more successfully and more consciously execute her heretofore unconscious inclination. Cohesiveness of being should not be singular but multiple and simultaneous. Health comes not from achieving singular reality but from embracing multiplicity.

The difficulties inherent in negotiating the difficult trajectories of contemporary society virtually mandate the double (multiple, actually) agency of the quantum personality. Modern culture, as

Hapgood seems eventually to realize, currently does not fully understand or endorse the necessity of such behavior. Science, perhaps cued by halting modernist declarations of fragmentation and schizophrenia in contemporary culture, has formalized a reifying alternative to simple despair; society would do well to understand, accept, and adapt the results gleaned from nature and articulated by the new scientists. Each discrete member of society must at times accept its "linear" particle reality (as self-interested, private individuals) but must also utilize its quantum potential. To a great degree we imprison ourselves in our outdated urges to be viable "Newtonian" individuals conforming to a traditional perspective of being either/or in whole (as with Blair) or alternatingly (as with Jekyll-and-Hyde Ridley).

This element of self-knowledge of the new possibilities of the world is exactly what is often missed by observers, critics, and participants of both postmodern life and the art it s(t)imulates. Unlike the absurdist paradigm arguing that the world is governed by chance, the quantum paradigm is governed by a belief in free-swinging choice among countless probable options, including the often necessary possibility of simultaneous choices. As counterintuitive as that may sound, it is nonetheless an option limited only by our limited sense of possibility, not a limitation imposed upon us by nature, if, that is, we can learn to accept the quantum paradigm rather than the Newtonian/naturalist paradigm. What we will see in future chapters is how the chaos paradigm more precisely defines the variety of choices suggested by the quantum paradigm. But the quantum paradigm is important nonetheless because it has opened the way to these further refinements, beyond the refinement already inherent in the quantum paradigm.

With *Hapgood*, Stoppard has clearly moved beyond absurdism, but in ways even more precise than Hersh Zeifman has suggested. In "A Trick of the Light: Tom Stoppard's *Hapgood* and Postabsurdist Theater,"[17] Zeifman argues that, despite entering "an absurdist nightmare" (p. 193) at the climax of the play (during the confrontation with and shooting of Ridley), Hapgood ends with a sense of optimism, symptomatic of her very name: "Chance may be positive as well as negative: Hap (defined by the *OED* as 'chance or fortune: . . . luck, lot') is specifically linked to *good*" (p. 197). But Stoppard is doing more than merely presenting a picture of hope against all hope; Hapgood is doing more than simply seeing good in some newly discovered happenstance circumstances. We are in fact looking at more than chance when we utilize the quantum paradigm. The quantum paradigm subscribes neither to chance nor to linear determinism, but to a system of probability, less secure than determinism/fate but more stable than randomness/absurdism. (This is the point that chaos theory will further help refine.) So Stoppard is presenting more than a tonal shift in his "postabsurdism"; he is doing more than suggesting we embrace or even accept a world of chance/absurdism. He is in fact arguing for an actual reconstructed order rising out of the absurdist gloom, less defined than Newton asserted but far more defined than randomness/absurdism suggests. Hapgood survives uncertainty to reclaim a renewed sense of how order actually operates; she learns to accept Kerner's model of extenuating uncertainty and simultaneous behavior/being. And through that lesson, she very likely will be able to regroup and re-enter the world freed from the fear of following Ridley to his doom. Zeifman, ultimately, is accurate in seeing *Hapgood* as a postabsurdist play, but he does not fully rise to see that Stoppard is playing with more than simply a *spirit* of optimism. In *Hapgood*, Stoppard has actually presented a valid *foundation* on which to base his optimism.

Willy Loman's Quantum Personality, and Others

In a restrospective look at early postmodern theatre, Enoch Brater observed that "[p]laywrights like Beckett now made us see as new things that were always there in front of our eyes, but never before in such sharp relief."[18] Beckett's follower, Stoppard, has with *Hapgood* provided a similar opportunity to see in sharper relief the works of other earlier playwrights, this time from a post-Beckettian, postabsurdist perspective. Having provided a working paradigm/metaphor, Stoppard has made it possible to review several significant previous studies of human personality and to reveal fundamental flaws in the self-perceptions of those personalities. Willy Loman, the tragic Everyman of Arthur Miller's *Death of a Salesman* (1949), is a good case in point.

The quantum paradigm would suggest that Willy needs to

accept personal validation *simultaneously* as both father and salesman, that subscription to one or the other ideal is insufficient, and that failure at both is of course disaster. Instead, Willy chooses the linearly simple and mythically/culturally inscribed (delusional) option of hoping to find both family and business success in one and the other line of behavior. We have in essence a culturally prescribed schizophrenia striving to find some unifying nexus. So Willy works to a degree to find success in business, as his role model Dave Singleman was apparently able to do in an earlier generation. (Recall that we only know Singleman through Willy's recollection.) But as Willy himself even admits, "Today, it's all cut and dried, and there's no chance for bringing friendship to bear – or personality."[19] Or, alternately, he strives to find business success within his family. For example, when Biff finally breaks down and confesses his love for his father, all that Willy can do is announce, "that boy is going to be magnificent" (*Death of a Salesman,* p. 133), and later, about the insurance money, "When the mail comes he'll be ahead of Bernard again" (p. 135). Like Stoppard's Ridley, Willy schizophrenically moves from one choice to another, never envisioning the possibility of embracing both options simultaneously.

Willy, however, is something more than a Ridley, though less than a Kerner. His tragedy is that he's ultimately less competent than a Hapgood to see the need for and the ways to change. It is true that in virtually every instance of interpersonal relationships, Willy wants to merge both ideals – family love and business success – in a single line of endeavor. Family should be "Loman Brothers," and work should be family. Ultimately, it's not that Willy's dreams are foolish; it's that he believes a single line of action, followed as a discrete personality could perhaps have followed in the past, could possibly succeed in the complex world that's grown up around him. He senses the thing Hapgood learns but doesn't know how to get what he desires, trapped as he is in his delusions of an idyllic, simple, and discrete past. Perhaps realizing the (post)modern necessity of being both here and there, both father and salesman, would have helped him at an earlier stage in his life onto the path of success at both, whereas his actual decision has resulted in double failure. Joking too much and striving, unsuccessfully, to be well liked on the road, he fails to develop the business acumen to succeed, while his blind commitment to business success ruins his relationship with his sons, whom he singularly hopes will find success where he failed.

Willy's boss, the modern businessman Howard, is only superficially closer to being both here and there than Willy is, by virtue of technology that allows him to bring his wife and children to work, in the form of taped recordings of their voices. Technology, however, the hope-opiate of our age, proves insufficient. Miller insists that change be more fundamental. Howard is actually only slightly more rounded than Stoppard's Blair since Howard has a family, but he ultimately lacks the simultaneity that would make him an integrated "quantum personality." Consider the fact that, like Blair, Howard deals with his employees (Willy) strictly as a business dealing. He is finally no better than alternately here and there himself. It is apparent that Howard, modern society's ideal of success, is not truly complete as a human being.

More fully capable of simultaneously integrating multiple realities are Charley and Bernard, the father and son who live next door, if for no other reason than that they are unencumbered by delusions of the past and can act accordingly. Bernard carries a tennis racket to Washington, DC, where he will argue a case before the Supreme Court, and Charley can offer his friend and neighbor a job regardless of that friend's qualifications. Charley and Bernard appear to have reached a point of integrated harmony found in Stoppard's Kerner and potentially in Hapgood. Mere schizophrenia, seen in Howard, is not what we see in Bernard or Charley. Rather, they engage in what quantum behavior suggests, again counterintuitively: a double agency conducted simultaneously. Charley and Bernard have both family (though the wife and mother is strangely absent) and financial success *and* have reached a point where each man's two (or more) behaviors coalesce and work seamlessly. Willy, aware of the necessity of multiple behavior, nonetheless only has past paradigms to follow, which tragically prevent him from ever being able to crystallize a cohesive quantum personality.

Willy is finally too committed to the myths of Dave Singleman and his brother Ben to realize or to adjust to this new paradigm. He could behave in a singular linear pattern, or perhaps in a schizophrenic, double linear fashion. But he doesn't approach an awareness of a nonlinear quantum option. Though an undeluded Willy might have learned to enter both slits simultaneously, he is too much a product of his culture, steeped in the myth of conventional, singular individualism, to accept this changing dynamic. That is Willy's failure, and it is apparently the cultural failing that Miller documents in general, the insistence that personalities have distinct, Newtonian trajectories, or, of a similar generic construct, that they require schizophrenic trajectories to survive the complexities of contemporary life. Society as yet has not considered the option suggested by the quantum metaphor, so solidly grounded as our culture is in the rationalist, Newtonian paradigm.

Critics often suggest that Miller is espousing a return to the idealistic tradition of "family" standards. Through the limited sighting of linear, either/or thinking, that critical positioning seems reasonable. But Stoppard, the quantum model, and the complexities of (post)modern existence all suggest a third alternative: deriving means of double agency amid the contemporary realization of growing cultural complexity. Miller demonstrates the modernist sources of tragic failure, Stoppard articulates a hopeful postmodern solution.

To extend this concept of quantum personalities and double agency, one need only look at the redoubled interest in "doubling" evident in contemporary theatre and performance. One particularly engaging discussion of the phenomenon comes from Una Chaudhuri, in her book *Staging Place: The Geography of Modern Drama*.[20] In her pursuit of a solution to the ubiquitous twentieth-century problems of place (including concepts of home, home-comings, exile, and immigration) – she coins the term "geopathology" – Chaudhuri locates a multicultural option within contemporary theatre. For example:

> The bilingualism of *The House of Ramon Iglesia* [by Jose Rivera] . . .
> is not the mark of an unbreachable difference but rather of an inviting pluralism. It is a demonstration of the possibility of entertaining two or more cultural contexts simultaneously, of inhabiting two or more homes simultaneously. (*Staging Place*, pp. 211–12)

The simultaneous existences Chaudhuri speaks of are not a suggestion of schizophrenia but quite accurately (though doubtless unintentionally) an advocacy of what has here been called the quantum personality. Elsewhere, summarizing an impressive list of multicultural works, she observes that "doubling" is a tool used throughout to "contribute to the construction of a model of multiplicity of identity that links the projects of multiculturalism and postmodernism" (p. 216), leading generally to what eventually "emerges as the definitional phenomenon of multiculturalism, namely the paradox of simultaneous sameness and difference" (p. 232) that ultimately "defines" us all.

At the boundaries of daily existence or at the intersections that challenge the illusion of singular, discrete identity, quantum reality posits a solution to matters of selfhood so violently deconstructed in the twentieth century. It is a solution untenable, perhaps, to a traditionalist frame of mind; but the lessons of the twentieth century, at very least, should have revealed the impotency of traditionalism.

Once again a question of influence arises, again left unanswered: could the twentieth-century politics and poetics of exile, placelessness, and immigration have encouraged quantum inquiries, perhaps even quantum conclusions?

2

Chaos and Theatre

Sensitive Dependence on Initial Conditions

N 1961, Martin Esslin reviewed European theatre and observed what he considered a revolutionary phenomenon, which he labeled, along with his book, *The Theatre of the Absurd*. In this landmark work, Esslin studied a substantial list of post–World War II playwrights, primarily European (Edward Albee being the notable exception), whom he reported presented visions of the world as governed by randomness, arguing against reason or orderliness of any kind. Quoting from Ionesco, Esslin agrees that the world of the absurd "is devoid of purpose.... Cut off from his religious, metaphysical, and transcendental roots, man is lost; all his actions become senseless, absurd, useless."[1] Rational thought, in essence, has failed to fulfill its goal of finding meaning in the universe, leading these artists to conclusions that challenge the possibility of a rationalist, classical- or naturalist-positioned vision. One of the stronger points in Esslin's argument distinguishes "existential" theatre from "absurdist" theatre. Whereas the existential theatre of Sartre and Camus presents an illogical, counterrational position by using essentially rational methods of construction and presentation, the absurdist drama of Genet, Ionesco, Beckett, and others reflects a counterrationalist vision by using a nonrationalist form. Absurdism practices what it preaches. So Ionesco's *The Bald Soprano* (1948), for example, lacks formal dramatic structure and so justly deserves its subtitle, "Anti-play." Ionesco's world is one of nonrational randomness, and so is his art.

These playwrights' visions, however, I would argue are limited

55

in scope. What we see in these absurdist dramatists is a presentation of existence in a purely chaos-as-randomness phase of human and natural dynamics, generalizing from their momentary – and sometimes extended – sightings of randomness that all existence is random. They are decidedly opposed to any thought that considers the world operating in a causally informed, rational manner, oblivious or resistant to any sense of possible order within human and natural dynamics whatsoever. These playwrights who fit into Esslin's scheme have concentrated on a world dominated by a chaos of actual randomness, not envisioning any sense of an orderly disorder within the chaos phases they present. According to them, chaos is nonrational, incoherent, and incomprehensible randomness, and so are their visions of the world.

What was revolutionary about Esslin's work was that he used current – 1960s – philosophical positions to make sense of a wild new brand of theatre formerly incomprehensible to most theatregoers, though many intuitively felt something vital and important to be going on in that theatre. As Ruby Cohn observes of those early days of Beckett and others, "I had a vague notion that transcendence and agnosticism meet theatrically when an absurd Everyman faces death, but it was Esslin's book that sharpened my focus."[2] In 1990, Ruby Cohn and Enoch Brater co-edited *Around the Absurd: Essays on Modern and Postmodern Drama,* in which they collected essays documenting the significance of this absurdist movement, both as influence on later generations of writers and as providing insight into re-visionary past works of theatre. (In the latter case, consider Jan Kott's *Shakespeare Our Contemporary,*[3] which predates yet works from an assumption paralleling Cohn and Brater's observation.) The sense of the absurd has pervaded our thinking on world theatre as well as on contemporary existence itself, and the conclusions drawn were very much in line with a mid-century existential philosophy that argued ultimate meaninglessness, verified by the horrors and senselessness of world war.

But as Arnold Hinchliffe has observed, "The theater of Nothing, if it is to develop at all, will have to move to Something – whether the conventions and subjects are artistic, political, social, or religious."[4] The absurdist vision did not remain on the field of Nothingness for very long, despite a popular pervading belief that it did. There are significant signs that even Beckett, the ostensible leader of the movement (though "leader" and "movement" imply a conscious grouping that even Esslin acknowledges did not exist among the absurdists), was moving beyond the absurd even as its initial position was being defined. This suggestion is not an effort to discredit either Esslin or Brater and Cohn; rather it is an observation privileged by a 1990s perspective that brings with it the opportunity to re-view recent theatre history with the tools of "postabsurdist" thought. As Brater observed that "Beckett now made us see as new things that were always there in front of our eyes, but never before in such sharp relief,"[5] so can we today see writers in sharper relief thanks to a new paradigm that extends Esslin's configuration of absurdist drama.

From the perspective of the new paradigm, it is my contention that Samuel Beckett does not cleanly fit into this confederacy of absurdists that Esslin has put together; indeed, perhaps none but the most limited of the listed practitioners may fit. In fact, in 1965 Esslin himself acknowledged the imprecision of his label, never actually wanting it to be a prescriptive phrase but rather "a kind of intellectual shorthand for a complex pattern of similarities in approach . . . of shared philosophical and artistic premises."[6] There is, after all, an order in Beckett's chaos, even a rationalism that belies the very definition of absurdism that Esslin has suggested. It is nevertheless valuable to see Esslin and absurdism as critics have generally (mis)represented them, for that perspective provides a valuable counterpoint to numerous alternative positions, including my own.

For example, Vivian Mercier challenges the position of Beckett as absurdist by observing how Beckett's strong neoclassical scholarly background has invaded Beckettian dramaturgic constructs. Seeing Beckett's art as an aesthetic invaded by oppositions, Mercier observes that one central opposition is classicism/absurdism.[7] In particular, Mercier highlights Beckett's interest in Racine, a playwright whose bloodless, actionless drama assumes a classical formalism that always returns to order following temporary turmoil. For Racine the neoclassicist, order inexorably triumphs in the end. Seeing Racine's influence on Beckett, as Mercier did in 1977, clearly undermines Esslin's argument that Beckett's drama is absurdist in both form and content, since in Beckett's work disorder is invariably invaded by a pervading order. Even though Beckett can be seen as forwarding a rather bleak assertion of impotent order struggling against a continually encroaching randomness, he seems more appropriately to achieve something less despairing and quite different from absurdism as it is currently understood, namely an urge toward an order–disorder interaction within his work.

Mercier suggests that Beckett is a postmodernist integrating classical assumptions, and to some degree he is correct. From a different perspective, however, derived from recent developments in chaotics, I would argue more forcefully that Beckett's work aims to create a new hybrid, an integrating vision of order and randomness/chaos – or order in chaos and chaos in order. If one considers that the idea of the absurd presupposes that chaos/randomness is the opposite or negation of order, then Mercier's dialectical scheme seems an appropriate one. But the chaos paradigm suggests something quite different. As Bohm and Peat have observed about chaos theory in science,

> Randomness is being treated not as something incommensurate with order but as a special case of a more general notion of order, in this case of orders of infinite degree. This may appear as a curious step to take, since chance and randomness are generally thought of as being equal to total *dis*order (the absence of any order at all). . . . But here it is proposed that whatever happens must take place in *some* order so that the notion of a "total lack of order" has no real meaning.[8]

Order and disorder do not operate in dialectic opposition to each other as Mercier suggests, nor is disorder the "total lack of order" previously suggested by apologists of the absurd. Rather order–disorder is a continuum wherein one should consider randomness/disorder to be, as Bohm and Peat suggest, "a limiting case of order," a concept that makes it "possible to bring together the notions of strict determinism and chance (i.e., randomness) as processes that are opposite ends of the general spectrum of order" (*Science, Order, and Creativity*, p. 132). The interaction between these "ends" of the spectrum – and everything in between – is precisely what chaos theory argues occurs in nature: order rises from disorder, and disorder originates in order. The new science has concluded "that randomness cannot be equated with a complete absence of order, which in itself has no meaning" (p. 128), because every actual instance of randomness has its origins in some higher degree of order. "Thus," say Bohm and Peat, "there is no need to fall into the assumption of complete determinism. . . . Nor is there any need to assume that chance and indeterminism rule absolutely" (p. 134).

And so, too, does Beckett's art depict an interplay between degrees of order, from the "highest" causal forms (though these rarely occupy much of Beckett's time or space) to the "lowest" richly disorderly/random forms. Beckett's is a chaos-informed rationalism, ultimately, one that leads neither to absurdist nor to existential drama, if these forms suggest that certain behavior or events exist which have no informing order. This integrated vision of order within disorder originating in chaos science is clearly not what Esslin meant when he used the term "absurdism." And it is much more than existential theatre would claim in its rationalist affirmation of the absurdist position. Neither is it Mercier's perception of a vacillating either/or world of chaos or order. Ultimately, Esslin's random absurdism as well as Mercier's position of either/or operants fail to explain the overriding vision that Beckett presents.

Windows of order reveal themselves in a Beckettian work when one considers, for example, how order rises up when Estragon and Vladimir engage in word games, slapstick routines, pantomime, and so on. Order rises out of the chaos of these characters' conditions, and, of course, chaotic randomness surfaces out of moments of order. As order is created amid chaos *within* the works of Beckett, one can also move up in scale and make a similar claim of Beckett's work in general, a metatheatrical observation that out of the chaos of existence his art creates order, though not of the type a classicist would expect. Repetition of events (and of whole acts) is one obvious example of this ordering/ordered pattern. What is revealed is a recurring repetition of pattern wherein windows reveal self-similar patterns of order and chaos from any number of scaled positions, reflecting, one can assume, processes of nature themselves.

I would agree in part with Una Chaudhuri's suggestion that Beckett's world is a denatured world where issues of identity and being draw support from sources that challenge traditional visions of nature.[9] That is not to say, though, that Beckett's vision does not reflect actual processes of nature. While they may challenge traditional views of nature, they seem interestingly to confirm the new visions of nature, especially the nature recently uncovered by chaoticians. What Beckett undertakes is a resolution independent of scientific enterprises which, ironically, evolve to reflect the conclusions that this other process has itself derived. Rejecting the old vision of nature, Beckett has hit upon the qualities governing our new vision of nature. This distinction, of course, between "natures" can be confusing and doubtless has been part of the source of confusion among Beckett scholars. Patterns within chaos pervade Beckett's art, a pervasiveness now evident in the new view of nature. But because the patterns often do not occur in any predictable fashion, they at very least appear random, even spontaneous, and certainly therefore "anti"-natural, a point that perhaps led critics such as Esslin to conclude that Beckett is absurdist, necessarily disassociated from a nature of cruel deception that teases us with order only to sink us with its disorder. Without benefit of the informing element of chaotics, this type of argument is perfectly understandable.

More precisely, however, with chaotics as a guide, one can see that such patterns are not actually unpredictably *random* but unpredictably *deterministic,* because hindsight can often verify the causes of their recurrence, though such knowledge cannot provide us with foresight into what comes next and when, since we cannot be certain which cause will rise up to produce what effects. Events in nature *and* in Beckett are determined by antecedent causes, but it is impossible to predict which causes will trigger what event. We have unpredictable determinism. It is something that appears cruelly deceptive from a traditional perspective, ultimately "un"-natural, but it turns out to be exactly and precisely natural. Our illusions have thwarted us, not nature. Recovering the traces of the true nature is the thing Beckett initiates for us even in his denatured world: an orderly disorder of the human mind that must adjust to unpredictable determinism.

As Mercier suggests, Esslin's vision of the absurd is the antithesis of the naturalist-classicist's vision of strict causal determinism. Beckett, misidentified by Esslin as an absurdist and of course never considered a naturalist-classicist, is in essence a fusion of both, but in an even more integrated way than Mercier's dialectical dynamic posits. Whereas Mercier argues that Beckett vacillates between two distinct world visions in his drama, Beckett seems more precisely to be asserting the existence of an integrated single world wherein these two forces – randomness/disorder and determinism/order – coexist not as incommensurate realities struggling for dominion but as extremes on a single sliding scale of order. The struggle for the triumph of order over disorder – a classical or naturalist inclination – is virtually as unacceptable as the absurdist presumption of the triumph of randomness. The "triumph" in Beckett comes with the recognition that both elements naturally coexist and interact and with the further observation that stasis results in one extreme (order) or entropy in the other (disorder), both being variations on the theme of death. Coincident regeneration and decay are the essence of life.

Recent scholarship on Beckett has tentatively challenged both Esslin's and Mercier's positions as incomplete, but none of that scholarship has seen the chaos model as an applicable paradigm, many simply because the paradigm was not yet readily available. Even David Hesla's tantalizingly entitled 1971 work, *The Shape of Chaos: An Interpretation of the Art of Samuel Beckett*,[10] argues for a dialectic analysis of Beckett's art rather than positing a nondialectical chaos model of integrated and interacting order and disorder. And although in the mid-1980s Esslin presented and published a lecture entitled "Samuel Beckett – Infinity, Eternity" in which he observes patterns of repetition, he nonetheless takes a different direction than I've suggested:

> Consciousness condemned to an eternal repetition of its last conscious moment – as represented in the final stasis of *Endgame*, the entropic recurrence of the same last thoughts in *Play*, the final landscape of eternal entropy in *Lessness*, the endlessly recurring streams of creatures moving through mud in *How It Is* and in many other Beckett works – all these are images of Hell, and we must never forget Beckett's deep preoccupation with Dante.[11]

Esslin's own recognition here of recurring patterns of action and behavior belie his 1960s idea of the absurd. These patterns in art say more than merely that somehow life's patterns recur, and they clearly move beyond an absurdist's position. But they also speak to us in ways that work beyond the tradition of Dantesque cosmography that Esslin here suggests. If we choose to apply the chaos model – the notion of integrated order and disorder – to

graphy, then Hell is perhaps knowing that order
ows in a chaotic/random natural existence but not
n order will arrive and not knowing how long it will
w brand of rational uncertainty within the realm of
and conditioned certainty.

ιιυ   ?" of both Esslin's and Mercier's interpretations very
likely lies in the fact that an articulated alternative vision of nature
was as yet not fully available. The difference is that even though
Esslin and Mercier did not have the foresight to envision new
models, apparently their subject of analysis – Beckett – did. Esslin's earlier position on Beckett is absurdist (Beckett's material is
antirational) and his later position suggests a postindustrial re-
creation of a Dantesque world (Beckett's material is a rationally
comprehensible entropic Hell), while Mercier creates a sort of
combination interpretation (Beckett's material is alternately nonrational and rational). From a chaotics perspective, what Beckett
has created is an art that presents the counterintuitive, though
visionary, precise, and rational (though this rationalism is informed by new, post-nineteenth-century adjustments) assessment
that chaos and order are neither distinct nor alternating opposites
in nature but integral elements of a single, coherent system, an
"order in chaos" vision of existence, a mitigated absurdism at best.
Esslin and Mercier, though rather ingeniously manipulating old
systems in new ways, have ultimately missed the full revolutionary vision of their subject's art.

Beckett's interest in the entropic realities of existence is a critical focus his works encourage. His early as well as later works
invariably end with the triumph of entropy, of disorder by dissipation leading to heat death. But Beckett's work also seems to be on
the verge of regeneration, a regeneration constantly displayed
within his works, amidst events of apparent inevitable and final
degeneration. Being merely on the verge of regeneration, however,
as most of his works could be seen to be, may be more a sign of caution, an unwillingness to speak optimistically of futures despite
subtle signs that optimism can be felt to be just around the corner.
In this regard, perhaps Hersh Zeifman is right when he observes
that Beckett differs from Stoppard, the postabsurdist, only in tone:

> [W]hile frequently exhibiting an absurdist outer shell, Stoppard's
> plays contain at their core a subversive "sweetness" that ultimately

bursts forth and cracks that shell; this unique blend of shell and core produces the distinctive postabsurdist tone of much of Stoppard's theater. The measure of Stoppard's departure from true absurdism can be gauged partly by comparing the humor of his plays with that of Beckett.[12]

Zeifman's suggestion here is that Stoppard is at heart a resistant absurdist, someone who accepts the absurdist position but *desires,* hopes for, perhaps even prays for, an order amidst irrefutable evidence of rising disorder. I would suggest, however, that we should reverse Zeifman's direction and look at Beckett more as we look at Stoppard than at Stoppard from the position we currently view Beckett. Beckett cautiously embraces a belief in order rising out of chaos; Stoppard more enthusiastically embraces that belief. For both of them it appears that out of an apparent pervasive entropy arises self-regenerating order. While Beckett more tentatively posits such a position, Stoppard has extended himself to fully embrace Beckett's first halting gleanings. If Beckett the absurdist is actually Beckett a postabsurdist, where did Beckett the absurdist go? I would suggest that proponents of absurdism have embraced only a limited part of Beckett's vision and consequently identified in Beckett a position that he never fully held. Caution is not denial, and the caution that Beckett exhibits presents a tentative optimism against a dominating sense of despair.

If Beckett was indeed suggesting a new philosophy, and given that Stoppard does indeed suggest such a philosophy, we must realize the human consequences that this philosophy presents. It encourages neither the existentialist's claim of total human freedom in an uncontrolled universe, nor, obviously, a naturalist's vision of total human foreordination and resulting human progression in a pre-established world pattern. From a new science and postabsurdist position, one can see that to varying degrees, given different circumstances, each individual is simultaneously free from and bound to predetermined consequences. Chaoticians James Crutchfield, Robert Shaw, et al., observe, "Chaos is often seen in terms of the limitations it implies, such as lack of predictability. . . . [But] chaos provides a mechanism that allows for free will within a world governed by deterministic laws."[13] Chaos theory may reveal certain human limitations, but it also argues for a good deal of offsetting privileges.

A Scientific Digression

The traditional, "Newtonian" scientific community has remained wedded to the assumption that any and all dynamic systems operate in a rationally causal manner. And through a sort of
feedback loop, traditional artists (and psychologists and other
social scientists) likewise have generally accepted the assumption,
following the rationalist-naturalist model of behavior which in
turn reinforced the assumptions maintained by the scientific community. Iconoclastic breakthroughs in quantum physics in the
early part of the twentieth century, leading to Heisenberg's uncertainty principle, rocked the rationalist scientific community and
even to a point called popular cultural attention to a sort of crack
in the causalist's frame of comprehension. But quantum mechanics ultimately showed only that this new and uncertain type of
dynamic behavior exists in the universe of imperceptibly small,
subatomic "particles" (or in extraterrestrial phenomena such as
black holes); our visible macro-universe seemed not to be affected
by these new doubts brought on by this rationally incomprehensible, noncausal behavior. As noted in Chapter 1, such insights could
only be metaphorically applied to our visible, macrocosmic world.

While absolute security in macro-universal causality in fact
met its tentative opponents as early as the nineteenth century
with developments in turbulence theory, the late twentieth century has perhaps delivered the death blow to our simplified
visions of causality and determinism. Problems began incontrovertibly to surface in macro-universal studies as groups of scientists, equipped in the 1960s and 1970s with computers and a
renewed skepticism, evaluated assumptions made about nature
based on linear expectations. While classically simple and strictly
causal systems like pendulum behavior closely follow linear
expectations (though even pendulum behavior has been called
into question of late), naturally occurring events are rarely brought
about by single forces but rather engage in varied interactivities,
influenced *nonlinearly* by multiple forces in numerous conditions. Testing laboratory conclusions against less controlled natural events, the new skeptics discovered that traditional scientists
oversimplified reality, creating locally "true" results in their labs
but not necessarily results that globally recur in "real" time and
space. For example, when a pendulumlike behavior occurs in

nature, we assume the behavior will settle into an orderly pattern until it runs out of applied energy. In reality, though it may display linear behavior and settle into an orderly pattern when sufficiently controlled, it can also be placed in extreme (though not unusual) circumstances and swing without a pattern or, more precisely, fall into a richly varied pattern, the effect of imperceptibly small influences that are generally considered inconsequential. Oftentimes in the past scientists accepted what they saw ninety-nine times out of a hundred as "law" and attributed the one aberrant event to testing error. These new skeptics, however, replicating events much more efficiently on computer, discovered that even the scientists' highly controlled events documented legitimate deviation from the assumed "laws" of behavior. They also concluded that the deviations should not have been ignored as aberrant conclusions resulting from poor procedure, though ignoring such deviations has historically been enforced by a cultural bias that insisted on orderly, universal comprehension of natural forces.

Given encouragement by the subatomic breakthroughs of quantum physics as well as, apparently, by weakening cultural resistance in the late twentieth century, the new skeptics focused on these aberrations and discovered that often the laboratory exceptions are actually the natural rule and that even basic lab-verified assumptions about billiard balls and pendulums cannot necessarily be expanded to natural law. As Briggs and Peat point out, even for the billiards player innumerable influences can alter expected behavior: "the air pressure, temperature, the nap of the table, the muscle tone of the billiards player, his or her psychology, the flight of neutrinos from a supernova millions of light-years away, the gravity of an electron."[14] In theory, behavior should be 100 percent consistent; in practice virtually "inexplicable" and definitely unpredictable deviations occur. And in the natural world the deviations are often the rule.

By concentrating on rather than ignoring the deviations, the new skeptics discovered a phenomenon known as "the butterfly effect" that explained that countless dynamic systems – all general fields of action or behavior – share a highly sensitive dependence on initial conditions that rationalist causal extrapolation never fully anticipated. Unexpected and significant effects occur as a result of minute deviations in cause. The traditional causalists regularly ignored such troublesome conditions, labeling them "noise" and striving to control or eliminate their influences. The new skeptics, however, did not look for controls because, as they discovered, they could not create controls that did not artificially affect results, a discovery parallel to the actor–observer dilemma in quantum physics.

Several examples may be helpful at this point. The issue of turbulence – how and when it begins, how it will proceed, and so forth – has been a center of mystery among scientists for generations and to some degree remains unsolved today. However, breakthroughs in general understanding have occurred in the latter part of the twentieth century. Consider a slowly moving stream partly obstructed by a stone. Steady, linearly comprehensible flow will occur at a certain low speed, but as the stream's speed increases, at a certain point eddies will begin to appear, points at which the stream will flow faster than the overall speed of the stream, as well as points where speed and direction reverse. Time-series graphs of steady and periodic (eddying-patterned) events will look like those in Figure 5.[15]

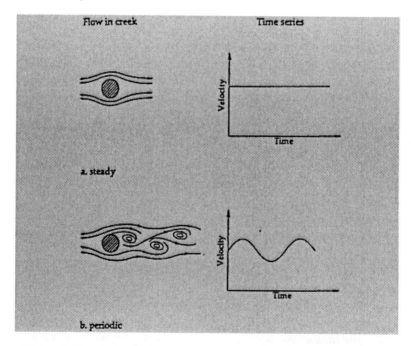

Figure 5. Flow/time series. From Stephen H. Kellert, *In the Wake of Chaos* (Chicago: University of Chicago Press, 1993). Reproduced by permission of the University of Chicago Press

State-space graphs represent the events as in Figure 6, with the steady phase simply attracting to a point of consistent behavior, and a mildly eddying though still periodic phase attracting toward an ellipse.

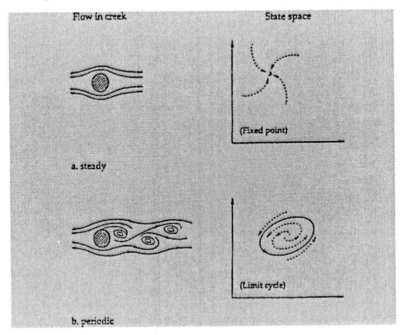

Figure 6. Flow/state space. From Stephen H. Kellert, *In the Wake of Chaos* (Chicago: University of Chicago Press, 1993). Reproduced by permission of the University of Chicago Press.

As the eddying increases, self-similar, downscaled eddying will occur within the initial eddies, creating quasi-periodic time- and state-space graphs as in Figure 7.

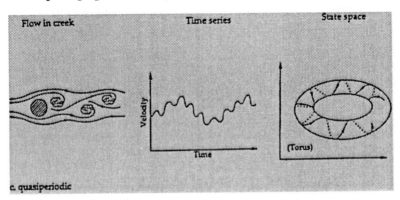

Figure 7. Quasiperiodic flow. From Stephen H. Kellert, *In the Wake of Chaos* (Chicago: University of Chicago Press, 1993). Reproduced by permission of the University of Chicago Press.

Though fairly complicated, even this stage of events remains comprehensible to the orderly Newtonian mind. But this bifurcation to two attractors will further bifurcate as speed increases, into a "torus" of virtually infinite embedded ellipses that will never fully replicate themselves as time passes. And here Newtonianism gets lost, seeing incomprehensible randomness at work.

However, pursuing this mystery of disorder and equipped with the calculating wizardry of the computer, recent science has discovered heretofore unnoticed phenomena. A complex, forever embedded model of multiple attractors unfolds, toward which countless events singularly but invariably settle. Turbulence may not be "orderly" in the old sense, but neither is it random; we have clearly a determinist pattern because the events attract toward some generally foreseeable state, but the complexities are such that no single moment can be fully anticipated, given the immensity (though not infinity) of the possibilities. We know what the stream is capable of doing, even what it might do, and definitely what it won't or can't do, but never what it will do. We have an unpredictable determinism at work.

Very specifically, mathematicians, uncomfortable with the unwieldiness of previous explanations, pursued the study of turbulent, quasi-periodical phases and discovered that a very simple formula could be derived to explain the complexities. This new model, known as the Ruelle-Takens-Newhouse model,[16] was further articulated and clarified in 1963 by Edward Lorenz,[17] who developed the Lorenz attractor, also called the strange attractor, to explain the unpredictable yet determinist dimensions of turbulence behavior (see Figure 8).

Lorenz described the full consequences of his simplified-yet-complex explanation of turbulent behavior:

> It implies that two [initial] states differing by imperceptible amounts may eventually evolve into two considerably different states. If, then, there is any error whatever in observing the present state – and in any real system such errors seem inevitable – an acceptable prediction of an instantaneous state in the distant future may well be impossible. ("Deterministic Nonperiodic Flow," p. 133)

Classical assumptions hold that small causes lead to small effects and that an initial cause would always be reflected in the subse-

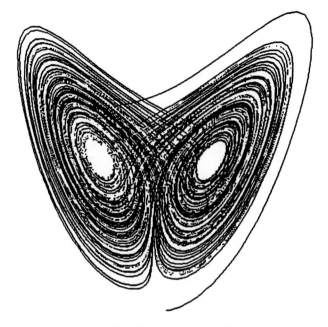

Figure 8. The Lorenz strange attractor.

quent effect. This is Newtonian linearity at work. Now, however, we find that small causes can produce momentous effects (or none at all) and furthermore that we can't be sure what those effects will be. The result is a likely significantly altered original arrangement of relationships: points once near each other could now be almost worlds apart while others have drawn closely together, creating a totally new and unexpected relational configuration. Today this is known as sensitive dependence on initial conditions, or the butterfly effect. The concept of sensitive dependence on initial conditions is the foundation of chaos theory, an acknowledgment of nonlinear behavior pervading countless dynamic systems, of which turbulence is one and of which we will see different varieties throughout this (and the next) chapter, each adopting a slightly different variation on the orderly disorder theme.

Because of the butterfly effect at work in the turbulent world, predicting future states is not possible. As a result of the insertion of such uncertainty into systems study, Kellert observes, "Lorenz used a qualitative approach to study his system" (*In the Wake of Chaos*, p. 13), conceding that quantitative prediction – the traditional goal of classical science – was impossible. We can be certain of qualitative *patterns* but never of quantifiably precise *behavior* from one moment to the next. At best we can outline a course of probable general behavior using such "maps" as the Lorenz attractor.

Perhaps the first expanded evidence of the global significance of this need to acknowledge initial sensitivity and to strive for qualitative rather than quantitative predictions occurred in meteorology; meteorologists during the 1960s and 1970s concluded they had amassed sufficient understanding of variable influences to develop a system for making long-term weather forecasts. This bold assumption seemed entirely plausible in the 1960s. After all, we had the instruments to track all but the (seemingly) least significant weather events in the earth's atmosphere; all that remained was to use that knowledge to determine precise causal connections. But in the process of developing the determinist system, a macrosystem discovery was made, similar to the turbulence data above since weather systems follow similar flow patterns. It is in meteorology, in fact, where the popular tag "butterfly effect" originated: the idea was that a factor as small and remote as a butterfly fluttering in China could affect the weather of the United States. Not knowing which events will ripple up to a level of significance leads to an inevitable uncertainty and to imprecise conclusions even when data are precise to a seemingly reasonable (scientifically acceptable) degree.

It should be noted here that scientific data are and will always be selective except in the most limited and controlled of conditions and as a result will always imprecisely reflect actual systems behavior. The only way scientifically to account for the butterfly effect is through comprehensive systems data accumulation – recreating or knowing *everything*. Creating an omniscient model would virtually require a process of actual and complete duplication of reality, a Faustlike overextension of human capacity.

If, in fact, this impossible obstacle were somehow overcome – if we could accumulate *all* data (still something of a dream of classical science) – we still would not be able to predict what degree of effect each cause would have, since we now know that causes can produce unexpected and unequal effects. This is where chaotics ultimately defeats classical assumptions of human rational potential, since the ultimate goal of predetermination as envisioned by the Newtonian scientific empiricists and the artistic naturalists is as likely as actually discovering the alchemist's philosopher's stone.

The conclusions to be drawn from the material above are significant: it is impossible to realize the Newtonian-naturalist goal of discovering deterministic patterns of systems behavior whereby future events can be solidly predicted. Rather, what chaos theorists describe are a variety of universal "patterns" that apply to any number of dynamic systems – from the weather, to population growth patterns, to heartbeat patterns, to disease patterns among discrete populations, to the stock market, even to the pendulum. Much as with the quantum physicists, chaos theorists conclude that they can uncover a pattern that leads to possible and even at times probable outcomes based on a delimiting of options. Chaos theory identifies systems of *unpredictable determinism:* there are causes and effects (determinism), but we cannot always know all the causes (butterfly effect) and so cannot anticipate future events (unpredictability) with anything near to the certainty we once felt we could.

This movement from certainty to probability is, of course, a direction that many philosophers have suggested in the past, and so is not a particularly new revelation, though we now have scientific data to support these assertions. As such, chaos theory confirms what has previously been posited. What the chaos theoreticians do contribute to Western thought, however, is a far more precise understanding of the probable options. As noted above, chaos theory does not conclude that the universe is random; rather it sees patterns where patterns were previously unseen or unexpected. As such, through a significant loosening of the goals and ambitions of classical science, this field (these fields) could still be considered roughly Newtonian – at least by way of extension – in several regards. Consider the following.

From the perspective of a linearly causal prejudice – that held by classicists-naturalists – events invariably settle into a pattern of stable, predictable behavior. We've all seen graphs of sloped lines (rising and falling), bell curves, and various types of oscillations (like heartbeat pattern recorded on an oscilloscope). These graphs each identify what is called an "attractor," a pattern in time and space that events settle toward in some diagrammatically predictable fashion. The graphs describing creek flow, the torus, and turbulence, presented above, are examples of attractors.

The "strange attractor" above identifies ordered patterns *within*

systems of apparent chaos. There is yet another model attractor
that applies to chaos theory, one that identifies order and chaos
arising out of each other. (The common thread here is the butterfly effect.) Population growth, for example, might settle into an
attractor that looks something like the graph in Figure 9.

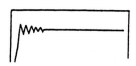

Figure 9. Steady-state line.

Animal populations will rise
and fall (boom or bust), depending, for example, on the
availability of food sources
and the presence of predators,
until they presumably reach
a steady state, a balance of
nature.

If the food source increases in equal proportion to predatory
increases, an attractor such as that in Figure 10 would explain the
growth pattern, reflecting something of a diminishing return on
environmental increases.

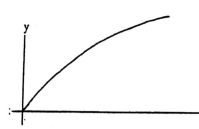

Figure 10. Steady-state curve.

The easy, traditionally prejudiced assumption would be
that growth would continue in
an orderly fashion, literally off
the graph. Generally speaking,
this kind of conclusion was
deduced by Newtonians as
sensible, logical, and therefore
a factual point.

However, as the chaos theo-
reticians have observed, if the parameters of such variables as food
and predation continue to increase and are eventually strained,
the traditional causalist-Newtonian assumption does not hold.
Traditionalists at this point would almost need to concede the
occurrence of an absurdist/random singularity. The chaoticians,
however, saw a pattern wherein a strange phenomenon occurs: the
steady-state line bifurcates and creates an oscillation pattern
between two possible "steady states" of behavior, suggesting the
equal likelihood of boom or bust based on the same causal conditions. If increases continue, the bifurcated patterns would themselves bifurcate into various middle-level steady-state conditions,
ad infinitum, into a condition of true chaotic randomness (see Figure 11).

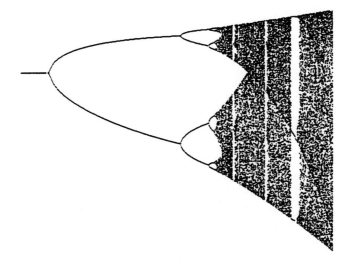

Figure 11. Bifurcation pattern.

This rather orderly movement into a chaos (or, more precisely, a disorderly/random phase) is similar to the turbulence models described earlier. But in the case of population dynamics, chaoticians found something different from the order within disorder concept revealed through strange attraction of the turbulence model. Here the incredible additional discovery is that within certain bifurcations into randomness, windows of order reappear. We have a condition where order turns to chaos and then returns to order, not merely where there is a perceived order in randomness as with Lorenz's strange attractor model for turbulence.

A new steady state develops, a self-similar though downscaled replication of the primary pattern. Within these replications, even further downscaled replications reoccur, again and again. Order arises from chaos. We see an unpredictable order since we cannot anticipate *when* order will occur, but a determined order nonetheless and not merely random behavior. This model differs from the turbulence frame, since the butterfly effect leads in this instance to systems that actually generate order out of disorder (see Figure 12).

Order leads to chaos, and chaos in such systems in turn leads to order without extraneous influence. The practical lesson is that population ecologists can predict population adjustments in a

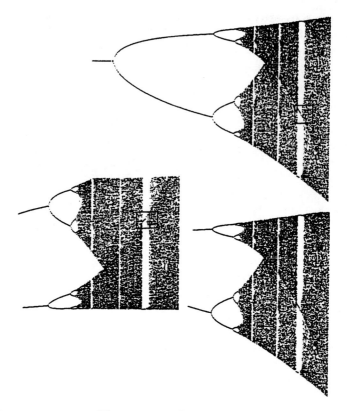

Figure 12. Windows of order.

classical vein if conditions are aberrantly controlled (as in lab rat populations), but if scale increases or conditions intensify, predictability evades scientists even as they witness nature's determinism. However, because of the deterministic features of the system, certain results – even a return to order – can be anticipated as probable somewhere within an expected period of time.

Patterns of rich and varied sorts pervade systemics in several unique but related – via the butterfly effect – permutations. Only the most simplistic systems are predictable, and they are systems that reduce the complexities of true systems dynamics to "comfortable," traditionally rationalist, linearly causal fictions. Patterns of chaos – a phrase once considered at best a witty literary-metaphorical paradox – exist in countless dynamic systems. What has been learned locally (in lablike, stable, limited environments) does not necessarily apply globally (in the world) beyond a certain very limited point in systems behavior.

Chaos theorists would likely agree with the assessment that classical science has been creative fiction-making, striving – and finally failing – to fulfill a cultural desire to see the world as humans chose to see it and to valorize human perception (human reason) in the process as capable of not just comprehending the world (what the chaoticians claim to have come closer to doing) but of being able to understand futures as well as presents. This latter wish is achievable only for the simplest of systems, and certainly human beings and human social structures are not the simplest of systems. The new chaotics breakthroughs, however, reveal the limited human potential for control of our universe, but they also forcefully argue against our succumbing to despair, given the vast new opportunities that it offers for understanding the world. Conservatively assessed, we have an adjusted Newtonianism; more enthusiastically, we have hit upon a brave new world of models through which to understand our world.

The Chaos Model Applied: An Early Crack in the Chimney of Causality

In 1978 Robert Brustein published an article, "The Crack in the Chimney: Reflections on Contemporary American Playwriting,"[18] in which he makes much of a point of logical inconsistency that arises during the action in Henrik Ibsen's 1892 play, *The Master Builder*. In the second act, Solness reveals to Hilda Wangel the event that was the breakthrough in his life, the event that led him simultaneously to fame and fortune as a master builder and to experience the severe guilt that would haunt him the rest of his life. Solness reports that he once discovered a crack in the chimney of his house but never got around to repairing it because of a feeling that a fire leveling the house would give him the opportunity to build on the property and thus to begin his ascent to the high rank of master builder. In fact, a fire did destroy the house, and indirectly destroyed his family as well, but Solness reports with certainty that the fire began in a clothes closet in a remote part of the house. Despite his being innocent of any complicity in the event, however, Solness's overwhelming sense of responsibility remains.

Brustein's conclusion about this strange turn of events is that Ibsen was rather perversely undermining his contemporary audience's expectations of a tight causal relation between Solness's present condition and the antecedent events and conditions that forged his life. Specifically, Ibsen challenges the very tenets he is best remembered for popularizing: naturalism in the theatre. Ibsen, says Brustein, is suggesting that the universe is so complex that it is a gross presumption to accept the naturalist's vision that all effects can be linearly traced to single causes, that all causes linearly lead to inevitable and predictable effects. Brustein points out that Ibsen's iconoclasm anticipates later movements in science, philosophy, and the arts – including the drama of Strindberg, Beckett, and Handke – and he proceeds to note that this non- or anticausal perspective fails fully to invade the American psyche until many decades after the European revolution in thought. (This latter point will be picked up in Chapter 3.)

Ibsen, says Brustein, may have initially accepted the naturalist model – in, for example, *Ghosts* – as, to some extent, everyone even today accepts it. Genetic and environmental influences do affect our lives, but the question is: to what extent can we identify and then predict or anticipate the actual effect of such influences? As the Newtonian physical model promised complete causal comprehension of the mechanical universe, so did the other "sciences" follow the lead and presume equally confidently that they could achieve complete comprehension of any "system," including the human system and the human social system. The art of such a culture should, of course, follow suit.

The problem for the iconoclast Ibsen was that, living in a culture dominated by determinist-naturalist frames of thought, he had comfortable access to no clearly articulated philosophical alternatives to use as a model in his assault on the traditionalist's status quo naturalist vision, and, likewise, no vocabulary to explain the sense of discomfort he felt toward the determinist-naturalist model, in all its arrogant complacency. I am not suggesting that he needed such a model, but it is often the case that artistic intuition, for all its virtues, is very foggy and incomplete. The sense of existence that Ibsen was presenting has indeed found bolder (and more precise) mouthpieces in subsequent generations of playwrights, practitioners, and critics, but even in these cases, the articulation has remained somewhat vague and the critical assessments imprecise. Mercier's and Esslin's assessments of Beckett (though not Beckett himself) are good examples. In fact, Brustein's own 1978 article suffers from a certain similar critical fogginess as well.

However, the fogginess of thought that Ibsen experienced at the turn of the century and that even Brustein experienced as recently as 1978 is not necessarily reflective of flaw; rather, these prognostic assertions of an alternative vision of reality, and others like them, very likely helped soften the soil of a culture encrusted by a spirit of neo-Newtonian reason that ultimately reduced our vision of existence rather than encouraged it to expand. As a result, very specific – and at last verified – visions have developed throughout the twentieth century that very likely are indebted to the cultural awakening inspired by artists like Ibsen, and in turn, when used retroactively, reveal the general accuracy of many of these visionaries. With the assertion of a chaos paradigm, science and art in the twentieth century in many ways have reunited.

To a large degree, the playwright, like the laboratory scientist – as opposed to the field scientist – can limit the uncertainties of the butterfly effect in his or her staged "experiments" by simply not allowing extraneous elements into the experiment. Some playwrights, on the other hand, have mastered reality by studying causes and their unpredictable effects – consider Shakespeare's *Hamlet.* Or at a more controlled level, the playwright can call attention to the havoc a particular butterfly effect can wreak upon a system by building a butterfly effect into his or her experiment and providing focused attention to it. Furthermore, given recent theories that have announced the death of the author, the autonomy that a text assumes allows for the rise of events in the experiment unforeseen by the playwright, much as experiments may take on unforeseen lives of their own despite all the attempts of a scientist to control the events. Any number of these possibilities may have taken place in the case of Ibsen with one exception: he did not work to eliminate or control the seemingly extraneous, and the result was a cultural crack in the bastion of traditionalist, linear logic that peaked with naturalism.

The crack in the chimney does, as Brustein suggests, undermine strict causal assumptions in *The Master Builder* in that it plays no direct role in either Solness's professional rise or his family's destruction. But it clearly has a bearing on Solness's less-than-robust conscience and destroys any hope of Solness finding happiness in his good fortune as a master builder. He can't accept his "nonlinear" good fortune because it belies his sense of causal reality. Facts notwithstanding, the crack becomes an alogical force in his life, and for him alogic, that is, nontraditional logic, is unacceptable. We once again see the urge for coherence sacrificing truth to achieve its ends.

This apparent alogical force is a verification, in fact, of Solness's own sensitive dependence on initial conditions. As with the butterfly effect in natural science, this crack is a causally distant factor that rises up to affect Solness's entire psychic condition in a manner that only roughly falls into the realm of naturalist causality. I say that it roughly applies because the chaos paradigm includes elements of determinism. It is "logical," though not linearly logical, as Solness assumes logic needs to be.

This assumption that the logic of determinism requires strict linear behavior is not merely a problem for Solness because it is very likely the assumption of Ibsen's audiences as well, even today. Again, subscribing to the logic of excluded middle, we presume to have *either* linear, undeviating logic/determinism *or* meaninglessness. But Ibsen strives to secure a middle ground, working to develop a complex, nonlinear logic that has meaning and even exhibits determinist tendencies, though not of the predictable sort. This standing on middle ground causes a problem of audience reception when it comes to Ibsen's craft, his effort to convey this middle ground stance. If, for example, an audience witnessed one of the iconoclastic anti- or nonrealistic *Ubu* plays by Alfred Jarry, it could easily understand that the logic of reality/realism was being undermined by a vision of illogic. When, however, one sees an ostensibly realist play on stage, one presumes the invocation of rationalist, linear logic as espoused by naturalism. One does not expect "middle ground." In fact, such an effort to produce something other than linearity will typically result in the critical charge of poor craftsmanship, and the play is generally critically censured, much as traditional scientists react to "noise" in their classical pursuits by ignoring it, assuming it is the result of poor preparation.

Add to this point the fact that because Ibsen has chosen to call attention to this negligible fact of the chimney's crack, it no longer remains negligible. Consider the impact of a scientist's decision to study the turbulence of a butterfly's flutter in China and ultimately identifying its actual effect on meteorological conditions in the United States. The actual decision to make this crack central to the overall system, notably through retrospection, could lead to a presumed conclusion that this butterfly's effect was inevitably profound. But because any number of variables could be studied and any number of causal conclusions could be drawn, each seemingly verifying a naturalist universe, how do we ever know that the cause in focus is actually *the* cause? Some playwrights, of course, identify the cause under scrutiny as incontrovertibly *the* cause in their work. But in the case of *The Master Builder,* even though Solness virtually identifies this crack as a "*the* cause" from among any number of causes that could be asserted, Ibsen pointedly undermines Solness's claim by identifying another source (the closet) and frustrates his audiences in the bargain. The source of the fire, however, is only a partial cause of Solness's doom, since several other sources rise up to contribute to his downfall. So though a naturalist posture could be imposed upon the play to assert the crack as a "*the* cause," it is primarily a matter of craft at work – of a decided choice to concentrate on the butterfly effect – that creates an impression of possible naturalism. Ibsen does work to dispel the impression but with limited results, stemming, it seems, from a determined audience's desire to see what it wants – a causal series of events.

If Solness alone may not change audience perception, Ibsen has given us additional opportunity to re-vision the events. Mrs. Solness, another victim of the fire, does not clearly conclude that the fire, much less the crack (of which she apparently remains unaware), was a primary cause at all for her personal suffering or her husband's success. She writes her sufferings down to "providence." Ibsen has cleverly presented two victims, experiencing the same events, who come to completely different conclusions. Like quantum physics, perspective, not objectivity, determines conclusions, leading to the point that the linear-naturalist cause is a comfortable and comforting fiction, a selecting/highlighting of any number of butterfly effects, all possible causes but none necessarily *the* cause. While a naturalist-traditionalist assumes the inevitable effects of causes within the human dynamic system, Ibsen suggests that such determinations are finally relative assessments. And chaos theory confirms that general assessment.

Take another matter of relative causality, Solness's first

encounter with Hilda Wangel ten years before the drama opens.
Solness, apparently engaged in play with the child Hilda,
promises her a kingdom when she grows up. That after a decade
Solness has forgotten the incident is entirely understandable. For
the young Hilda, however, the early encounter with a great man
becomes a pivotal moment in her life. And again, although the
suggestion of a naturalist pattern of causality may apply to Hilda
in this case, the event has become a "*the* cause" for Hilda because
she has chosen to make it one. It was not an inevitable and necessary force until the causalist in Hilda determined to make it one.
For Solness, on the other hand, the minor incident could – and
probably should – be of no consequence. But, again, the butterfly
effect rises. Solness's incidental, momentary contact with Hilda
ten years ago reverberates, builds, and clearly unexpectedly returns as a spectre to haunt and finally destroy Solness. That Ibsen
chooses to concentrate in his drama on this past incident may create an illusion of inevitability, but again it is not entirely clear that
that momentary contact ten years ago was necessarily destined to
reverberate as it does. Like a small wind storm, this contact could
very well have died out – as, no doubt, so many others have –
without ever having grown to the tempest it has become in Hilda's
psyche.

Of course, if Ibsen had chosen to dramatize inconsequential
contacts in Solness's life, he would have created a non- or
antidrama, something that actually occurs in the works of playwrights like Ionesco. So the fact that we have here a sense of
inevitability is more a case of Ibsen requiring his art to focus on
consequentiality to make his important but subtle case for a disorderly order, an argument against deterministic predictability – as
well as against the randomness which Ionesco's antiplays later
assert – but for unpredictable determinism. Splitting hairs – working against excluded middles – as Ibsen does, is no easy task, but
it is an important one and the heart of his efforts. Ibsen generalizes
the matter of unpredictable consequences (as Beckett, but not
Ionesco, also does) even as he is forced to concentrate on events
that *imply* predictable consequences (which he, though not Zola,
challenges).

Here we must recall several key distinctions not often realized.
Retrospection can produce an illusion of linear causality, can
work backward to presume a forward-moving possibility of pre-

dictability. And that element of seeing inevitability can be considered support of the naturalist presumption. But nowhere does Ibsen endorse the naturalist element of future-looking predictability, as he has worked to present any number of interconnecting causes of which it is impossible to predict which cause will become *the* cause. This major adjustment to naturalist belief is Ibsen's key consequential challenge to naturalism as a whole, and a consequence that conforms precisely to the chaotics process.

Solness's life has involved a turbulent "pattern" that his traditional causal mentality can't comprehend because it cannot comprehend the more general notion of patterned turbulence. One can see, however, that Solness's turbulent, postfire life follows the pattern anticipated by the strange attractor: a repetitive, self-similar series of building followed by a continued sense of unfulfillment. But instead of having Solness realize the strange attractor in his life, what Ibsen has Solness do is "explain" the inexplicable by attributing the chaos in his life to the literal presence of "trolls." Solness and Hilda directly refer to the mysterious impact of trolls throughout the play, impish creatures whose actions follow no predictable pattern of behavior. As a result, no one who falls under their influence can prepare against them since it is impossible to anticipate their next actions. This invocation of trolls in an otherwise rationalist play parallels the invocations of strange sprites by any number of prerationalist, mystery-based systems when chaotic understanding evades human grasp. The process of personifying the forces becomes the last, ultimate attempt to justify nonlinearity within a linear perspective.

In Ibsen's case, the invocation hearkens back to Ibsen's own prenaturalist career and to his *Peer Gynt* (1867) in particular. It appears that in the course of his career Ibsen replaced mysticism (*Peer Gynt*) with scientific certainty (*Ghosts*), only to realize that traditional scientific rationalism (or naturalism) could only incompletely explain the world (the course his later works would follow). In his first effort at rational accommodation via ironic realism, rather uncomfortably, Ibsen has Solness attempt a return to a prior – though postlapsarian – mystical innocence, having Solness insert a ghost into the machine of his existence. Calling up the trolls, of course, is no longer satisfactory for Ibsen or Solness, though Solness himself clings to that explanation of his life, that trolls had overtaken his existence. This "philosophy" does come rather surprisingly close to the truth if one considers that even trolls must have some sense of order, a sense actually akin to the strange attractor. This last-gasp attempt at comprehension through "mystery" reveals the full extent of the antinaturalist posture that Brustein sees Ibsen assume. But having no clear alternative explanation, having only a clear intuition of the incompleteness of rationalist linear causality, Ibsen offers the only alternative that he knows, an offering he does not fully accept even as he inserts it.

In some ways, though, it's the only alternative that Brustein himself knows, a foggy generalization that linear causality is an incomplete process for comprehension of human dynamics. Foggy or not, however, Ibsen's and Brustein's intuitions reflect chaos theory surprisingly well. In fact, from the point of the fire – the crack in the chimney – to the moment of Solness's death, Ibsen presents a process that precisely fits the order–disorder pattern of chaos.

Solness's existence takes a turn toward advancement immediately after the fire. Following an urge kindled in adolescence, he builds his reputation creating edifices honoring his Christian God. The country churches he builds honor God, but only incompletely. According to Solness, God destroyed everything in Solness's life but his urge to build in order that Solness might concentrate on God's glory more fully. Into Solness's life enfold events designed to torment him into submission to God's will. The dedication of the tower at Lysanger – precisely ten years ago, when and where he met Hilda – marked a critical juncture in Solness's life. Atop the tower in Lysanger ten years ago, Solness reached out toward God and announced, "Hear me, Thou Almighty! From this day on, I'll be a free creator – free in my own realm, as you are in yours."[19] Breaking from a clean Christian causal teleology, Solness falls into an increasingly free, disorderly natural order, one that parallels the robust, "chaotic" spirit of the Viking forebears he so admires. At this point his linear, steady-state existence bifurcates – between the Christian guilt springing from his betrayal of his past and the robustness of the Viking heritage he can't quite attain. The trolls are loosed, and he vacillates between the two bifurcated options. This bifurcated existence is further exacerbated by his recurring guilt into continuingly bifurcating bifurcations (each level "remixing" the degree of guilt and robustness Solness feels), until his life slips into a randomly disordered phase altogether.

A decade later – the actual time of the play – stability amid randomness, the order within disorder/chaos, momentarily returns as he feels he's escaped the trolls. Order returns in the form of Hilda, herself something of a refined troll, offering actual vitality against Solness's efforts to reduce his life to mechanistic simplicity and encouraging him to rise and meet God once again. He gains a certain peace at this point, followed, tragically, by a renewed urge to linearly "control" his destiny. Rather than comprehending a natural pattern that he had been resisting his whole life, Solness musters up his strength once more to insist upon linear control. At this point, considering chaos the foe needing to be vanquished, Solness's rigidity positions him to be crushed by his declared foe.

Given the long life of resisting the natural pattern of order-to-chaos-to-order, Solness has virtually ensured a violent consequence once he chooses an all-or-nothing confrontation. To counteract Solness's unnatural effort to place control upon the processes of chaos, the impending chaos phase is forced into a violent swing that destroys Solness in the process. The lesson here is not that chaos must be prevented or resisted, as might conventionally be deduced (by, say, a Victorian mentality), but that one must allow the pattern to develop as it will, which will thereby prevent the violence of the transition from one phase to another. In essence, it is Solness's unnatural control and restraint, not the natural forces, that doom him. If Solness had initially accepted the patterns of chaos into his life, if he had allowed for robustness, vitality, life itself, the chaos pattern would have provided him with a life fulfilled, though not controlled as expected, but certainly not ruined.

Solness's death marks an end to Solness but apparently not to the self-similar pattern set up in the play, since Ragnar is there to replace the fallen master builder. Here, too, Ibsen's schema follows the chaos model. If Solness's struggle was with God, Ragnar's will likely be with the ghost of his father, Knut. The pattern very likely will recur, but it will be within a window of order within the chaos of Solness's model. And if Ragnar allows the pattern to follow its natural course, Ragnar's fate will not take the violent turn Solness's took. Note here that Solness was a master builder, not an architect, leaving open the possibility of assuming that Solness's pattern of chaos began as a window of order within an even greater master's pattern of chaos. (His or her success or failure in dealing with the pattern, however, is not presented.) The scale in each case may vary, but the pattern remains self-similar. The chaos pattern, relabeled to reflect the pattern in *The Master Builder,* would look like Figure 13.

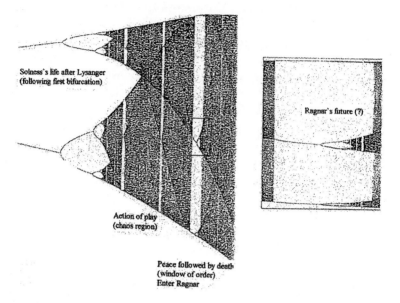

Figure 13. *The Master Builder* and windows of order.

Ibsen – and even Brustein – did not have the scientific model before them, but their insights clearly anticipate what chaos theoreticians have since verified: a breakdown of predeterminable causality, replaced by patterns of bifurcation, chaos, and finally windows of order within the chaos phase. Determinism does exist – confirming one aspect of naturalist doctrine – but predictability does not – rejecting another naturalist presumption. Ironically, it should be noted that not only Ibsen but Solness himself came close to explaining the very process of chaos theory. The butterfly effect is in fact a scientific counterpart to Solness's trolls. Solness's tragic turn – not Ibsen's, however – was that he believed he needed to defeat the trolls, to dominate the uncontrollable. In the process of resistance, he set himself up as antagonist of, rather than conformer to, the uncontrollable, and that antagonism directed his doom. It is this very point of failing to embrace uncertainty and to engage in unpredictable vitality that causes his ruin. His resistance converted the benignity of chaos into the malignant cause of his destruction, ironically setting up a causal connection he could understand. Solness's tragedy is that he does not choose to accept benign chaos.

Here it would be of value to note that while Ibsen as proto-chaotician is perhaps unique/original in late nineteenth-century drama, I am not necessarily arguing that he is universally unique. Note, for example, that earlier I suggested the chaos model could very well apply to *Hamlet*. Rising up to resist forces of uncertainty, struggling to control our environment, is obviously one type of tragic action. Tragedy could in fact be generally read to be a form that depicts humanity's resistance to the chaos process, which becomes all the more tragic if one realizes that the chaos pattern models for us an existence that suggests that order will eventually arise out of disorder provided we allow nature appropriately to run its course. There are many works both pre- and postdating Ibsen, tragic and otherwise, to which this model can apply. Comedy itself may be re-visioned as an ultimate endorsement of behavior that encourages humanity to accept the chaos model in the certainty that such acceptance of natural flow eventually leads to order.

This newly confirmed paradigm additionally engages the age-old philosophical question of human free will, with results not entirely new to human thought. Given the fact that all events are part of a determined system, so too then are humans in part victims of their origins. However, since linear determinism does not exist in this model, humans must also accept responsibility within the parameters of the nonlinear choices afforded them. No one in Ibsen's drama, or presumably in the real world, is either completely free and responsible or completely determined and guiltless.

Stoppard's "Arcadia": Studying the Humanity of Chaos

Tom Stoppard's 1993 play, *Arcadia,* pointedly utilizes chaos theory in ways that Ibsen's *The Master Builder* only intuitively utilizes. Stoppard creates characters who discuss and describe its various implications, and he actually uses chaos patterning to structure the work. As such, the play is the first mainstream theatre product consciously designed to be a "chaos" play. Chaos theory, as Stoppard reports through his character Valentine in *Arcadia,* is a theory that revolutionizes our understanding of "[t]he ordinary-sized stuff which is our lives,"[20] unlike the twentieth-century revolutions of relativity and quantum physics, which only "explain the very big and the very small" (*Arcadia,* p. 48).

The play is set in a single room but in two centuries, 1809 and the present. The latter time period capitalizes on the practical possibility of introducing a character, the graduate-student chaotician Valentine, who is actually able to articulate chaos theory. However, refusing to be bound to simple regurgitation of scientific formulae, Stoppard utilizes the former period to suggest a connection – even a kindred spirit – between twentieth-century chaos thought and the eighteenth/nineteenth-century Romantic frame of mind, both of which oppose the rationalist, eighteenth-century Newtonian frame of mind. The connection is valid, as I've suggested earlier, and is evident from reviewing the course of "chaos" throughout Western philosophy, art, and letters.

In his essay "Turner Translates Carnot,"[21] Michel Serres in part anticipates Stoppard's thesis, suggesting the cultural permeation of Newtonian scientific thought into the aesthetics of the Enlightenment painter George Gerrard, which faces eventual opposition from a revised scientific, nineteenth-century vision of dynamics captured by the Romantic painter J. M. W. Turner. Turner's is an aesthetic that, according to Serres, in many ways anticipates and parallels nineteenth-century breakthroughs in thermodynamic studies, which themselves undermine the eighteenth-century mechanistic world order. Serres describes and analyzes a 1784 work of Gerrard, "something like an advertising sign showing the warehouse of the brewer Samuel Whitbread" ("Turner Translates Carnot," p. 54). Serres describes the piece:

> The collection of objects put on display is the *recapitulation* of a perfect world soon to disappear: men, horses, tools, ships. A wooden shed stands on the dock where a three-master with furled sails has just tied up and is being unloaded: flawless timber woodwork, tie-beams, lintels, and rafters which overhang and cover the scene. . . . Obviously, it is the equipment that is supposed to stand out. . . . The point is to lay out the set of tools and to omit nothing, to tabulate all the products of mechanics, static and dynamic. (pp. 54–5)

The picture is one of "[l]ines, points, circles – geometry" (p. 55); it parallels in spirit the 1788 work of the French Newtonian mathematician Joseph-Louis Lagrange, *Analytic Mechanics*, which, according to Serres, "*recapitulates*, by its story and in its system, a perfect world that will soon disappear, totally overthrown when fire and its power supplant wind and water, horses and men, as source and origin of force" (p. 55). A 1772 painting, *An Iron Forge*, by Joseph Wright of Derby (Figure 14), shows the Enlightenment urge to have "the paddlewheel, the hammer, weights, strictly and geometrically drawn, still triumph over the ingot in fusion" (p. 56).

Figure 14. *An Iron Forge* (1772), oil painting by Joseph Wright of Derby (1734–97).

As Serres observes, the historical and cultural moment depicted in these works is at an end: "From Gerrard [and Wright] to Turner, the path is very simple. It is the same path that runs from Lagrange to Carnot, from simple machines to steam engines, from mechanics to thermodynamics – by way of the Industrial Revolution" (p. 56). Turner "*enters into Wright's ingot*, he enters into the boiler, the furnace, the firebox" (p. 56, italics in original).

Serres goes on to observe that "Turner is not a pre-impressionist. He is a realist, a proper realist. . . . The first true genius in thermodynamics. . . . Turner sees the world in terms of water and fire, as Gerrard saw it in terms of figures and motion" (p. 57).

Turner's 1832 painting *Staffa, Fingal's Cave* (Figure 15) displays the painter's understanding of the triumph of thermodynamics over simple mechanics, revealing a sense that "[t]he cosmos is a steam engine, and inversely" (p. 59).

Figure 15. *Staffa, Fingal's Cave* **(1832), oil painting by J. M. W. Turner (1775–1851). Reprinted by permission from the Yale Center for British Art, New Haven, CT.**

Tonally, Turner's work captures the spirit of entropy, the second law of thermodynamics, which proclaims a natural tendency toward dissipation and universal heat death.[22] Of an early (1797) Turner watercolor, *Iron Foundry,* Serres observes:

> Disorder is everywhere. . . . Theorem: beneath the forms of matter, stochastic disorder reigns supreme. To smelt is to rediscover chance as fundamental. The furnace is the engine for going back towards chaos. The foundry is where creation starts over at zero. (p. 61)

Bohm and Peat make similar observations concerning the visionary nature of Turner's work, observing,

It is curious to note that these paintings were made some three decades before J. C. Maxwell published his electromagnetic theory of light, which replaced the Newtonian order of linear trajectories and rigid forms with fields in constant motion and eternal rotation.[23]

They add, referring to Turner's *Regulus:* "The painting seems, therefore, to symbolize a movement toward a new order in art that at least tacitly and implicitly aims to replace the old" (*Science, Order, and Creativity*, pp. 168–9).

Both Serres and Stoppard see the beginnings of chaos theory breaking through the cultural fabric during the industrial and Romantic revolutions, each concurrent revolution in its own way striving to undermine the eighteenth-century mechanistic universe of enlightened Newtonianism. Stoppard reminds us of thermal power in several instances throughout *Arcadia:* a steam engine is put to good use in replacing the country estate's eighteenth-century formal gardens with Gothic/Romantic landscaping, and a fire consumes the orderly world of the aristocratic family housed on the estate, which is the object of transformation and center of the play's attention. Very specifically, Stoppard has the young Thomasina of the nineteenth-century world grasp the significance of her own growing skepticism toward Newtonian order when she properly evaluates an obscure text actually from the period ("A prize essay of the Scientific Academy in Paris" [*Arcadia,* p. 81]) and concludes that the text "contradicts determinism" (p. 81). She in turn applies this "equation of the propagation of heat in a solid body" (p. 81) to Noakes's steam engine (the one working on the estate), and essentially discovers entropy. This second law of thermodynamics is typically regarded as the first full challenge to the triumphant Newtonianism of the age because it establishes the irreversibility of time, which contradicts Newtonian assumptions that all natural processes can be conducted both forward and backward in time: for example, the process of one billiard ball striking another can be reversed and lead to a return to an original state.

Irregularity in systems behavior, however, cannot be reversed; the process of heat dissipation, for example, is irreversible. There are no laws that allow for regrouping of lost heat to an original condition. As Thomasina rightly concludes, in rather simple yet profound terms, if you stir a bowl of rice pudding and jam, "the spoonful of jam spreads itself round making red trails like the picture of a meteor in my astronomical atlas. But if you stir backward, the jam will not come together again. Indeed, the pudding does not notice and continues to turn pink" (*Arcadia*, pp. 4–5). Thomasina's demonstration is Stoppard's apt illustration of irreversible entropic dissipation. Hence, Thomasina proves Newtonian law to be incomplete at best. Furthermore, by demonstrating that, as her tutor Septimus Hodge later concedes, "atoms do not go according to Newton" (p. 81), Thomasina realizes how thoroughly her budding thermodynamic ideas challenge Newtonian determinism. Things don't happen as Newton proposed they did, at least not all (or even most) things. Complexity must be ignored for Newtonianism to succeed.

But it would take another century, with the advent of quantum physics, to discover true undetermined behavior in microcosmic nature, and nearly two centuries, with actual chaos theory, for science actually to confirm the tenets of unpredictable determinism in the macrocosmic universe. Essentially Stoppard's Thomasina is equivalent to Serres's understanding of Turner: they were both revolutionary in their understanding of the consequences of thermodynamics.

While thermodynamics gets a certain degree of attention in the play, it is only a starting point in an agenda that Stoppard makes clear includes a second visit to the Romantic movement, a period that reveals important critical contours (clinamen-like disruptions) in cultural thought and attitudes. In *Arcadia*, Stoppard sets up a contrastive paradigm between classical, eighteenth-century sculpted gardening styles and the Romantic/Gothic picturesque wildernesses that would supersede the earlier style. The proposed conversion of the grounds at the country estate Sidley Park are described by Lady Croom, the resistant lady of the manor:

> Here [in a sketch] is the Park as it appears to us now, and here [in another sketch] as it might be when Mr. Noakes has done with it. Where there is the familiar pastoral refinement of an Englishman's garden, here is an eruption of gloomy forest and towering crag, of ruins where there was never a house, of water dashing against rocks where there was neither spring nor a stone I could not throw the length of a cricket pitch. My hyacinth dell is become a haunt for hobgoblins, my Chinese bridge, which I am assured is superior to the one at Kew, and for all I know at Peking, is usurped by a fallen obelisk overgrown with briars –. (p. 12)

Responding to Captain Brice (Lady Croom's brother), who observes "It is all irregular," Mr. Noakes confirms, "Irregularity is one of the chiefest principles of the picturesque style –" (p. 12). Figure 16 is a contrastive illustration of an early style of landscaping replaced by the Gothic or picturesque style, not unlike Lady

Figure 16. Comparative scenes from Richard Payne Knight's *The Landscape* (1795). Reproduced from Russell Noyes, *Wordsworth and the Art of Landscape* (Bloomington: Indiana University Press, 1968), by permission of Indiana University Press.

Croom's contrastive descriptions. Irregularity prevails in the picturesque style rather than the former mode of tight order.

Irregularity is the significant nexus term in the play, for irregularity is one of the principles of nature that Thomasina is pursuing in her iconoclastic studies. She glowingly calls Noakes "The Emperor of Irregularity" (p. 85). Working herself on a "new" geometry designed to capture her iconoclastic musings, Thomasina sees Noakes's landscaping work as the inspiration for her new math, which she calls a "New Geometry of Irregular Forms" (p. 43). The connection allies her pursuits with that of Noakes's picturesque style. Seeing the irregular, picturesque, or Gothic style as a sort of model for her own intellectual pursuits, Thomasina makes a cultural connection between a rising (though often resisted) Romantic predisposition and her own scientific endeavors. Culture in this case has influenced and encouraged science – at least Thomasina's science. Specifically, Thomasina's "Geometry of Irregular Forms" becomes an effort to demonstrate that algorithmic iterations charted on a graph reveal the structure of naturally occurring objects such as leaves, rivers, and arterial networks in animals. This process today is known as fractal geometry, and it is yet another significant path of entry into chaotics, a butterfly-effect engagement of the study of morphology.

Newtonian linearity reveals geometric forms not precisely found in nature (for example, cones resemble but do not duplicate mountains); Thomasina is in the process of uncovering fractal functions that reveal order out of the irregularity, or chaos, of nature. As she says, "I will plot this leaf and deduce its equation" (p. 37) – a fractal-based procedure that would be formally developed almost two centuries later, greatly assisted by computers. Stephen Kellert explains fractals as follows:

> A jagged coastline provides a useful example of a fractal-like object. Observed from afar, the coastline reveals some peninsulas and bays; on closer examination, smaller juts and coves are seen, and these again reveal jagged borders when surveyed more closely. If we can imagine the coastline so jagged that with each new level of magnification new details of the terrain appear . . . this is a fractal.[24]

Generally speaking, nature does not create straight edges but rather fractals, increasingly diverse and rich configurations revealed as one upgrades or downgrades the form's scale. What is important (and what has been noted of chaos theory in ways discussed earlier in this text) is the surprising self-similarity that nature utilizes throughout these scaled levels, self-similarity betraying duplication because of small though rising adjustments at each stage. Once again, we see the butterfly effect at work, here as the source of nature's morphological diversity. Tiny initial deviations result in natural diversity, but this does not concede randomness because this morphological butterfly effect produces self-similarity even as it produces diversity. No snowflake is the same though all have convergent similarities.

Fractals and fractal geometry were actually introduced in the mid-1970s by Benoit B. Mandelbrot.[25] The irregular yet self-similar qualities of fractals have since been found to explain/reflect countless physical phenomena far more accurately than previous geometrical applications were able to do. Fractals can be generated by computers using relatively simple reiterative mathematics, resulting, for example, in landscape "pictures" wherein boundaries forever replicate a ragged *pattern* at ever-decreasing scale. The natural parallels include, among other things, actual shorelines whose patterned complexities are seen to generally replicate each other as one moves from, say, a satellite camera's view to an airline passenger's view to a view from a nearby cliff. Discovering the appropriate reiterative equation can actually lead to replication of patterns in nature. As Gleick points out, "The act of writing down a set of rules to be iterated randomly captured certain global information about a shape, and the iteration of the rules regurgitated the information without regard to scale" (p. 237). Apparent random and relatively simple computations eventually reveal ordered, self-similar, scaled patterns actually produced in nature. The need for computers stems more from the need to make *so many* computations, not from any inordinate complexity in the computations. In fact, the complexity fractals describe is mathematically quite simple. Complexity arises from simplicity, as order arises from disorder.

One might recall that strange-attractor chaotics argues for a pervasive order or pattern amidst apparent randomness within countless dynamic systems. Likewise, fractal geometry argues for order amidst countless morphological systems and identifies patterns previously believed to be random. The symmetry may not be the

symmetry our high school math classes taught us, but a sophisticated symmetry of self-similarity – articulable and relatively simple – exists nonetheless.[26] This is precisely Thomasina's argument,
an argument contemporary science has only recently verified.
Through fractal geometry, reconstruction of leaf formation is possible simply by doing what Thomasina suggests, "deducing" the
equation and then plotting iterated solutions (see Figure 17).Quite

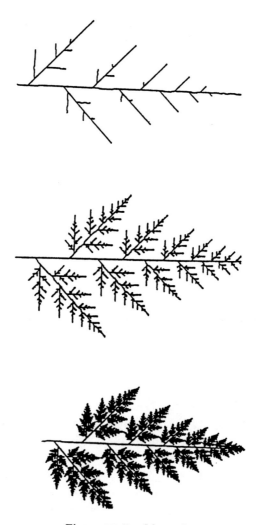

Figure 17. Leaf fractal.

significantly, Goethe (1749–1832), an actual nonfiction contemporary of Thomasina, contemplated precisely the same things contemplated by Thomasina. (Significantly, he was also an influence on Turner.) Goethe's studies led him to the notion of an *Urpflanze*, or original plant, from which he argued all other plants are morphologically derived. Differences occur in the infinite minor variations nature permits (the butterfly effect or clinamen at work), a point fractal geometry today actually describes.[27] But, as in Thomasina's case, Bohm and Peat observe of Goethe's ideas: "Because most of the prevailing ideas concerning the development of form were, at that time, expressed in terms of Euclidian geometry and sequential order, Goethe's notion found little resonance in the science of his day."[28]

Thomasina, too, complains that Newtonian geometry produces "equations [which] only describe the shapes of manufacture" (reminiscent of Gerrard's eighteenth-century art) and that if this is God's mathematics, then "God could only make a cabinet" (*Arcadia*, p. 37). Her tutor, Septimus, brilliant but nonetheless fundamentally Newtonian, replies that God "has mastery of equations which lead into infinities where we cannot follow," to which Thomasina replies, "What a faint heart, We must work outward from the middle of the maze" (p. 37). She chooses to strive for a mastery that will reveal God's mystery to her.

From Thomasina's (and Goethe's) perspective, her contemporary mathematics reduces existence to formulae comprehensible to humanity, and nature must be molded to fit the model. She, however, wants to discover formulae that fully describe nature, without needing to reduce it to conform to human desire. Back to landscape architecture: the eighteenth-century practice entails reducing nature so that it conforms to the limited/limiting prescriptions of existing formulae. Long, sweeping curves and controlled planting are the rule. The picturesque/Romantic style, however, encourages breaching the boundaries of those prescriptions and therefore encourages minds like Thomasina's to uncover the formulae that organically describe the naturally occurring irregularities that have thus far been prescriptively controlled.

Indeed, while Thomasina's perspective – and the picturesque style – encourages a widening view of existence, the actual cultural perspective of her contemporaries argues for a reductionism.

The cultural perspective is so ingrained that God is indeed described as Newtonian. When Lady Croom nearly apostrophizes her park, she essentially makes just this connection:

> The slopes are green and gentle. The trees are companionably grouped at intervals that show them to advantage. The rill is a serpentine ribbon unwound from the lake peacably contained by meadows on which the right amount of sheep are tastefully arranged – in short it is nature as God intended, and I can say with the painter, "*Et in Arcadia ego!*" "Here I am in Arcadia." (*Arcadia,* p. 12)

The delusion is obvious. Nature has been regularized to conform to a human vision of what God's creation should be. Irregularity is deemed unnatural and clearly not part of God's ultimate design. The ironic reality, of course, is that nature uncontrolled does not produce such regularity; rather, it obeys fractal necessity, irregularity created by an "order" that allows small points of unpredictable and unexpected deviations to effect an infinity of self-similar opportunities. Lady Croom's Arcadia is an Arcadia from an eighteenth-century perspective that argues that humanity needs to assist nature in fulfilling God's design. Nature needs to be regularized, something apparently it strives for; but it requires humanity's perfecting, controlling touch in order actually to achieve its final end. Thomasina does not accept such an Arcadia, looking instead for an expanded vision and encouraging nature to reveal its own design of irregularity, unfettered by Newtonian restrictions that lead to reductive Newtonian fictions.

The significance of the nineteenth-century section of the play is pronounced. As Hayles has argued, "*Issues become energized in theories because they are replicated from and reproduced in the social*" (italics in original).[29] Stoppard has made this very claim in his work, suggesting that a Thomasina *could* have existed in 1809 because the necessary information was available and because the social inclination toward "irregularity," as attested by the picturesque style, was also culturally available, though not pervasive. We should add that the existence of Turner and Goethe also confirms the possibility of a Thomasina. That Stoppard's young genius is intellectually exceptional cannot be denied, but Stoppard is very clear in making her a product of her culture: she is ahead of her age as any genius is, but she is very much a part of her age in much the same way Galileo, Newton, and Einstein were part of theirs. This observation, of course, contradicts the prevailing notion that science is "pure" and "unpolluted" by cultural influences, but the history of science continually verifies the claim that culture influences science and science influences culture. Stoppard, apparently, likewise agrees with this theory of scientific–cultural entwinement.

Unlike Galileo, Newton, and Einstein, however, Thomasina was not equipped with the proper apparatuses fully to confirm her theories. As the twentieth-century Valentine observes, for chaos theory "[t]he electronic calculator was what the telescope was for Galileo" (p. 51). So until the technology could catch up to the thought, thought remained in the realm of abstraction, mere philosophy.

With this obstacle in mind, Stoppard introduces the late twentieth-century counterparts to the nineteenth-century cast, including Valentine, the student of nonlinear mathematics, who provides regular commentary on the chaotic nature of nature. He concludes rather straightforwardly, "The unpredictable and the predetermined unfold together to make everything the way it is" (p. 47), a now commonplace observation among chaos scientists but the very thing Thomasina was groping to conclude. And while Valentine believes that Thomasina's documents verify that she was only "playing with the numbers" (p. 47), he confirms that she was at least approaching a procedure whereby algorithmic values are charted, and parts of their values are fed back into a new algorithm and charted, and so on ad infinitum (hence the need for a computer), until the initial value and its infinite feedback create a figure. With the correct initial value, one could reproduce the shape of a leaf; in fact, with infinite minor variations one could reproduce every leaf form that nature ever produced, as Goethe suggested, introducing minor initial conditions (of which these systems are sensitively dependent) to reveal the infinite variety seen in the general form "leaf" as created by nature.

So Valentine confirms that Thomasina's goal of understanding the mathematics of her leaf is presently possible:

> If you knew the algorithm and fed it back say ten thousand times, each time there'd be a dot somewhere on the screen. You'd never know where to expect the next dot. But gradually you'd start to see

this shape, because every dot will be inside the shape of this leaf.
(p. 47)

This description (illustrated in Figure 17) provides something of a sense of the rising order out of chaos, an order that will in fact be reproduced in larger scale in Noakes's picturesque style, a landscape initially created by Noakes but then permitted to rise on its own, a wild (but not random), verdant Arcadia. Without maintaining it, without keeping it "regular," as a Newtonian or eighteenth-century mentality would insist, the actual results of Noakes's initial conditions are impossible to deduce, beyond certain chaotics-described parameters, that is. Noakes's landscape is a chaotics paradigm ripe with unpredictable determinism and highly sensitive to initial conditions whose ultimate influences we can't fully predict beyond what the probability of strange attractors allows us to predict, which, of course, is far below traditionalist desires for strict control.

This uncontrolled free flow parallels the irregularities discovered in twentieth-century chaotics. As Valentine observes, "We can't even predict the next drip from a dripping tap when it gets irregular. Each drip sets up the conditions for the next, the smallest variation blows prediction apart" (p. 48). Romanticism may have introduced (reintroduced?) Western thought to irregularity, but without the equipment and scientific confirmation, the full consequences would not be felt. Now they can. Again Valentine observes:

> When you push the numbers through the computer you can see it on the screen. The future is disorder. A door like this has cracked open five or six times since we got up on our hind legs. It's the best possible time to be alive, when almost everything you thought you knew is wrong. (p. 48)

His is an enthusiastic statement echoed numerous times today in the publications of contemporary scientists caught up in chaotics possibilities.

But Valentine's enthusiasm for a new world paradigm is not shared by others in the play – except for Thomasina. Lady Croom's general disapproval of the irregularity of the picturesque style is an initial sign. Her mind is configured to accept the regularities of Newtonian order, and so are the minds of others. Reading Thomasina's essay on heat death, even her tutor Septimus responds, "You should not have written it. . . . It will make me mad as you promised" (p. 92), and later, "So, we are all doomed" (p. 93). Being Cambridge-educated and therefore programmed to a traditional view, even the apparently free-thinking genius tutor resists Thomasina's evidence. In fact Septimus appears to have gone mad shortly after Thomasina's death, retreating to the hermitage (one can assume he's the mysterious hermit of Sidley Park) and producing piles of paperwork with mysterious scribblings left on them, apparently having become a human computer and apparently having pursued a lifelong struggle either to prove or to disprove Thomasina's theory, a struggle he seems to have lost, though the play doesn't fully fill in the details. (An uncompleted fractal beginning?)

That even twentieth-century minds have Newtonian configurations is verified by the separate endeavors of Hannah and Bernard, inhabitants of the play's contemporary set. Hannah uses her mind to try to prove that Sidley Park is paradigmatic of the nineteenth-century "decline from thinking to feeling" (p. 27), intimating a desire to use orderly thought to prove it superior to the chaos/picturesque/Romantic model, which she describes as the irregularity of sentiment. And Bernard's enterprise is to prove that in 1809 Lord Byron was involved in a murderous duel at Sidley, which would solve the mystery of Byron's self-imposed exile thus far unexplained by scholars. In both cases, but especially for Bernard, evidence presents itself not in a regular and linear fashion, but much as the leaf reveals itself on the algorithmic graph – unpredictable dot by unpredictable dot – to reveal a reality/truth that belies every effort at "regular" thought. Bernard nevertheless proceeds linearly to his ultimate academic embarrassment. Likewise, Hannah's premises lead her to conclude that a minor nineteenth-century author deserves acclaim because of that author's craftlike sense of order, as opposed to the irregular "ramblings" of her more famous contemporaries. In the process of individual awakening, Hannah learns the value of "feeling," and Bernard learns that a "logical" reconstruction of the past reveals unforeseen trackings on his graph of reconstruction. What their minds have been configured to expect is fractally undermined by nature and reality itself. At different levels, they both learn something of the value of chaos, of the truth that unexpected order rises out of moments of unpredictability.

Bernard sees his personal search for scholarly fame dashed

when he attempts to complete a picture of Byron's visit to Sidley Park by following traditional procedures of inquiry. He accumulates data apparently sufficient to deduce a linear progression that concludes that a duel must have occurred in 1809 and that Byron was involved. Ingeniously, Stoppard sets the evidence before his audience so that it too can make similar linearly informed conclusions. Given the evidence, it is reasonable to chart out the conclusions as Bernard has done. But as with the algorithmic leaf, one cannot surmise where the next dot will be charted. We must be prepared *not* to draw extended conclusions from limited evidence because the unpredicted must be expected, anticipated, though in ways that prepare us to brace for the mysteries of the unexpected. For Hannah, one lesson is that had she tapped into the unpredictable realm of feeling, as Bernard suggests, she "might have written a better book. Or at any rate the right book" (p. 63), referring to her earlier, reductive attempt to write a definitive biography of Caroline Lamb. The same reductiveness is currently being applied to her research on the landscaping history of Sidley Park. And Bernard learns a similar lesson, to let evidence reveal itself rather than to try to squeeze the evidence into an ill-fitting prescriptive thesis. As with nature, history too provides its own fit, though invariably of an irregular sort.

That very few of the characters embrace chaos is, of course, not surprising. It appears very appropriate for Stoppard to have created intelligent twentieth-century characters who self-similarly (though fractally far from precisely) behave like their rational nineteenth-century counterparts. Despite the undermining of regularity, people, even today, fiercely cling to the illusion of regularity. Hayles echoes Valentine's earlier-cited sense of excitement when she observes, "Many scientists have commented that working on chaos has allowed them to renew their sense of wonder" (*Chaos Bound,* p. 292). But she adds, "The innocence of chaos is an assumption that is most tenable when one believes that the self is not itself constructed by the same forces that are replicated in theories and in the social matrix" (p. 293). When these new discoveries suggest that humans themselves are products of chaos/irregularity, traditional views of identity and personal control are challenged to the discomfort even of many of chaotics' greatest supporters, a challenge rarely based on evidence but on desire.[30] Hence, Newtonian regularity and determinist control frequently remain a comforting point of retreat. However, perhaps as Stoppard (and Hayles) suggests, our culture should see regularity as a movement that actually harmfully separates us from nature, placing us dangerously above nature, while the chaos paradigm encourages us to take the more healthy path of re-engaging nature. As Valentine observes:

> When your Thomasina was doing maths it had been the same maths for a couple of thousand years. Classical. And for a century after Thomasina. Then maths left the real world behind, just like modern art, really. Nature was classical, maths was suddenly Picassos. But now nature is having the last laugh. The freaky stuff is turning out to be mathematics of the natural world. (*Arcadia*, pp. 44–5)

Renaturalizing humanity and human thought has perhaps occurred in the most unexpected of ways. What we once considered the work of lunatics, lovers, poets, irregular geniuses, and fantasists, now appears to be the work of consummate realists. Resistance to such a perspective, of course, persists, in favor of Newtonian order, but the need to convert individual and cultural thought is critical – and the opportunity has now arisen.

Stoppard's play focuses on the confused humanity of his characters, the fact that they are *not* in control of their lives as they publicly try to verify. Chloë, an innocent twentieth-century girl who is a simple mind amidst intellectuals, pondering the nature of universal determinism and seemingly out of her realm as she does it, makes perhaps the most telling observation of all: "The universe is deterministic all right, just like Newton said, I mean it's trying to be, but the only thing wrong is people fancying people who aren't supposed to be in that part of the plan" (p. 73). Valentine puts it in more formal terms: "Ah, the attraction that Newton left out. All the way back to the apple in the garden" (p. 74). If Chloë is right, humanity's engagement in the universe involves a desire for mechanistic determinism washed over by unpredictable but nonetheless determined and totally natural inclinations. Human emotions are the strange attractor in human dynamics, the deterministically unpredictable side of humanity that allows us to engage in nature rather than to try to dominate and control it. "Declining to feeling" and accepting the chaos pattern in our lives will allow us to appreciate "Arcadia" as no traditional rational enterprise can. While one could see order as thought-imposed control over the disorder of indulgent feeling, one could/should perhaps more generally accept the chaos paradigm as a life model embracing both thought and feeling. When one informs the other, the result may very likely be a life well lived, in scaled harmony with the disorderly order of all existence.

Moving from Thomasina's leaf to Noakes's picturesque ecosystem, we move up in scale from one organic system to another, and they are fractally self-similar in pattern. So, too, does the play work on presenting self-similar realities on various scales. Valentine describes unpredictable patterns as pervasive in nature: "It's how nature creates itself, on every scale, the snowflake and the snowstorm" (p. 47). And later, from size to time, he describes scale, referring to weather patterns: "Six thousand years in the Sahara looks like six months in Manchester, I bet you" (p. 48). Apparent patternlessness is controverted when scale is considered. In the play, we have instances of self-similar repetition between 1809 and 1993, between leaf and park, between the formation of Thomasina's leaf and Bernard's Byron story, between Septimus's hermit project and Valentine's computer calculations. Even the algorithmic graphing of the leaf (the smallest-scaled system in the play) finds self-similar parallels in the very nonlinear, seemingly chaotic structure of the play (the largest-scaled system), wherein each scene is separately graphed with little concern for linearly presented chronology but so as collectively to reveal, scene by scene, a whole picture. We ultimately have before us a self-similar pattern of the accumulated totality of the nineteenth- and twentieth-century cast of characters and stream of events (though the latter time frame is not yet completed).

Even out of the tragedy of Thomasina's death (sadly though fittingly by fire) arises the regenerative self-ordering of thought and life that, in chaos terms, belies the gloom of the second law of thermodynamics by arguing for the rise of order even from the greatest of disorders, death itself, for Stoppard's art provides regeneration even as he presents us with the knowledge of Thomasina's death. Heat death is a universal inevitability, but in the face of that inevitability occur countless natural and human actions of significant, if impermanent, self-organization. Life – the paradigm of self-organization – literally defies an otherwise pervasive universal movement toward disorder. What we have of life we should revel in rather than merely strive to control or prolong. Life should inspire living in the face of inevitable physical disintegration. Beyond this point comes the additional assurance that, as Valentine observes, chaos theory gives us the necessary information to live in confidence that "the next [world] will come" (p. 78), even as we verge on losing the present one.

Stoppard's romanticism is not a romanticism of its sometimes-recognized logical extreme and classicism's opposite. That would be absurdism. Rather, his romanticism lies between the classical and absurdist either/or, occupying a both/and landscape of interacting order and disorder eternally at play. Ultimately, in *Arcadia* we have a fractal play demonstrating an orderly disorder and reflecting chaotics existence at every scale.

In *Arcadia*, we see a renaturalizing of human experience and thought that parallels what Una Chaudhuri calls "ecotheater."[31] The chaos paradigm works to reconnect humanity with nature, redirecting the course of contemporary thought, which has striven to highlight our natural exile. Using Spalding Gray as her example, Chaudhuri notes a turn toward reunion, a solution to our sense of dislocation through a theatre that establishes "a new relationship between itself and its world" (*Staging Place*, p. 82). Chaudhuri's discussion of Gray in many ways parallels mine here on Stoppard, though without using chaos. The point is that the chaos paradigm may be the paradigm embedded in numerous potential resolutions to the dilemmas facing late twentieth-century culture. The following chapter will work to unearth such embedded chaos parallels in the American theatre.

3

Intuitive Intersections

American Drama Confronts Orderly Disorder

ONCE AGAIN we return to the observation that naturalism and absurdism have been two strongly influential movements that have polarized modern Western theatre, arguing respectively for a linearly causal global perspective of human behavior and for a local vision from which ultimately no human behavioral patterns can be abstracted. We have standardly been left to choose between existence represented as strict linear determinism or utter randomness.

In his 1978 essay "The Crack in the Chimney: Reflections on Contemporary American Playwriting,"[1] Robert Brustein extended the naturalism–absurdism debate specifically to American theatre. In the essay, Brustein chastised twentieth-century American dramatists for their allegiance to tightly causal and linearly constructed works whose logical assumptions "belong to the eighteenth century, which is to say the age of Newton, rather than to the twentieth century, the age of Einstein" (p. 148). In contrast to this allegiance, Brustein observes that absurdism never became a force in American thought or theatre, agreeing with Martin Esslin, who succinctly observes, "In the United States the belief in progress that characterized Europe in the nineteenth century has been maintained into the middle of the twentieth century."[2] American drama for the most part has even to this day remained linear and progressive, refusing seriously to acknowledge the randomness, stagnation, and entropic doom embodied in absurdist drama.

But while Brustein notes the general adherence to causal progression of plot in the work of such playwrights as O'Neill and Miller, he is perhaps the first to observe a more recent and growing intent on the part of contemporary American playwrights to overturn the standard methodology and its attendant linearly causalist philosophy. Here Brustein loosely anticipates a direction in American drama, not quite absurdist or naturalist, but a blending of the two that Samuel Bernstein would later identify in the title of his study *The Strands Entwined*.[3] A hybrid form, naturalist/realist in appearance but absurdist in sympathies, according to Brustein and Bernstein, has come into existence. Enoch Brater has likewise come to realize that the realism of contemporary American playwrights is of a new sort: "The possibilities we now find in that elusive term *realism* . . . are really quite different from those stable qualities we were once told were there."[4] However, seeing realism – new or old – on stage has resulted in a problem of audience reception, since the appearance of realism suggests the attendant philosophy of an extreme realism, namely naturalism. But to these new playwrights, the appearance itself is critical because it is the very thing that these playwrights are undermining. Creating a realist front is essential in the movement to challenge all it represents.

Rabe's 1976 play *Streamers* is an excellent example. *Streamers* concludes with a sequence of violent, seemingly senseless and bloody events. New York audiences, for one, were clearly repelled by the events before them, for reasons explained by reviewer Walter Kerr: "What the audience asks for is a pattern, a design, a shape that will embrace what they are now looking at and place it in significant relationship to what has gone on before and what may come after."[5] The concluding events of the play shatter causal expectations, confusing an audience prepared for unity and design. While a play with a clearly nonrealist premise, acting style, and set – as an absurdist playwright might present – would better prepare an audience to expect a vision of randomness, a realist format invariably leads an audience to expect "Ibsenesque" causality. But Rabe refuses to present such an order (though, ironically, his play *is* Ibsenesque if we accept the revisionist position of the previous chapter), creating a work that insists we question traditional visions of order and begin to consider the inescapable cracks in our assumptions that such order and design are universal natural constants.

That Rabe and others have experienced such audience and critical resistance is not necessarily surprising,[6] for such resistance to the new is typical in art as well as in science. As Bohm and Peat observe, speaking specifically of the scientific community, "[U]nless the mind is free of rigid commitments to familiar notions of order . . . it cannot provide a context within which basically new orders might be perceived."[7] They add more generally,

> Just as a paradigm is realized when scientists develop fixed habits of mind that leave them insensitive to subtle changes and overemphasize certain obvious differences, so in a similar way can the artist and the viewer become rigid in their responses. (*Science, Order, and Creativity*, p. 167)

Of course, when such resistance is broken down, then "[l]ooking at a work of art [becomes] a creative act which leads to an order similar to that which the artist had in mind when the original work was created" (p. 171). Introducing such a new order – cracking the old paradigm – is precisely what Rabe is attempting, but the shift is not so great that it should be considered ultimately what Thomas S. Kuhn would consider "incommensurate" with the past orders,[8] for such art as Rabe's is a crucial extension of rather than a break with visions of the past. From this perspective, it becomes easier to see Rabe as not needing to be so revolutionary that he challenges the old order by simply embracing the apparent opposites of disorder/randomness/chaos; rather, he has the option of envisioning a continuum that includes disorder as a crucial, intregated element along the general spectrum of order–disorder. Though audiences may feel that they are in the midst of a revolution in art, this revolution nonetheless has strong and necessary evolutionary contacts with the past.

Though violating strict naturalist philosophy in *Streamers*, Rabe is in fact subscribing, as Esslin would describe it, to naturalism's legacy of experimentally exploring the realm of reality with a scrutinizing, "scientific" eye. In Rabe's particular case, what is explored is not the linear science of Newton but a science of nonlinear dynamics. Certainly strict Newtonian causality is abandoned at the conclusion of *Streamers*. Yet Rabe also presents something more than an absurdist embodiment of inexplicable, unpatterned randomness. His theatre presents something that incorporates both the classically closed causality of naturalism and the open-ended randomness of absurdism. The play scatters events that amount to seemingly unrelated causes of the play's final effects, but these causes rise to reflect and follow principles increasingly significant in contemporary scientific thought, especially the butterfly effect.

Rabe is, at least intuitively, a chaotician; this is a point that Bernstein's work *The Strands Entwined* approaches, but once again the chaotics position is never actually reached. Bernstein instead sees at work in Rabe and others "the relations of realism to Absurdism, the two major strains in each of the works" (p. xii), suggesting only that these playwrights capitalize on the familiar realist form to present an absurdist vision. This, I believe, is also Brustein's basic understanding of recent shifts in American drama. I am suggesting, however, that keystone aspects of both naturalism *and* absurdism coexist in such plays, but they argue for a dynamic interplay between order and disorder rather than, say, either an alternating emphasis of one over the other or the use of one merely to convey by negation the "true" essence of the other. One must recall a crucial observation by Bohm and Peat that places these intuitive encounters with chaos in a critical cultural matrix. They observe of twentieth-century scientific breakthroughs: "As the old framework was gradually dropped and new notions of cause, motion, and matter evolved, science underwent a major transformation in the way it looked at the world, a change which was absorbed into the new tacit infrastructure" (*Science, Order, and Creativity,* p. 29). This institutionalizing of a new tacit infrastructure within a science discipline can be said likewise to have occurred in art throughout history: consider, for example, the nineteenth-century resistance to Impressionism (an example Bohm and Peat actually use; see pp. 170–1), now accepted as a conventional way of representing and viewing the world. In fact it is very nearly cliché in its familiarity. One could in turn suggest that what Rabe is undertaking is a similar infrastructural transformation, having tacitly absorbed a twentieth-century, possibly scientifically derived, infrastructural pattern and utilizing that tacit infrastructure, which is familiar to specific intellectual elements of our society but not yet fully accepted in popular culture – though it could be argued it is fast becoming tacitly institutionalized with the assistance of Rabe and other popularly connected artists and media.

While straightforward naturalism or "classic" realism in general may lead audiences to expect a single line of causality to determine ultimate outcomes, something akin to a butterfly effect intrudes into the events of plays like *Streamers* to produce determined, yet unpredictable, behavior. Hindsight will reveal that causes were indeed present, but attempts to anticipate which causes will have lesser or greater effects will only produce probable conclusions at best, which finally may or may not occur. This brand of realism in the theatre would seem to embody a new vision of reality similar to that provided by chaos science. Unpredictable determinism, an almost inconceivable concept for an audience trained to expect causal linearity, begins to permeate the fabric of popular American theatre.

Rabe articulates this concept of unpredictable order in his "Afterword" to *Hurlyburly* (1984), where he describes

> the "realistic" or "well-made" play [as] . . . that form which thinks that cause and effect are proportionate and clearly apparent, that people know what they are doing as they do it, and that others react accordingly, that one thing leads to another in a rational, mechanical way, a kind of Newtonian clock of a play, a kind of Darwinian assemblage of detail which would then determine the details that must follow, the substitution of the devices of logic for the powerful sweeps of pattern and energy that is our lives.[9]

According to Rabe, traditional realism has buried "the powerful sweeps of pattern and energy that is our lives" (chaotics) under an avalanche of Newtonian "devices of logic" (naturalism). Put another way, our culture and its theatre has never acknowledged such sweeps in favor of the devices it could more easily comprehend.

Though never actually hitting upon chaotics, Rabe's notion of sweeps of pattern and energy strongly echoes the concept of causes fluctuating nonlinearly and leading to unexpected and disproportionate, though still causally predicated, effects. He has in one way or another internalized the concept of the butterfly effect. Note, especially, that Rabe argues for "pattern" and therefore cannot be considered absurdist; but since his visioning of pattern is not directed by devices of conventional logic, he is anything but a traditional causalist.

Though perhaps not his most successful effort at displaying orderly disorder, Rabe's 1986 play *Goose and Tomtom* indicates Rabe's tentative awareness of advances in science. Rabe chose three epigraphs for the published text,[10] the first a short, reverentially metaphysical fable showing humanity enslaved by its fears, the third a quote by Sonny Liston: "I'd rather be a lamppost in Denver than the mayor of Philadelphia." The second epigraph – appropriately "middle" – is from the quantum physicist Werner Heisenberg: "Not only is the Universe stranger than we think, it is stranger than we can think." Though Heisenberg is speaking of the subatomic universe, the passage appears to appeal to Rabe on the macrolevel of human existence as well. The strange attractors of chaos pervade existence in ways not fully comprehensible to Rabe – or, presumably, to any of us – because too much involves the unthinkable, certainly from a traditional perspective. So to present the vision of the logically unthinkable, Rabe inserts apparently extraterrestrial beings into the world of *Goose and Tomtom*. They speak from a position "alien" to our own current existence, but they also speak the words the characters Goose and Tomtom are trying but unable to articulate:

> The sea was blue as the sky, and in this we saw a uniformity in the design of all things in which our place, should we ever come to understand it, would be equally harmonious. That this time of understanding had not yet come did not dismay us. (*Goose and Tomtom*, pp. 116–17)

If "uniformity" were replaced by the more specific synonym (for chaos theory) "self-similarity," these beings could very easily be speaking of fractals, a key to chaos theory's effort to find a roughly patterned (though certainly not linear) harmony in all things.

Consider the fractally generated landscapes in Figure 18, for example, as evidence that fractal geometry may be exactly the tool to assist these beings in their search for a comprehensible design. In addition to using fractal equations rather whimsically to create hypothetical natural landscapes (a process often used today to create movie backdrops), science can also work from the other direction, one of viewing actual natural landscapes and deriving

Figure 18. Landscape fractal. From Benoit B. Mandelbrot, *The Fractal Geometry of Nature* (New York: W. H. Freeman and Co., 1977). Reproduced by permission of the author.

explanatory fractal equations (as Stoppard's Thomasina anticipates). Such a process comes tantalizingly close to Rabe's sought-after grand design. Fractals can be derived for geological landscapes as well as the landscapes of human faces, for morphologies of leaves as well as the trees on which they grow, tributary systems as well as circulatory systems, and countless other systems. Fractal geometry, the math of chaos, makes it quite reasonable to assume that developments in chaotics have brought us one significant step closer to the understanding that Rabe's extraterrestrial incarnations and Rabe himself is searching for, in which case otherworldly beings such as Rabe invokes (and which are like Solness's trolls in *The Master Builder*) would no longer be necessary.

Despite Brustein's and Rabe's imprecision in articulating ideas that have become more exact in the wake of chaos science, it is clear that science and theatre are fast approaching agreement on new, more sophisticated, and subtle ways of viewing and representing the world around them. A crucial aspect of this shift in how to model reality is the way information is conceived. Realism and naturalism have been both praised and condemned for the techniques they use to manipulate the knowledge and information they provide. An objective, documentary rhetoric and an emphasis on recording the data of experience with acute detail and verisimilitude is, of course, the hallmark of all realistic art. The question of realism's status as an object of knowledge, a source of information, has thus been crucial in critical assessments of the form. The information that early realist theatre amassed was judged complete and accurate, and the technologies that made the communicative task complete – from stage design to acting technique and appropriately realistic dramatic texts – were lauded for their ability to describe systems of reality exactly and completely, with Newtonian precision.

More recent critiques of realism, however, have emphasized the duplicity inherent in its claims to objective, complete representation and perfect information, though one can actually return to Zola to uncover similar cracks in the pervading objectivist confidence. As a recent example, we have William Worthen's insightful critique of realism's attempts to assign a "'scientific' transparency" to its practices by "attenuat[ing] the medium," thereby positioning the audience as objective and unstaged so as to "legitimate its private acts of interpretation as objective."[11] European naturalism, manifested in particular by Ibsen and Chekhov, created dramas in which the direction of causality was toward a kind of moral, economic, or physical heat death, an entropic decline from order to disorder. American dramatists, however, generally resisted this entropic paradigm in favor of an optimistic, progressive vision of existence as rising order.

Perhaps because of their closer experience with cultural decay, Europeans more generally accepted visions of universal entropy while American optimism, enforced by a vision of "successful" American progress, chose more positively to see the naturalist universe as something of a perpetual motion machine, constantly revitalizing and rejuvenating itself. For example, though Clifford Odets was strongly influenced by Chekhovian style, his works constantly regenerate energy in a typically American pattern of rejuvenation. Consider, as one example from a nearly bottomless canon of hope, the conclusion to Odets's 1935 "Chekhovian" play, *Awake and Sing!*, where against all reasonable indications the young Ralph generates the self-confidence to challenge the world and look forward to the future. Perhaps because they were culturally unprepared and generally unwilling to accept the more sobering likelihood of inevitable decadence deriving from the entropic paradigm, Americans have adjusted to the pessimistic perspective more slowly and with a resistance that would never fully result in absurdism.

One upshot of the paradigm of dissipation/decadence confronting American optimism is that disorder is regularly seen simply as the point of reality existent prior to a return to order. Likewise, rising suspicions concerning objectivist validity have nonetheless led to something less than a radical, absurdist rejection of rational possibilities. A modified stance on the possibilities of objectifiable posturing has been taken, at least in the theatre, and at least by such playwrights as Rabe and Sam Shepard: qualitative, patterned generalities rather than quantitative, controlled/controllable precision has been the result. And absurdist randomness, though occasionally indulged, is never a pervasive American thought.

Rabe and Shepard Reconsidered

Although it is unlikely that Rabe or any other American playwright is well versed in specific recent trends in the scientific community, Rabe's work demonstrates a keen awareness of the limitations of a dramatic form like naturalism, or any other form that carries the burden of reproducing reality in such a way that linear clarity and order are singular goals. His plays explore the possibility that higher levels of knowing are produced when precise control is destabilized, when information degrades and consequently creates noise or disorder, from which a new order may generate.

While *Streamers* may have been an appropriate starting point in following Rabe's assault on order, and while *Goose and Tomtom* is an interesting extension of the assault, *Hurlyburly* (1984) is Rabe's most sustained and rigorous assault on naturalist causality. The words "logic," "logical," "syllogism," "deduction," and "induction" pervade the play's dialogue, set up only to be undermined by the disorderly sweeps and nonlinear patterns that energize the lives of the characters. That the theatre establishment, apparently even at the highest levels, was not prepared for such an assault is evident in audience responses to *Streamers* as well as in *Hurlyburly*'s original Broadway production, where significant cuts were made to Rabe's text. Mike Nichols, the director, "cut everything about Phil [a central character] that could make him interesting or complex or vulnerable and tried to turn him into a total creep," according to Rabe.[12] The production essentially eliminated the complexities of chaos, reducing the play to a linear narrative, more easily accessible to its audience, and failing to incorporate the flood of uncertainties and ambiguities present in the original text.

In the text, each character handles these floods of uncertainty in a spectrum of ways, creating a range of order–disorder on a sliding scale from naturalist reductionism to absurdist randomness. Phil is a character struggling to control or at least understand the uncertainties that engulf his life but lacking a clear position on this sliding scale of perspective. Eddie offers one extreme, reductively utilizing cool abstractions both to explain himself, when possible, and to discard untidy material when it fails to fit his self-conception. Mickey, on the other hand, sees randomness as the "order" of the day and uses that posture of total freedom as an excuse to behave as an ethical egoist: cut free from a meaningful, rational world, as he sees it, what is now right is that which provides him with the greatest gains.

Phil's life becomes something of the experimental material wherein to test various possible ways of now viewing existence. His self-doubts reach their articulated peak in the following exchange, which additionally affects Eddie's own visions:

PHIL: . . . I mean, we got these dark thoughts, I see 'em in you, you don't think you're thinkin' 'em, so we can't even nail that down,

how we going to get beyond it? They are the results of your unnoticed inner goings-on or my gigantic paranoia, both of which
exist, so the goddamn thing in its entirety is on the basis of what
has got to be called a coin toss.

EDDIE: I can figure it, I can – It's not a goddamn coin toss.

PHIL: You think I'm being cynical when I say that? Nothing is necessary, Eddie. Not a fucking thing! We're in the hands of something, it could kill us now or later, it don't care. Who is this guy
that makes us just – you know – WHAT? . . . THERE'S A WORD FOR
IT – . . . IT'S LIKE A LAW. IT'S A LAW? WHAT THE FUCK IS LAW?
(*Hurlyburly,* p. 70)

Eddie's desparate response notwithstanding, the two men are
grappling with something that does appear to be an ethical coin
toss. Like Einstein insisting to quantum scientists that God does
not play dice with the universe (or like the more positively posi-
tioned coin-tossing scene in Stoppard's *Rosencrantz and Guildenstern Are Dead*), Phil recognizes that something exists besides randomness, that there is an order, even a law, governing existence.
But what law is it? In his way, Phil grasps at anthropomorphizing
that source, calling it a guy (recalling Solness's trolls), as one
might expect given his male consciousness. But this "guy" can just
as easily be the nonhuman forces at work under the name of chaos,
an order perfectly comprehensible if and when Phil could transcend to the new paradigm of understanding as outlined by the
new sciences, a process Rabe demands even without a clear grasp
of chaotics.

Trapped in a world formerly controlled by a masculine ideal of
domination, these men (like Miller's Willy Loman) are now thrust
into a world where past processes and beliefs are no longer acceptable. The delusional patriarchy is crumbling, and they can neither
reinforce the crumbling foundations nor find a satisfying linear
replacement. Themselves products of manipulated logical devices
that formerly granted them power, they are now struggling in
something even greater than a gender war, trying to comprehend
the forces that have replaced those devices and stripped them of
their privileged positions of power. Mickey has basically gone
underground and modified his avenue to control through guerrilla
tactics of random egoist subversion. Eddie, more conscientious
and perhaps even more sincere, strives to hold onto his rationalist

infrastructure while shifting to a new and growing, but as yet foggy, cultural reality. But for Eddie such a move does not provide any significant sense of contentment. He remains basically out of orbit.

Eddie works within the old logical paradigm – a master of its rhetoric – but his logic basically proves nothing because, as an audience soon realizes, Eddie can manipulate it to validate whatever he chooses, albeit unsettlingly and uncomfortably. For example, trying to console the distraught Phil, who is on the verge of losing his wife (and his mind), Eddie moves from the emotions of Phil to his own abstraction of logic:

> She hates you, she hates me. She hates men. . . . It's a goddamn syllogism. . . . The fucker's irrefutable, except that's not how it works, GODDAMNIT. . . . You start from the particular in something. . . . Oh, my god, do you know what it is? . . . Science! What goes the other way is science, in which you see all the shit like data and go from it to the law. . . . We have just verified, and I mean scientifically, the bitch has been proven to basically hate all men. (pp. 22–3)

The devices of science are irrefutable, at least so claims Eddie. But Eddie's science is a classicist's science, striving to verify the unverifiable. We must here recall the recent scientific concession that science regulates/fictionalizes results by the very elements it chooses to observe and by the means with which it observes them. But the objective *appearance* of truth, manifest in the tools of linear logic, is for Eddie objective truth itself. Eddie's ramblings, of course, don't undermine the scientific process; they merely call into doubt the capacity of science to prove what he wants it to prove, and what it once thought it could prove.

Phil is less obsessively looking for controllable or manipulable truth. Though in many ways he is confused into believing that that is exactly what he wants, what surfaces is that Phil is looking for a meaningful and lasting relationship, something not predicated at all on a sense of control. Seemingly willing to let nature reveal itself rather than desiring to manipulate it, Phil actually comes close to moving one step toward chaotics. But at last unable to find the meaningfulness both he and Eddie look for, Phil commits suicide, leaving Eddie lost. Eddie comes to realize that he is impotent in the face of a reality that does not operate by the laws he once believed in.

Interestingly, Mickey jokingly selects precisely the right description of the hurlyburly events of the play, but the description falls without comprehension. He actually uses the phrase "the pattern in the randomness" (p. 89) derisively, as he watches Eddie and Phil grope for meaning.

The pattern in the randomness is nonetheless independently pursued by Eddie after Phil's death. Phil leaves the suicide message "The guy who dies in an accident understands the nature of destiny" (p. 142), suggesting that he had somehow come to understand reality but could not face the truth about the chaotics he's confronted. His epiphany is unbearable because it fails to offer the rock-solid comfort he has learned to hunger for. Properly attaching to "accident" (randomness) and "destiny" (determinism), Eddie nonetheless continues to struggle for meaning, which ironically is now in his hands, though – as Phil apparently despairingly realized – it's a less certain, qualitative meaning rather than the manipulable quantitative one he fruitlessly pursues. Life is continual interplay between randomness/"accident" and determinism/"destiny." However, not yet freed from his own devices of simple, linear, Newtonian logic, Eddie cannot comprehend and finally dismisses the message: "[I]f it is an anagram, it wouldn't be cryptic. The cryptic element would have been, you know, more than handled by the fact that it was in a fucking anagram to begin with, right? . . . [F]ollow the logic of what I'm saying. It's logical" (p. 149). Though Phil's message is lost on Eddie and the rest of the *Hurlyburly* cast, Rabe's apparent hope is that the message won't be lost on the audience.

One can hope with Rabe that if this message may not initially have been well received, then perhaps the accumulation of such messages within the theatre and other cultural venues may eventually produce Rabe's intended effect. And such accumulation may very well occur because a similar sense that realism must go beyond such strict linear causality informs the work of other playwrights, not the least of whom is Sam Shepard. Applications of chaos theory to Shepard's work reveal strong affinities between the playwright's expanding vision of the world and science's changing perspective. Shepard's titles to his recent plays, *A Lie of the Mind* (1986) and *States of Shock* (1991) – similar in sentiment to Rabe's *Hurlyburly* title – suggest an explicit awareness of the turmoil attendant on this shift in paradigms.

The very fact that Shepard has difficulty with closure in his dramas reflects his resistance to the tidy, self-contained traditions of classic realism and naturalism: "Endings are so hard. Because the temptation always is a sense that you're supposed to wrap it up somehow. You're supposed to culminate it in something fruitful. And it always feels so phony, when you're trying to wrap it all up."[13] Shepard here seems at least intuitively aware of the scientific fact that information exists in an orderly state (the only kind that permits comfortable closure) only in systems rarely existing in the natural world itself. As twentieth-century science began investigating dynamic systems, the implicit closure of the Newtonian paradigm could no longer be located. Nature itself has proved to be dynamically open-ended. Similarly, strictly linear and causal realist theatre has begun to give way in America to drama that attempts to reveal the indeterminate, open-ended, and chaotic nature of the world.

Shepard's 1986 play *A Lie of the Mind* dramatizes the results of a particularly brutal case of domestic violence in which the husband, Jake, has assaulted his wife, Beth, to such a degree that she has become brain-damaged. Ironically, Beth's injury liberates her from "sane" deliberations on life and leads her to greater insights into life than could ever be achieved by her deterministic, linearly obsessed husband or by their respective family members. Jake looks very specifically for the actual cause of his violent eruption, seeking linear connections between his motives, his actions, and their results. His mother, Lorraine, suggests one linear link between cause and effect by establishing a genetic logic, recalling her husband's (Jake's father's) own violent nature. Beth's father, Baylor, works in a business-as-usual manner to conclude that Beth's problems are typically "female" and evidence of a fundamental incompatibility between the sexes. Jake's brother, Frankie, rationally goes to Beth's family to find logical answers only to fall prey to the family's linear process of revenge. Beth's brother, Mike, seeks to order events by responding to a code of honor, moving a step beyong searching for logical causes (the object of Frankie's search) and sinking to more primitive and vengeful, though no less linear, reactions to the event. They are all, to one degree or another, linearly deterministic causalists.

While there are numerous ways to apply the title *A Lie of the Mind* to the play, one application seems most inclusively appropriate: the rational application of linearly deterministic causal patterns to human events is itself a lie of the mind, a categorical reduction of reality to fit convenient configurations designed by human desire to explain and even anticipate existence. Linear determinism, in short, is a lie created by the mind in its efforts to delude itself into believing it is in control of its surroundings.

Taken to this level of understanding, the play fits nicely into Brustein's observations about postmodern American drama. Shepard is clearly revolting against the tyranny of linear models of inevitability. But he is not merely concluding that existence randomly produces the results that it does. He is not merely an absurdist turned to the realist form. Unpredictable determinism seems best to describe what Shepard presents. In Scene One, Jake asks, "Why didn't I see it coming?"[14] The answer is simple: as chaotics explains, there is no way to predict future events within complex systems subject to multilinear or nonlinear feedback. An audience may presume that Beth's decision to accept an acting job led to Jake's jealous eruption, and to some degree it did. But there is no way to presume Beth's decision predetermined Jake's reaction. In fact it could be a case of Shepard inserting "noise," information that ultimately has no causal bearing on the subject under scrutiny, despite possible clues to the contrary. Jake could very well have erupted even if Beth had chosen another course of action. Lorraine says Jake's genes predetermined his actions; after all, Jake is like his father. But, again, there is no way to presume that that genetic influence predetermined events. One might recall that the brother Frankie is of the same genetic stock but is not violent at all. Mike presumes he has only one course of reaction, to follow a code of honor and seek revenge. But the fact that he does subscribe to such a code does not mean that he must do so inevitably. Almost nothing, finally, is inevitable in the action of the play. And even less is predictable.

The fact that much of Shepard's dramatic output seems nonlinear has often been ascribed to Shepard's own carelessness as a craftsman. From the perspective of a traditionalist critic/audience, careless or poor craftsmanship almost necessarily has to be the answer, since certain lines of action lead nowhere while other actions seem to have no lines of origin at all. From the perspective of chaotics, however, it can be seen that Shepard's apparent carelessness reveals a highly crafted, orderly disorder. The various dead-ends Shepard sets up in his landscape reflect the butterfly effect at work, producing "noise" that often forces detours in our errant pursuit of linear comprehension. Such linear pursuit is itself a "lie of the mind," the theme of so many of Shepard's dramas, which almost without exception strive to unearth self-delusional behavior and the unattainability of grandiose human goals. Writers like Shepard and Rabe force realism to confront the contradictory nature of its own semantic status and to recognize that the tools of communication – what Rabe calls the "devices of logic" – are not objective and absolute but rather culturally determined and imposed. This is an important lesson, for as Worthen states, the politics of theatre "emerge not only in the themes of drama but more searchingly in the disclosure of the working of ideology in the making of theatre, in the formation of the audience's experience and so, in a manner of speaking, in the formation of the audience itself" (*Modern Drama and the Rhetoric of Theatre*, p. 146).

Traditional realism, like traditional science, strives to maintain a mastery over nature and asserts objective validity in its description of nature. Chaos theory and the emerging chaotics theatre of Shepard and Rabe play another game. Shepard and Rabe question the status of language and its powerful logic as purveyors of truth, presenting instead their currently veiled function as manipulators of truth and oppressors of alternative visions. As a result, perhaps even more evident in Shepard than in Rabe, the playwrights' various breaks from a seamless, linear presentation signal a responsiveness to the need for change rather than some flaw in craftsmanship, as traditionalist critics would argue. Even the acting style Shepard prefers in his work – "controlled anarchy"[15] – argues for a re-visioning of audience expectations.

Controlled anarchy, in fact, is a term applicable to most of Shepard's work, a characteristic that distinguishes his work from earlier American dramatists whose instincts tend toward envisioning a world or culture that *controls* anarchy/chaos, ironically – and surely unintentionally – to the point of not only subjugating it but of eliminating its creative potential as well. Language, logic, and dramatic form are chief among the instruments of that control. In contrast, Rabe and Shepard turn language, logic, and form in upon themselves in the process of questioning their authority. They serve a meaningful function of calling doubt upon themselves. But as they implode into disorder, they also open up new vistas of change and opportunity. So though this questioning of authority is a hallmark of absurdism, the absurdist's extreme of simply rejecting language, logic, and form can be said to be seen by Shepard and Rabe as merely counterproductive radicalism. Language, logic, and form must be recognized for what they can do as well as for what they can't do. If they cannot achieve their former goals of providing completely secure, objective truth, then perhaps we can accept them more conditionally into a more tentative qualitative construct. If they can't provide true, precise, quantitative comprehension of total order, then we must accept the disorderly order that they can accurately, qualitatively, and generally describe, a reflection of the controlled anarchy that chaotics suggests is possible. And if they can't control, perhaps they can be retooled to create and regenerate.

That earlier American dramatic sense of a need for order reflects an American cultural desire for control in general. America needs to maintain order in its pursuit of its "manifest destiny," a cultural imposition of a sort of predictable determinism on the events in which it engages. The temporary triumph of this position is evidenced by the twentieth-century triumph of humanity over its primary foe – nature. In the case of America, a dominating cultural juggernaut has tamed "the West" and has apparently achieved its manifest destiny. That such a victory has borne anything but productive fruit is suggested in *Buried Child* (1978), a play that argues for a readmission of naturally flowing processes into our cultural fabric. America, Shepard seems to be suggesting, needs to loosen its grip on control, needs to allow the natural processes of disorder to re-emerge among our longings for order and to revitalize a culture that has become "triumphant" over disorder but that has paid the price of stagnation and sterility. One must recall from the lessons of science that the re-emergence of chaos is inevitable, so America must adapt and prepare for stages of disorder, embracing its promise of a reconstituted order (that is, moments of order within the order–disorder paradigm) rather than fearing and resisting what the old order insists will be the result if we give up our control – a downward spiral of chaos-as-randomness leading to inevitable doom. Ironically, it is a failure to prepare for and embrace such heretofore unpredicted inevitability that will result in an inevitable doom, since efforts to resist will only result in a delaying of the inevitable, producing in the process not a natural transfer from order to disorder and vice versa but a cataclysmic adjustment radically reacting to the prior constricting controls. We can accept evolutionary change or must brace for a self-generated revolutionary cataclysm, but change will prevail.

Shepard's implicit argument is profound and reverberates to the very foundations of our cultural edifice. We must release ourselves from an order boldly pronouncing the need of humanity to linearly pursue its destiny, rejecting or subduing disorderly "interference." The new "order" that Shepard is positing is one that sees the dynamic necessity of welcoming a balanced interaction between disorder and order, a decentered vision of the notion of order as control and randomness as death or decay rather than potential. Order–disorder must be given room to develop.

True West (1980) is an excellent case in point, a play whose very title suggests its cultural engagement. Austin is a product of a culturally triumphant "real" West and Lee of a declining, "untamed" West. The two brothers are paragons of the culturally prescribed, false dichotomy set up between human order and naturally occurring disorder. From a chaotics perspective, the flaw of such a prescribed dichotomy (actually a set of dichotomies: humanity and nature, and order and disorder) is obvious. Separately, the two men – one a cultural success, the other a cultural pariah – have stagnated into sterile, unproductive existences. It should be noted that while several critics have seen the play as a psychological study of two halves of one self, Shepard has rejected such an interpretation because in many ways Austin and Lee are not "selves" at all. Only inasmuch as Shepard argues for a dynamic interaction between the two can psychology even peripherally enlighten the subject. What Shepard is arguing is that the culturally prescribed dichotomy must be broken down, that the real West – developed, paved, orderly – must re-engage with the untamed West – vital, wild, disorderly. The fact that Austin and Lee reverse roles suggests that neither position alone is acceptable because even the much desired reversal ultimately satisfies neither. Once again, we are not looking at an either/or proposition. Rather, Shepard is suggesting a both/and proposition. The dynamic between order and disorder, between culture/humanity and nature, will guarantee the necessary vitality for continued cultural *and* natural health.

The play's conclusion, with the two brothers bound together in a death grip, can be taken two ways. *True West* leaves open the possibility of a self-destructive decision to fight or a regenerating decision to embrace a new integrated vision. One conclusion could lead to a triumph of the real West wherein the entire landscape would turn into a Palm Springs development and the vitality of the wild would be eradicated. But it would be an eradication that would also inevitably lead to the eradication of humanity, which would only belatedly, if at all, discover its essential interrelationship with nature. Another conclusion could lead to a triumph of the untamed West wherein the resistant real West would be ultimately overrun by a patient but persistent natural West, destroying resistant humanity in the process. Or – the apparent hope of Shepard – the stand-off could lead to the revelation that both "opponents" need to re-engage in a dynamic interchange, a transcendent order of continuous change resulting from rising and changing states of order–disorder.

Culturally speaking, it is not entirely surprising that such re-evaluations of our cultural suppositions have occurred during and after the Vietnam era. After all, that era was a time when America needed to reassess its linearly prejudiced, previously unshaken belief in its universal "rightness" within the world community. Most of Rabe's plays, of course, connect directly with Vietnam. Even *Hurlyburly,* a Hollywood play, has a Vietnam connection, offering a Vietnamesque landscape among its scenery and essentially bringing the disorienting horrors of that world to America's shore, in fact to Los Angeles, America's dream factory. While all of Shepard's drama can be said to be a product of a Vietnam-era spirit of reassessment, in *States of Shock* (1991), Shepard, too, brings Vietnam – or a suggestive facsimile thereof – to the stage.

In *States of Shock,* Shepard forcefully emphasizes the point that America can no longer adhere to its rationalist, Newtonian vision of reality and behavior, certainly not in a post-Vietnam, post–Cold War, post–Desert Storm world. The chaos, randomness, and uncertainty of the current world order is pervasively inserted into the play by way of an upstage scrim, behind which the efforts of two percussionists and through which the silhouettes of scenes of war invade the action taking place in the foregrounded "Danny's," a family restaurant. In the restaurant sits a couple who would fit nicely into a "West Palm Beach" milieu, well-off, "civilized," generally unperturbable, except for the poor service of the waitress and rude behavior of the other pair in the restaurant. This other pair includes a wheelchair-ridden veteran of some unnamed war, Stubbs, the middle third of whose body was blown away in battle by a shell that passed through him and killed, apparently, the son of the other member of the pair, the Colonel. The Colonel has taken Stubbs out of a VA hospital and to this restaurant on the first anniversary of his son's death, ostensibly to uncover the truth about the events that day.

Stubbs's mental capacities have been damaged as well as his body; the Colonel explains, "He's suffered a uh – kind of disruption. Temporary kind of thing, they say. Takes some time to unscramble."[16] A thorough American, the Colonel intends precisely to unscramble Stubbs's mind, by way of rational inquisition, once again reminiscent of the scientific process:

> I want to reconstruct everything up to that moment. . . . What I'm trying to figure out is the exact configuration. The position of each element. A catastrophe has to be examined from every possible angle. It has to be studied coldly, from the outside, without investing a lot of stupid emotion. . . . What we're after is the hard facts. (*States of Shock*, pp. 13, 14, 15)

The Colonel is in many ways similar to Eddie in *Hurlyburly*, as Stubbs is in many ways like Phil. Stubbs, of course, cannot review his catastrophe free from "stupid emotion," and his emotion-filled, "unscientific" conclusion is that on that day, "America had disappeared" (p. 20). For Stubbs the logic of America was shattered by the senselessness of the events of that day, shattering his belief in America even as his body was shattered. The Colonel immediately responds: "DON'T TALK FOOLISHLY! That's a blasphemous thing to say! It's a disgrace to the memory of my son!" (p. 20). Clearly for the Colonel, America could not have been in error, and finding the truth about that day should verify his point. Blending nationalism with an apparently interchangeable rationalist linear fervor, the Colonel adds: "The principles are enduring. You know that. This country wasn't founded on spineless, spur-of-the-moment whimsy. The effects are international! UNIVERSAL!" (p. 20).

But the Colonel's insistence on order, linearity, Manifest Destiny, is immediately undermined by the play's stage action: "*Immediately the percussionists and war sounds join in full swing. The cyclorama explodes with bombs, missiles, and blown-up planes*" (p. 20). This drowning of the Colonel's speech in sounds of war hints strongly at Shepard's challenge to the order the Colonel espouses, and an opposing perspective evolves. While the Colonel strives to overlay meaning onto events that have evaded explanation, Stubbs is the living result of at least momentary randomness, ironically observing throughout the play, "I was the lucky one." We have at this point an absurdist (Stubbs) confronting a traditional realist (the Colonel). The Colonel insists on control, believing no action goes wasted in the grand design; what he needs to do is uncover how his son's life was invested in that grand design.

Espousing a nineteenth-century naturalist's obsession with order, the Colonel gives a lesson to the waitress, Glory Bee, who is having trouble balancing water glasses while delivering orders. First, he shows her how to balance the glasses, and then explains: "Always [remind] yourself that the human body is little more than a complex machine and, like all machines, can be trained and programmed to fulfill our every need. Through repetition and practice" (p. 32). Onto this mechanistic perspective of life, reminiscent of neo-Newtonian conclusions, the Colonel adds:

Repetition and practice. Slowly, a pattern begins to emerge. Slowly, through my own diligence and perseverance, this pattern takes on a beauty and form that would have otherwise been incomprehensible to my random, chaotic laziness. Now I become master of my own destiny. . . . I understand my purpose in the grand scheme of things. There's no longer any doubt. Fear takes a backseat to the certainty and confidence that now consumes my entire being. I am a God among men! (pp. 32–3)

There is here an uneasy sense of chaos. But as would be expected, the Colonel circles around to the conclusion that chaos must be recognized only as disorder; it is finally an undesired other and yet another enemy – or perhaps the summation of all his enemies – that he must destroy. Constantly set up in oppositions – friend or foe – the Colonel's world view sees order as friend and disorder as foe. Once he "orders" his laziness, he can control the randomness apparent in the world out there.

This concept of order as positive and chaos as degenerative is one that Shepard ascribes to the American psyche throughout his work, in which ordering the wilderness into civilization figures as America's singular task and singular triumph. The natural processes of a rising order have been superseded by an impulse to control, to be "gods" dictating order to nature. But the effort to dam up natural flow leads only to a temporary triumph because the forces of disorder will work away until artificial control breaks down, leading to a flood of ensuing disorder that may very well destroy its former oppressors. Essentially, in an act of self-fulfilling prophecy, it is America's own actions that channel nature and its chaos pattern into the devastatingly destructive force we claim it to be. Allowing natural flow would minimize negative impacts. It would certainly minimize cataclysmic impacts.

In essence, claims Shepard in the play, today we have become victims of "friendly fire." As Stubbs concludes that his wounds came from friendly fire, so does Shepard suggest America's own falling away (either perceived as currently under way or as soon to be under way) has been the result of friendly fire, namely a debilitating unwillingness to see the world in any way other than oppositionally and in the process forcing an otherwise benign world, an ostensible ally, to malignly fire back at us. Even Glory Bee suggests that we've been hit by our own friendly fire:

> The thing I can't get over is, it never occurred to me that "Danny's" could be invaded. I always thought we were invulnerable to attack. The landscaping. The lighting. The parking lot. All the pretty bushes. Who could touch us? Who would dare? (p. 40)

Almost a parody of the neoclassical park in *Arcadia*, Danny's, in its triumph over nature (paradise paved into parking lots), has instilled in Glory Bee a sense of invulnerability. But the invasion is internal, since the domestic "friendly fire" assaults of which she speaks can only actually be metaphorical. Her Arcadia is imploding, falling in upon itself as a result of the inevitable crumbling of the bastions imposed to create that seeming paradise and to prevent unruly nature from invading. She even muses, "I missed the Cold War with all my heart" (p. 41). Having clearly defined oppositions was of course instrumental in maintaining a rationalist control over all the ethnic, racial, and nationalist disorders lurking beneath the apparently orderly surface of the Cold War world. With the thawing of the Cold War, chaos has returned and with a vengeance barely imaginable before the thaw.

Before his accident, Stubbs, too, was much like Glory Bee and even the Colonel. On the assault beach on the day of his horrible injury, he worked to control both his fears and his growing sense of meaninglessness in ways the Colonel's eschatology would fully endorse. Says Stubbs of his recollections on the beach, rather ironically spiced:

> Keep thinking of "home." That's the way to pull through this. . . . Think of what we've achieved! The "Trail of Tears"! The Mississippi! Samuel Clemens! Little Richard! The Dust Bowl! The Gold Rush! The Natchez Trace! It's endless! A River of Victory in all directions! Flooding the Plains! Hold to an image! Lock onto a picture of glorious, unending expansion! DON'T LET YOURSELF SLIP INTO DOUBT!! Don't let it happen! You'll be swallowed whole! (p. 38)

Stubbs saw himself as part of a greater purpose, and perhaps he would have continued to believe so except for the friendly fire that destroyed his body. He apparently begins to see the shell that wounded him as equivalent to the cultural lies that likewise have left him one of the walking wounded even before the physical wound. Not only do they no longer offer him a reasonable defense (a benign mental/emotional self-delusion), they now reveal themselves as a fundamental source of his physical debilities, walking into the actual line of fire as he has done.

The Colonel's control over his world likewise crumbles, but the result is reactionary entrenchment. Shortly after the random, chaotic laziness speech, the Colonel loses both Stubbs and the girl he dreams of marrying (Glory Bee), and he never gains a satisfactory explanation of his son's death. He can't accept the friendly fire explanation, and he won't accept any suggestion of cowardice on his son's part. Responding to the possibility that Stubbs will leave him, the Colonel observes: "I can easily do without. It's a question of training. Repetition and practice. All those days. All those horrible long days without the enemy. Longing out the window. Staring at the stupid boredom of peacetime. The dullness of it" (p. 39). Wedded to an oppositional perspective on life, the Colonel comes alive only in war. The subtle complexity of peace is incomprehensible to him; in fact, it is apparent that through "repetition and practice" he has trained himself into a mechanistic existence void of any life-affirming qualities. He does not engage; he can only confront. As he says, "Aggression is the only answer" (p. 39).

Stubbs, however, has begun to re-enter life, both literally and figuratively remasculated by his newfound understanding of life and existence. He makes contact – also literally and figuratively – with Glory Bee, and together they become a pair searching to fathom the mysteries of a world no longer able to be molded by the old American, linear, Cold War frame of thought. Stubbs cannot dismiss his own engagement with randomness; his emotional attachment to those deadly events blocks him from recomprehending an old, useless order, as the Colonel insists of him. Chaos cannot be ignored or dismissed, and it can no longer be overpowered or subdued. Rather, its reality and inevitability must be accepted, and strategies to cope with it must be newly developed. But he moves out of a purely absurdist posture, seeing chaos not solely as randomness but as an order in disorder reminiscent of a point found in Stoppard's *Arcadia*. Uniting with Glory Bee, Stubbs has discovered what Stoppard's Valentine describes as the attractor Newton left out. When one engages life by allowing emotion to enter, order–disorder may operate once again.

The Colonel is absolutely wrong in his last speech when he both takes an aggressive posture and subscribes to his own version of American isolationism, which even he appears no longer fully to accept:

We've got to keep our back to the mountain, Stubbs. At all costs. You can see our position. We've got a perfect vantage point from here. We're lucky in that respect. There are certain advantages to isolation. After all, we're not in exile. This is our domain. We've earned every inch of it. Surrounded by water. Engulfed by the prairies. Marooned. (*Pause*). MAROOOOOOOOONED!! (pp. 44–5)

The Colonel has perhaps a perfect vantage point from which to *observe* life, but he is indeed marooned not merely by geographical realities but by an overweening fear of increasing, encroaching, advancing uncertainty.

Stubbs and Glory Bee embrace that uncertainty; they appear willing to accept the patterns of nature, to look for an orderly disorder, and, in the process, to live. When Stubbs blasts out his last "GOD BLESS THE ENEMY" (p. 46), I would suggest that it be spoken differently from the earlier occasions in that this final blast is an ironic speech of actual thanks, that the enemy has blasted him out of his incapacitating ignorance. Has Vietnam perhaps helped America to blast out of the same? Will America be able to transcend its own incapacitating ignorance? These seem to be Shepard's ultimate, unanswered questions.

In a recent article Gary Grant discusses "Shepard's aesthetic belief in the transcendental power of theatrical images and language to actualize a paradigm shift in consciousness."[17] Shepard's struggles in the theatre are cultural struggles, and frequent, recent use of realism is the appropriate venue for these struggles, embedded as realism is in so much of our traditional cultural assumptions. Realism is not obsolete by any means, but its task – to provide a "scientific" description of reality as it is experienced by human beings – has been altered by the dynamics of modern life and by what science and culture now make possible. American new realist playwrights are recently discovering that to turn away from the linear causality of the mechanists and to turn toward the dynamic, nonlinear, and evolving chaos of life may provide American culture – and indeed all of postmodern civilization – with a more accurate depiction of nature and a clearer vision of how to function within that universe.

Marsha Norman's Conceptual Challenge in "'night, Mother"

Thus far, discussion has centered exclusively on male-created drama. Perhaps one of the most significant points about chaos theory is that, as Hayles points out, "Chaotic unpredictability and nonlinear thinking . . . are just the aspects of life that have tended to be culturally encoded as feminine."[18] Our culture's increasing (though often begrudging) valuation of "the feminine" and the rise of feminism in general may have conributed in ways not yet studied to the rise of chaotics itself. In its subtle way, Marsha Norman's *'night, Mother* (1981) both highlights the potential for chaotics realism and suggests that chaos belongs to the feminist frontier.

It has been over a decade since Norman's play was first produced and shortly after won the Pulitzer Prize (1983). During that decade, feminist critics have both praised it and attacked it as a discourse on the condition of women in (post)modern society, disagreeing among themselves on whether to applaud the play's positive virtues of presenting female entrapment in a male-centered ideology or to condemn the play's defeatist resolution of suicide in the face of that entrapment. Moving a step beyond this character-based debate, an equally heavily debated, more general criticism has arisen: female/feminist playwrights who utilize the realist format, it is argued, are implicitly permitting the feminist message to be subordinated to a restrictively dominating, male-constructed mode of presentation. While some critics challenge this position and defend Norman against the charge, others have virtually dismissed her precisely because of her format choices.

Critics outside the feminist dialectic similarly have both lauded the play and condemned it, on a point that in several ways relates to the above. The central issue here involves the concept of universality. Stanley Kauffmann, for example, observed in his 1983 article/review "More Trick than Tragedy":

> If the hoopla about Marsha Norman's new play were credible, the current state of American drama would be better than it is. . . . Because the play has only two characters, is in one long act, and ends with a death, some commentators have called it classical and have invoked Aristotle. I envy their rapture; the play itself keeps me from sharing it.[19]

Invoking Aristotelian criteria in an effort to accord the play universal status, such critics reveal in the process an unfortunate urge to seek safe, secure traditions in their efforts to "understand" new works of art. Though Kauffmann may or may not have a valid justification for disliking the play, he is certainly justified here in questioning other critics' invocations of Aristotle. The play's formal allegiance to Aristotelian principles, even regular assertions of the play's cathartic results, appear little more than well-intentioned, though misdirected, Procrustean efforts to find a place for *'night,*

Mother in the American dramatic canon. If, however, Norman's play presents a chaos theme, then Aristotle would in fact be an inappropriate (though not totally incommensurate) invocation and a sign of exactly how mistaken critics have been in their viewings of the play.

As is the case with Rabe and Shepard, critics of Norman have not yet pursued the possibility of an alternative vision, working rather to ascribe more traditional assumptions to the work. Jill Dolan[20] has traced the male-dominated American theatre industry's efforts to find reason to include the play in its canon. She shows that in that effort the industry has found ways to see the play as essentially unthreatening to the male dominion and its ideology. It has found ways to disarm any potential feminist message and as a result has granted Norman "token" status by allowing her to be considered a good but – by its standards – not a great playwright. Dolan's cataloging and analysis of myriad male reviews of the play impressively support her case, demonstrating how Norman has been neutralized, made safe to enter the male-dominated, traditional canon. In fact, the play's vulnerability to co-optation by the dominant power structure is a primary reason Dolan rejects the play as possibly feminist, concluding that "Norman's play can be considered for canonical membership because Norman is still writing for male spectators under the guise of universality" (*Feminist Spectator,* p. 39).

Jeanie Forte[21] has crystallized the more general concern that any play that adopts a realist format such as Norman's has cannot be genuinely feminist, observing that "classic realism, always a reinscription of the dominant order, could not be useful for feminists interested in the subversion of a patriarchal social structure" ("Realism, Narrative, and the Feminist Playwright," p. 116). However, because realist plays like *'night, Mother* at least find an audience, whereas alternative women's texts rarely do, Forte concedes that at least " *'night, Mother* may be perceived as a feminist text, in that it challenges on some material level the reality of male power" (p. 123).

While both Dolan and Forte agree that the play in part presents a challenge to the reality of male power, neither can accept Jessie's suicide in the play as a viable challenge to that power. And rightly so, for the "heroic" gesture of defiance appears so obviously defeatist. In fact, this ultimate message of defeat that troubles Dolan and Forte is what they see as central to the male gaze's reassuring sense of comfort in the play; after all, if female defiance leads simply to feminist self-extinction (leaving only those who accept the status quo), then the challenge is not at all threatening to patriarchal social order.

The fact of Jessie's suicide is just that – a fact – and the attendant response that it signifies defeat is unavoidable. So, too, is the fact that Norman utilizes realism, a form that signals suspicions of submission to a dominant hierarchy (hence the invocations of Aristotle). Both facts, in turn, lead to the documented fact that male critics are reassured that the play's message is not rebelliously threatening. Though I don't pretend to have a resolution to the ambivalent – at best – feelings that many have toward the play, I would like to suggest a more benign reason why critics, patriarchally inclined and otherwise, could and should ascribe universal status and canon consideration for the play. Such consideration need not be a cowardly bow to pressure to include at least one woman among the patriarchal pantheon nor to consider Norman for such selection because she's "safe" (though my ideas may upset those who endorsed Norman for those reasons). I suggest that it is possible to see the play as utilizing the chaos paradigm that is becoming more and more theatrically and culturally prevalent. The play transcends gender-specific considerations even as it speaks to gender-specific issues. While our culture as a whole grows more open in recognizing the new paradigm, the paradigm is also, as Hayles suggests, of a uniquely feminine significance as well. And as has been suggested earlier, realism is an appropriate form to utilize in conjunction with chaos theory, itself a new brand of realist thought, though this brand works to challenge the assumptions inherent in classic realism. Ultimately, Norman's play presents a heretofore unseen, legitimate challenge to dominant hierarchy.

In considering the appropriateness of realism for Norman, consider by contrast Samuel Beckett's 1976 work, *Footfalls*. *Footfalls* involves a failed mother–daughter relationship and a totally despairing daughter in virtually every manner that *'night, Mother* does. The only "plot" deviation – an admittedly significant one – lies in the fact that in *Footfalls* the despairing daughter, May, continues her incessant, empty pacing and doesn't commit suicide as Jessie does in *'night, Mother;* but May doesn't do anything else, either, certainly nothing positive or productive in any traditional sense. It is clear that the pair of women in *Footfalls* is similar to the pair in *'night, Mother,* the younger members (daughters) of each pair desiring but not finding means of personal redemption, the older members choosing to avoid despair by accepting much less out of life. Beckett's play, however, is generally studied from an absurdist/existential perspective with little commentary on how materialist social conditions lead to the women's situations, while *'night, Mother* seems to be exclusively confronted by critics with little more than social considerations in mind at all.

There are several possible reasons for the focus on social conditions in *'night, Mother.* Norman does not have the absurdist/existential reputation that Beckett does. Her socially defined, realist milieu does not readily encourage intellectual abstraction in the way that Beckett's nonrealistic, theatrical presentation does. Plus, Norman is a woman, so one seems "naturally" to assume, as so many critics have verified, that she's probably writing about real women, just as Beckett may be assumed "more profoundly" to be writing about abstracted archetypes.

It is helpful, however, to see Norman with the same critical eyes with which we see Beckett. Though use of realism does encourage us to assume the play is planted in a social context and operating only on a social plane, it is nevertheless possible to look at the set of *'night, Mother,* with its white light intensity, and at the play as a whole in the same abstracted way that we look at, say, *Waiting for Godot.* As Norman's stage directions indicate, and as Dolan confirms, Norman clearly intended the play to have a nonspecified locale, reflecting neither regional nor particular socioeconomic limitations for the women. Dolan, however, points out that set design decisions and actor selection on Broadway (often the monolithic arbiter of decisions for subsequent productions) ignored Norman's wishes and chose to reflect regionally limited, socioeconomically specific conditions. In these matters, though, we are speaking of productions rather than of the play; if we hold to Norman's prescriptions, we move one major step away from "kitchen drama" and perhaps one step toward acknowledging in Norman's work a sort of post-Beckettian, chaotics realism, placing her in a camp that includes Rabe and Shepard (a fact that alone may discredit her among some feminists). And while post-Beckettian realism *may* present something of an absurdist argument, I would suggest that in Norman's case (and Rabe's and Shepard's) it presents a chaotics vision instead.

Dolan excerpts a particularly telling passage from a review by Mel Gussow that observes that Norman's "dark view of life comes not from a Samuel Beckett, but from an affable, determined and *petite* [emphasis is Dolan's] young woman who looks more like a graduate student than a serious playwright wrestling with profound emotions" (*Feminist Spectator*, p. 38). Dolan rightly attacks Gussow for his sexist assessment of Norman's art based on her physical appearance (a strategy rarely applied to male playwrights), but Gussow's attitude may be little more than a reflection of a large group of viewers' reductive assessments of *'night, Mother,* assessments based on the play's "domestic," petite (e.g., "realist") appearances rather than on what occurs beneath its surface. Also, while Gussow is at least literally accurate in stating that the play is not authored by Beckett, a Beckettian strain is clearly evident once we look past the theatrical expedient of seeing the play clothed in realist trappings. The final point, of course, almost needn't be made: women, even affable, petite women, have minds capable of profound thoughts that transcend "kitchen" concerns. The simple, commonsense truth of this assertion needs no further explanation.

As we have done with Shepard and Rabe, with Norman we need to move beyond the traditional/classical visions of realism as being a realm reserved for social philosophy and social commentary and to slip out of standard visions of what realism typically does in order to understand what Norman's realism has actually done in this case. If for Forte realism is an obstruction to her appreciation of the play, for me Forte's sense of it being an obstruction is itself the obstruction, for it restricts our vision into the heart of the play.

This type of chaotics realism responds to the several assumptions about the realist form itself. While the assumptions are part of the specifically patriarchal–feminist discussion above, the discussion takes another fruitful direction when it moves into the domain of epistemology and ontology rather than sociology or gender politics. *'night, Mother* is essentially a realist play that challenges traditional realist assumptions. On stage, the direct challenge to this causal system takes the form of a dialectic between the two generations of women in the play, the conservative, traditional, classically minded mother, Thelma, and the "new"-thinking daughter, Jessie. Throughout the play's clash of generations, Norman argues not simply feminist stances invested in social critique, but broader philosophical conceptions that combine to create a debate on the nature of perception and existence. We must look at the play as we look at a work by Beckett, that is, from a metaphysical perspective that takes into account issues of ontology and epistemology.

It is at this epistemological and ontological level that *'night, Mother* operates at its most radical. It challenges the dominating, patriarchally inspired order at what has become its most vulnerable point, its epistemological roots. As noted earlier, this is the level at which Rabe's and Shepard's dramas operate, and it is the level at which Norman's best operates as well.

'night, Mother essentially pits two positions on perception against each other. The new, chaos-informed order espoused by Jessie wins out in the play despite the urgings of an old, naturalist-based creed that Thelma adheres to and that has convinced some among the play's audiences but not Jessie herself. Thelma speaks from the old grounding of naturalist order, presuming that every action provokes an equal and opposite reaction. Jessie, on the other hand, speaks from a position that challenges these pervasive concepts of linear causality and essential predestination. Unwittingly challenging classical scientific assumptions of inevitably deducible, ordered action, Jessie has inadvertently become a proponent of the "new science" vision of reality, which is of course a challenge to the classical, Aristotelian-derived order that is the source of naturalism, or "classic realism."

Jessie's own world view, and Norman's, too (though like Shepard and Rabe, her familiarity with the actual chaotics paradigm is uncertain), is that a faith in linear "scientific" certainty or ultimate destiny and causality is no longer possible. It is at best a mutually agreed-upon monolithic fiction that Jessie no longer needs to accept. So while the *likely* results of events can be reduced to a realm of probable results with relative qualitative confidence, there is no concrete, objective, quantifiable way to determine/presume particular actuality, as classical science previously aimed at doing. The best one can do is to see that, within certain parameters of probability, an agent is free to complete an event in any number of ways. Out of a random (absurdist) phase of infinite possibilities, ordered moments of unpredictable but determined *options* arise. Jessie has options before her, options informed by determinist forces that lead to greater or lesser degrees of probability of outcome. But which of the available options is actually chosen becomes a *free* decision for Jessie. The extent to which *'night, Mother* actually presents this new vision is the extent to which it (1) undermines the ideological tenets of "classic" realism and (2) undermines the foundations of dominant, patriarchal order itself.

Following Jessie's actions reveals the process described by this new vision of reality. The given set of parameters, as tightly drawn as humanly (scientifically) possible under this new chaotics formula of human understanding, would allow her the latitude to choose to live or die. Either choice could be calculated to be a probable choice. In a world permeated by the butterfly effect, there is no inevitability, no linearly predictable quality that permits us to guarantee one outcome over another. Accepting suicide as one among several possible or probable choices seems the central issue of the play. Norman herself noted that the point of the play was not that Jessie chooses *to die* but that she *chooses* to die.[22] According to the new sciences, and according to Jessie herself, freedom exists within a generally determined (and determinable) set of probable options, but the actual option remains unpredictable. Until the actual event occurs, we cannot be certain of its "inevitability." This sequencing, of course, denies the concept of predictability and strict linear (genetic, environmental, or other) inevitability.

The play's action dramatizes this abstracted dialectic between old and new perception in the form of Thelma's struggle to persuade Jessie not to commit suicide, continually asking "why" and finding reasons designed to instill into her daughter hope in a pre-destined linearly prescribed future. The daughter counters each argument, insisting that there is no single reason or cause for her decision, observing that she's just lost hope in the future. She's finally decided that after a lifetime of being told what to do (and doing it badly), the one action she can do without outside influence or interference is to commit suicide. While Rabe's Phil commits suicide because he can't face the truth about chaotics, Jessie's choice is a welcoming embrace of the modified chaotics freedom she's discovered. The choice is made, but even after Jessie's continued explanation, it is a choice that still unsatisfactorily lacks a strict, linearly "causal" justification from Thelma's perspective.

If, as naturalism argues, all human beings are products of their genes and their environment, then Thelma would be right in continually demanding reasons for Jessie's choice. From that linear perspective of existence, there must be a reason, or else Jessie is just insane, a nicely circular, culturally acceptable reason when no other reasons arise. The list of possible causes is indeed lengthy. Jessie is an epileptic, though the attacks haven't occurred for some time now, and many of her personal failings stem from this often debilitating condition. The fact of Jessie's epilepsy is significant; when afflicted, she is quite literally in a randomness phase of a physiological chaos paradigm. So when Jessie denies that epilepsy is a cause of her current decision, insisting that she's planned on this night exactly because she's been unafflicted for a good period of time, she is acknowledging that she has entered a window of order within several phases of randomness/disorder that afflict her. She is choosing the options, not during an irrational, despairingly random phase of her life, but during a moment of rational clarity rising out of the random/epileptic moments of her life.

Other suggested causes are perhaps less significant, but for Thelma they are all potentially relevant. Jessie's marriage has failed, and her son is a delinquent, but Jessie says she's made private peace with these demons. Her life with Mom is unproductive, a tedious routine, but she refuses to blame her mother or this "entrapped" lifestyle. She is tired of her brother and sister-in-law's invasion of her privacy, but that's not cause enough to die. She's even tired of events in Red China, yet one more level over which she has no control, but it's not enough for her to end her life over. Dolan has pointed out another of the critics' "reasons" for Jessie's suicide: Kathy Bates, the actress who first played Jessie, is overweight, and that attribute has been added to Jessie's list of reasons despite the fact that weight plays no part in the text of the play. Jessie blames no event and no agent in her choice, insisting it's her free decision simply to stop the bus that is her life and get off.

Thelma, on the other hand, insists at different points that every one of the above factors is a cause, or even *the* cause for Jessie's decision. For many who don't accept that Jessie is making a qualified free choice, as anticipated by the chaos paradigm, Thelma's position is convincing. Each clue in the play is for them a reason.

But Norman is actually highlighting naturalist arguments not for us to accept but in order to suggest their flaws. To give the play's debate credibility, Norman needed to present as strong a traditionalist counter-case as possible: Thelma is indeed a strong opposition voice to Jessie's (and Norman's) insistences. But either Thelma has grown in production and on paper as too strong a voice or audiences have chosen to side with Thelma as a result of empathy with her world view. If, as I believe, the latter matter of choosing to remain naturalists is what we see in audiences and among critics, then it is the spectator – and Thelma – not Norman, who is entrapped by a safe creed and unwilling to consider new options. So critics and audiences who attack the play are here clearly registering a predisposition to accepting a creed outworn and finally called into question by contemporary science itself, refusing as they do to realize or accept that Jessie's decision could be a free, unpreprogrammed decision. Several critics have even followed a direct line of naturalist "reasoning" in the purest form when they chose to look back and see Jessie's escapism as a result of her being of her father's seed, a man who "went fishing" every opportunity he had. But that is clearly not the line of reasoning Norman wishes us to follow, though we are apparently free to do so.

It appears that critics and audiences need to begin more freely to accept the fact that realism can be used to do more than present a linearly naturalist creed. That audiences are at least in part prepared and even predisposed to accept the new paradigm is evidenced, at least, in audience reception of Beckett's even more radical-seeming and absurdist-seeming agenda. That audiences have trouble with the new realism, however, is evidenced in Norman's reception as well as Rabe's and Shepard's.

Norman's play has been validly viewed as a social drama. From this perspective the feminist assault on the play as at least in part reinscribing dominant ideologies seems justified. On the other hand, if we move away from the social level and see it utilizing a post-Beckettian chaotics realism, then 'night, Mother offers its audience something quite different, an argument that subtly (a fact that may not please all) but clearly attacks dominant order. In the process, this argument asserts that it is ultimately unjustified to assault realism as a form that, without exception, embraces an inevitable, linearly naturalist dogma – either positively or negatively asserted. Realism can present something other than the dominant ideologies standardly ascribed to it.

In *'night, Mother*, Norman has allied the realist form with a new vision of human experience, one that denies understanding as centuries of male-dominated inquiry have striven to formulate and perfect it. This assault seems exactly the kind of approach feminist thinkers have been looking for. Other critics as well, those who attack realism as an outmoded form presenting outmoded thought, should likewise reconsider *'night, Mother*, as well as the works of Rabe, Shepard, and others. Perhaps work such as Norman's, suggesting a new foundation of understanding, may help us to create a yardstick (a feminist yardstick as well as others) whose assumptions are, finally, truly relevant to our age.

4

Theatre of Chaos, Past and Future

BSEN'S *The Master Builder,* discussed earlier, provides us with an excellent example of Enoch Brater's observation that recent developments in the theatre (such as Beckett's works, he says) "made us see as new things that were always there in front of our eyes, but never in such sharp relief," as well as the point that the possibilities of realism "are really quite different from those stable qualities we were once told were there."[1] The earlier discussion of *Death of a Salesman* similarly demonstrates Brater's point, as does the general re-visioning of absurdism from the perspective of postabsurdist chaotics. From these examples, one can generalize to make the larger point that much of our dramatic canon could be re-viewed from our contemporary chaos paradigm and that the result would be a revitalized perspective of contemporary relevance. Jan Kott, in *Shakespeare Our Contemporary,* made a convincing case for revisiting the works of Shakespeare using contemporary events, philosophy, and sentiments to reread the Bard, suggesting that with *Hamlet,* for example, "Many generations have seen their own reflection in this play."[2] Speaking of Martin Esslin's *The Theatre of the Absurd,* Ruby Cohn has made a parallel claim regarding Dadaism, Expressionism, and other early twentieth-century movements: outlining the elements of the absurd, Esslin's book provided her "with a wedge into unfamiliar pre-absurdist drama."[3] Kott uses the totalitarian world of his native, then-Communist Poland to reflect upon *Hamlet,* and he uses his postmodern sense of the grotesque and absurd to reflect upon *King Lear,* while Cohn uses Beckett to reflect upon the sur-

139

realists and others. These backward glances can both connect us
with our past and assist in our push to understand our futures
while coming to terms with the past and our debt to it.

Using the chaos paradigm, one may look again at the works that
so intrigued Brater, Kott, and Cohn, among so many others. And as
their fresh perspectives have given new relevance to these old
works, so can chaotics suggest even fresher perspectives, moving
in these instances beyond Eastern European totalitarianism and
the absurd and seeing patterns relevant to a new vision ushering
in the twenty-first century.

"Shakespeare Our Contemporary":
Revisiting Kott

In "Hamlet of the Mid-Century,"[4] an essay collected in *Shakespeare Our Contemporary,* Jan Kott observes that every generation
since the creation of *Hamlet* has found a way to make that play its
own and that while historical precision may have its virtues – generating productions that capture a Renaissance spirit – *Hamlet* continues to live best when we use it to "get at our modern experience,
anxiety and sensibility" (p. 49). From his own experience, Kott
recounts a production in Poland in the 1950s, "a few weeks after
the XXth Congress of the Soviet Communist Party," calling the play
"a political drama par excellence" (p. 49). He confesses the obvious when he acknowledges that this *Hamlet* was one of innumerable possible *Hamlet*s, observing, "*Hamlet* is like a sponge. Unless
produced in a stylized or antiquarian fashion, it immediately
absorbs all the problems of our time" (p. 54). Kott likewise
acknowledges another obvious point, that *Hamlet* is more than a
political or social play, that its philosophical dimensions are as
rich and culturally movable as its political or social dimensions.

Kott asks of Fortinbras, "Who is this young Norwegian Prince?
. . . What does he represent? Blind fate, the absurdity of the world,
or the victory of justice?" (p. 61), but confesses that Shakespeare
gives no answer. The answers that one can offer, of course, are
never complete. Kott's reading of the play suggests, for example,
that the eventual restoration of order in Denmark initiated by
Hamlet and continued by Fortinbras could "be understood as the
restoration of moral law, or as the 'neue Ordnung in Europa'" (p.
60). What this *neue Ordnung* is is open to interpretation from

every generation, and I would suggest that this new order could very well be assessed to follow the chaos paradigm. A destructive human-generated version of chaos-as-randomness reigns for a time, but with the defeat of that destructive human-generated tyrannical order that instigated destructive disorder, nature reinstates its own natural *Ordnung,* which is orderly disorder. Though Hamlet is the instrument that brings this order – ironically though appropriately through a flood of increased disorder – he ultimately succeeds only when he gives in to that "providence" which is seen even in the fall of a sparrow. His tragedy is that he initially works so hard to defy providence as he struggles to understand it, in fact to control it. To one degree at least, Hamlet's actions are of the same manipulative order as Claudius's actions, and so neither will triumph for long. Only in relinquishing control to that natural order he calls providence does Hamlet provide Denmark with the opportunity for regeneration.

In essence, the tragic carnage would not have resulted had Hamlet, Laertes-like, accepted nature's charge and only temporarily destabilized matters by immediately avenging his father's death. It is Hamlet's resistance to the patterns of disorder rising to reorder, or rather his willful interruption of the patterns to insert his own "Wittenbergian" pattern, that leads to his doom. Hamlet should have listened to his father's ghost, nature's emissary. But in the process of coming to terms with his duties, Hamlet interrupts the chaotics pattern of life. And this interruption becomes an opportunity for Shakespeare to cut through the seamless pattern of the chaos paradigm, for to disrupt a pattern is perhaps the only way actually to see it. That is the brilliance of Shakespeare's craft, as it is of all good tragedians' craft: he provides an instance where humankind disrupts natural operations to see precisely how the operations re-establish themselves, a process that simultaneously reveals nature's secrets and unearths human vanity, believing as humanity does that it's in control. Despite Hamlet's efforts, the play moves on with a natural impetus equivalent to the forces of metaphysical fate itself. Hence, the invocation of providence. But fate, to draw from the spirit of Jan Kott, can even more appropriately be seen today as the chaos pattern at work.

Hamlet puts his academic, scientific skills to work to understand the forces he confronts, but Hamlet's "scientific process," exhibited here in its modern infancy, shows its failings from the start. It strives, as Hamlet strives, to make man a god above nature, in control of it, whereas the new science paradigm advocates a nurturing renaturing of humanity. There seems to be a consciousness in nature, as Prigogine and Stengers would suggest, that Hamlet resists in his mechanistic, rationalistic, generally linear search for comprehension. Hamlet strives unsuccessfully to reduce the complexities he observes so that he can manipulate them. But even as early as Shakespeare, we see the goals of this process being called into doubt. What we see in Hamlet is a misguided process that would actually later evolve into the objective discipline of traditional, classical "science." Prigogine and Stengers observe of the procedure that it

> revealed to men a dead, passive nature, a nature that behaves as an automaton. . . . In this sense the dialogue with nature isolated man from nature instead of bringing him closer to it. A triumph of human reason turned into a sad truth. It seemed that science debased everything it touched.[5]

So, too, does Hamlet debase everything he touches. In essence, he has lost touch with his own burgeoning humanism through the very process typically held up to be the cornerstone of humanity: his reason. Shakespeare seems very much to anticipate the unfurling treachery of reductive and manipulative rational processes, of the laws of excluded middle, that everything must be either/or.

"To be or not to be." Hamlet operates through rational dichotomy whereas the case can be made that "To be *and* not to be" is actually the answer to Hamlet's question. Hamlet must accept his discrete individual self ("to be") but must also work to integrate or to enfold himself into the pattern ("not to be"), into the unpredictable inevitable that sweeps through his life as well as through the entire life of Denmark and the cosmos. Almost mystically, "to be" in its truest sense (not as Hamlet considers the term but as Shakespeare does) entails "not to be" in the standard, personal Renaissance sense of giving oneself up to the processes of life and death. Only when Hamlet accepts the paradoxical and allows himself to fall into the sweeps and patterns of a spontaneous nature fully capable of self-organization and independent regeneration, of a nature capable of rising and organizing out of its own disorder, only then does Hamlet fulfill his "destiny." The turn occurs late, in Act V, scene ii: "There is a special providence in the fall of a sparrow. If it be now, 'tis not to come; if it be not to come, it will be now; if it be not now, yet it will come. The readiness is all." By discarding a sense of excluded middle, by being a not *being,* by giving up his rationalist will to control, Hamlet actually *becomes* a renatured element, part of the natural force rising up to re-establish order out of disorder.

None of what I'm suggesting should sound terribly new. What I'm suggesting is that our new paradigm can explain the universal actions of Hamlet as effectively as former, prerational systems of thought could, but now with a language and a system appropriate to postmodern experience. Hamlet's central problem is that he is a modern man in a medieval world trying to mold it according to his new vision of how it should operate; Hamlet is a proto-Newtonian in a world of alchemy and mystery. From our new position, we see a man who comes to realize that his efforts to stand outside of nature and to predict it deterministically or ultimately to control it – all of which are modern, postmedieval urges – are futile. Even the premodern medievalism, alchemy, and "mystery" are better-suited systems of comprehension than the system Hamlet embraces, since they accept an integrated vision of man and nature. But despite Shakespeare's apparent warnings, Newtonian-ism has developed even into the twentieth century, a sure sign of our resistance to *Hamlet*'s lesson. The solution, one sighted from our current cultural position, is to accept the chaos paradigm.

Accepting a premodern, medieval, or alchemical unknown is not necessary for a contemporary audience because the world can be more appropriately interpreted to the postmodern mind through chaotics, which acknowledges an ongoing mystery – the result of probability over certainty – but which provides us a closer comprehension of the likelihood of events. The ebb and flow of existence has a "scientific" explanation but one that is much more tentative and less controllable than Hamlet chooses to consider. Hamlet arrives too late to the point where he compre-hends the limitations of his reason. And because his sensibilities do not comprehend the limitations, he challenges the conse-quences of his own growing awareness of his limitations – until the play's very end. That is Hamlet's tragedy.

While Kott's treatment of *Hamlet* invites a discussion of meta-physics, it does not move to such a level itself; however, Kott does utilize contemporary metaphysics in confronting *King Lear.* In

"'KING LEAR,' or ENDGAME,"[6] Kott interprets *King Lear* as an absurdist or grotesque play similar in many regards to Beckett's *Endgame*. As Kott notes, "Grotesque means tragedy written in different terms" (p. 105): "In the final instance tragedy is an appraisal of human fate, a measure of the absolute. The grotesque is a criticism of the absolute in the name of frail human experience" (p. 105). Connecting the grotesque with the absurd, Kott observes:

> In the world of the grotesque, downfall cannot be justified, or blamed on, the absolute. The absolute is not endowed with any ultimate reasons; it is stronger and that is all. The absolute is absurd. Maybe that is why the grotesque often makes use of the concept of a mechanism which has been put in motion and cannot be stopped. Various kinds of impersonal and hostile mechanisms have taken the place of God, Nature and History, found in the old tragedy. (p. 106)

Kott later adds:

> [T]ragedy lies in the very principle of choice by which one of the values must be annihilated. The cruelty of the absolute lies in demanding such a choice and in imposing a situation which excludes the possibility of a compromise, and where one of the alternatives is death. The absolute is greedy and demands everything; the hero's death is its confirmation. (p. 108)

The only way to give oneself at least a fifty-fifty chance of success against the absolute, says Kott, is to surrender to the devices of the absolute. As he notes, in a game where one chooses heads or tails and plays against a machine that guesses against and then records its human opponent's choices, the machine will eventually prevail by breaking the code of its opponent's behavior, no matter how creative that human opponent's "pattern" choices might be. The only alternative for the human victim – whose patterns will inevitably surface – is to toss the coin and leave the results to chance, a pattern that places the machine and the human on even terms. The answer to the grotesque condition is to give up the fight and in the process to become less than human, at least as we currently define that term. But this is a crucial qualification.

Lear challenges the absolute, says Kott, and loses; only the Fool, aware of man's folly, survives. One must recall, however, that Lear's unnatural choices at the outset of the play have been the cause of his alienation from nature. In essence, he has "chosen" to challenge the absolute, fighting resistant fire with equally resistant fire. From Kott's position, Lear has basically no choice other than to challenge the absolute by asserting his own idiosyncratic rules *or* to give up the struggle altogether. Lear's determination to challenge merely results in the triumph of the grotesque: "All that remains at the end of this gigantic pantomime is the earth – empty and bleeding" (p. 118). But at least Lear's choice grants him a certain humanity, which would be lost if he simply surrendered. Or so goes Kott's argument.

But from another perspective, one should emphasize that the earth did not invite Lear's destruction. After all, the options for Lear are not simple blind alley choices: either to be destroyed for defiance or to succumb dumbly to the singular absolute. Rather, "succumbing" to the absolute could be seen instead as a choice that would permit Lear to make various decisions from among a limited number of "natural" options. From a chaotics perspective, the absolute – or nature – is not a tyrant until it is challenged. Work with it, and it is essentially benign; challenge it, and a seeming malignity arises. It does limit choice to certain free and appropriate options, albeit not totally free choices (which is the absurdist/existentialist position). Lear essentially asks for more than nature (the family, the state, the cosmos) can grant; he desires more than chaotics determinism permits, willfully shifting himself into a grotesque, absurd world of unlimited options and inviting the absolute to "crack his code" of behavior and crush him for his insolence. As with Hamlet, Lear chooses the unnatural, to separate and denature himself and to strive to triumph over the absolute. Part of the failings of both Lear and Hamlet is that they misconceive the nature of the absolute, and they opt to confront it as an insufferable, perhaps even evil, tyrant. From this perspective, death seems the more noble outcome.

However, the choices made here are based on false assumptions concerning the nature of the absolute. As the chaos paradigm grants unpredictability within a determinist frame, it also allows for any number of directions in its move to regain order out of a destabilized condition. Hamlet could operate within given parameters; so could Lear. There's both freedom and determinism at work. However, looking upon the absolute as monolith, neither tragic character realizes fully the nature of nature; both choose to defy nature as they see it, creating and confronting a foe which itself never chose to be a foe.

Though Kott sees *King Lear* as confirming the triumph of a

grotesque, meaningless absolute, that position does not necessarily have to be the message for a postmodern audience. Rather, the play presents the tragic failing of Lear to see the variety of legitimate options, the degree of freedom that absolute nature affords. Lear and Hamlet suffer from hubris, but their actions show less an ennobling spirit of humanity faced with impossible conditions and show more fully cases where blind determination to work against and not with nature has resulted in self-destruction. This self-destruction *would* be noble if the absolute were a monolithic tyrant. But life is open to choice, albeit limited choice. Accepting this conclusion requires a surrender of willful human inclinations that many cultures (including our own) have frequently seen as positive qualities leading inexorably to our triumph over an equally willful nature.

The mystery of life that prevailed in the medieval world placed humanity in awe of nature, in fear of its unpredictability. The rise of reductive, predictive rationalism initiated a conflict between humanity and nature, with humanity trusting this new tool ultimately to assist in the human triumph over nature. The chaos model suggests that humanity must coexist with nature, is codependent upon the natural world; humanity must envision and then accept the parameters within which it can operate. Hamlet, Lear, the traditional rationalists (total order/control), and even the existentialists/absurdists (total lack of order/control) have yet to discover this option. They have yet to dislodge themselves from the choices permitted by either/or thought. But in *Hamlet* and *King Lear* we see Shakespeare's work as cipher from which our new visions can be decoded.

So despite something far less than total agreement with Kott on the particular matters at hand, I completely agree with him that Shakespeare remains a perpetual contemporary, even one relevant to a postabsurdist chaotics paradigm.

The Clinamen, Plague, Cruelty, Alienation, and Chaos

Shakespeare, Shepard, and Stoppard all argue that humanity has fallen out of the natural order in large part because it does not understand natural order. As a result, in its subsequent efforts to dominate nature, humanity verges on its own destruction. While it is perhaps still possible to reverse the human tendency toward self-destruction and turn toward a redeeming chaotics paradigm, prospects for this reversal dim as one considers the history of disregard.

Lucretius was one of the first to warn against human arrogance. For Lucretius, the plague – described as any devastating natural epidemic – was the ultimate clinamen, the disruptive challenge to civilization warning humanity of the need for change. When the plague arose, the attendant hysteria provided, as Lucretian scholar Charles Segal observes, "the release of aggression that . . . was inhibited as a necessary stage in the development of civilization but is never fully extirpated from human history."[7] The plague forces us to "accept our own end not only in the terms of our personal mortality . . . but also as part of the processes of the universe, in which death is the inevitable concomitant of life" (*Lucretius on Death and Anxiety*, p. 231). The plague is the disruptive opponent of unnaturally orderly civilization, cataclysmically mandating adjustment and change to a system grown linearly stagnant and arrogantly struggling against its own natural mortality. While it would seem that from a social and moral perspective the plague and its disorder must be opposed, one perspective suggests that humanity's very opposition to disorder is the cause of plague itself. Humanity's desire to secure control of nature leads to a violent loss of the very order and control it seeks. Such an argument may appear at first glance to have only metaphysically religious bearing at a perhaps metaphoric level, suggesting that ethical/moral decadence results in a god-sent plague. But there is another way of looking at the Lucretian picture: moral/ethical decadence leads to an arrogance that makes humanity disregard its natural environment and disrupt nature as it strives, godlike, to control that nature. Clearly, advances such as improved sanitation have minimized the threat of many types of epidemics that have plagued humanity, but our increasing urge to control, sterilize, and even dominate nature – to disregard natural forces – has led to disruptions whose future consequences have not been fully considered. These disruptions lead to nature becoming unbalanced and to the possibility of even more violent plague conditions.

Recent "new" science perspectives have suggested the accuracy of this literal suggestion, that human manipulation actually *effects* plagues. Laurie Garrett, in *The Coming Plague: Newly Emerging*

Diseases in a World Out of Balance,[8] reports recent scientific evidence that humanity's tinkering with nature has almost invariably preceded every historically documented outbreak of plague. She reports, for example:

> University of Chicago historian William McNeill outlined the reasons *Homo sapiens* had been vulnerable to microbial assaults over the millennia. He saw each catastrophic epidemic event in history as the ironic result of humanity's step forward. As humans improve their lots, McNeill warned, they actually *increase* their vulnerability to disease. (p. 6)

As new trade routes in the Middle Ages paved the way for European and, later, New World plagues, so may future plagues be the result of human advances on biological, ecological, and other related frontiers.

One conclusion could be that to escape the plague one must limit human advancement, a solution that is clearly less than fully desirable. Traditional, linear triumphs over nature, after all, are responsible for enormous advances that humanity is not prepared to do without. The triumph of medicine over countless diseases and advances in agricultural production, among so many breakthroughs, have increased lifespans and improved living standards. But one must consider the consequences of an uncontrolled Newtonian juggernaut, not only for what it is doing to our ecosystem but also for what it has done to the human spirit, instilling an arrogance begging for a fall. Is there not a way to recognize that the plague is not so much a call for humanity to do battle with its natural foe as it is a signal for humanity to return to natural orderliness after perhaps having ventured too far from that system of order? Is it not possible to see "plague" as an extreme natural reaction/defense launched as a signal that humanity and nature have fallen out of balance and that humanity needs to readjust its systems of dominion in order to return to the natural system? Lucretius's vision is that society needs to recognize the validity of this natural perspective.

Though he never invokes the concept of the clinamen, Antonin Artaud has in the twentieth century reintroduced the moral and physical nexus found in plague visitations as initiated by Lucretian thought, influencing generations of modern and postmodern thinkers, particularly in the theatre world. In his essay "The Theatre and the Plague," Artaud observes, "beneath the [physiological] scourge, all social forms disintegrate. Order collapses,"[9] resulting in "every infringement of morality, every psychological disaster" ("The Theatre and the Plague," p. 16). Here physical plague catalyzes moral plague, but Artaud suggests also that moral decay can instigate physical equivalents as well. Even more forcefully driving home the interconnectedness between a plague of body and one of spirit than Lucretius did, Artaud suggests, "I believe we can agree upon the idea of a [physical] malady that would be a kind of psychic entity and would not be carried by a virus" (p. 18).

Like Lucretius, however, Artaud sees the plague not as a scourge necessarily to be feared but as a liberator and cleanser of unnatural controls. The result of this psychic plague, stimulated by and stimulating the physical plague, is that "[i]t releases conflicts, disengages powers, liberates possibilities, and if these possibilities and these powers are dark, it is the fault not of the plague nor of theatre, but of life" (p. 31). This, too, is what Artaud sees as the mission of his theatre of cruelty, to reveal the destructive existence that invites plague and the productive, natural alternatives that, if embraced, can eventually vaccinate us from the plague.

Lucretius helps us to adjust Artaud's dark vision somewhat, to clarify a point Artaud seems to have passed over. Artaud clearly interconnects body and soul, the physical and the spiritual. And, as he notes, if the powers in the soul are dark it is because our lives are dark. Lucretius unsentimentally concludes the obvious, that death is inevitable and that the darkness of this fact surfaces only if we fear death. As Segal observes of Lucretius's view, "By seeing how the smaller fears [of existence] grow out of the fear of death, like branches from a central trunk, we gradually liberate our entire life from fear and from the violence, folly, and suffering that fear generates" (*Lucretius on Death and Anxiety,* p. 237).

The central point here is that an understanding of nature seems a critical priority, the antecedent to any valid approach to or philosophy of human existence. The idea of plague as disruption, as a radical manifestation of the Lucretian clinamen or the chaotics adjustment to disorder, is likewise crucial. Actual "cruelty" notwithstanding on the discrete individual level (where death is seen as an end to be avoided), the plague works well on a collective, social level (where death is part of a process of continuation), as a call for the human necessity of acceding to natural processes of orderly disorder. Moving from an individual level of ordered control and manipulation to a social or communal level of integration and acceptance of orderly disorder is the option humanity must consider.

Peter Weiss's *Marat/Sade* of the 1960s depicts the aftermath of something like a culturally incited plague – the French Revolution. The play offers insights into the concept of orderly disorder and how our visions of nature regulate our visions of personal existence, which affect our larger vision of social existence. Peter Brook's 1964 landmark production of the play was, as Ronald Hayman observes, "partly Brechtian, partly Artaudian."[10] Hayman continues: "This was apt because the central conflict was between a man who wanted to change the world (as Marat and Brecht did) by political action, and a man who wanted to change human nature (as Sade and Artaud did) by making it truer to itself" (*Artaud and After,* pp. 147–8). One must first realize the conceptual significance of the Brechtian/Artaudian connection in this play. Brecht the material rationalist confronts Artaud the spiritual anarchist, an appropriate integration of formerly orderly–disorderly opposites. The play itself moves from chaos to reorder and vice versa, suggesting a necessary fusion of the two extremes, what Marvin Carlson has called "diametrically opposed [positions], the one associated with a theatre stimulating the spectator to reason and analysis, the other with one regarding discursive thought as a barrier to the awakening of the body's inner spirit."[11] Either agenda alone – that of either Brecht or Artaud – seems likely doomed to failure as an agenda to change either the world or human nature. As the chaos paradigm suggests, they must play together or fail to succeed. We reveal again the limitations of either/or in an integrationist advocacy of both/and.

Working at various levels reveals the full integration of numerous positions validated by the new scientific perspective of integrated orderly disorder. Writing a play set just after the French Revolution that includes a play-within-a-play about the Reign of Terror provides an orderly–disorderly historical opportunity. The period itself, the same as Stoppard's 1800s set in *Arcadia,* occurs at a moment in Western history when predictable order and unpredictable chaos come into immediate contact. The whole performance of *Marat/Sade* takes place in an asylum, a location intended either to restore order to damaged souls or to lock those souls away from the order rising beyond its gates in a civilization trying to reconstruct itself after the "chaotic" Revolution. Within this confine, the debate on the nature of reality and possibilities of human behavior unfolds.

The asylum keepers, especially Coulmier the asylum director, are controllers of the "insane." Curious guests may be invited to witness insanity under control, but control is the critical element. Controlled chaos, locked-up insanity, is at most tolerated as a curiosity, and even that limited degree of disorder is frequently given censure by calls to exterminate the inmates. Coulmier is a protector of a rejuvenated Enlightenment, a member of the post-Revolutionary reactionary order that is working to restore control and propriety to France, a neo-Newtonian manipulator of actual as well as human nature.

In contrast to Coulmier are Sade's dramatic creations for the *Marat* asylum entertainment. Charlotte Corday, played by a somnambulist from the asylum, is the idealist unattached to human realities (having been raised in virtual isolation by nuns), who envisions "[a] society / in which every man is trusted with the right / of governing himself himself,"[12] a possibility only if humanity radically and fundamentally changes, a point the character Charlotte does not comprehend.

Sade's Jean-Paul Marat is more of a realist. But unlike Coulmier, he is not "Newtonian," since as "that eminent scientist Lavoisier" has concluded, "He wants to pronounce / the whole of firm and fixed creation / invalid" (*Marat/Sade*, p. 69). Advocating a thermodynamic view of flow rather than a mechanistic view of being, Marat has a sense of the volatile, chaotic, unpredictable, and nonlinear nature of existence. He also has a sense of body/soul not unlike Artaud's own. As Sade's Voltaire reports in the play-within-a-play, Marat claims "that the soul exists in the walls of the brain" (p. 67), that the material world and immaterial "self" interconnect. Through this configuration Marat argues that nature and human thought (and spirit) are intertwined, that there is an active interaction, the discontinuation of which is apparently impossible despite human efforts to do so. But Newtonian order has done just that, attempted to separate man from nature by granting humanity the illusion of control over nature. "Soul" cannot be part of nature; it must be other than nature if humanity is to be superior to nature. It is no wonder Voltaire laughs at Marat's proposal; an Enlightenment mind would simply find such interconnection laughable.

Marat perhaps best understood how the world operated – as evidenced by the catalog of fulfilled prophesies outlined for him before his murder on stage – but his intellectualized perspective coupled with his physical disabilities prevented him from actually living life, engaging in existence. That is ultimately his failing, creating a revolution that has lost its passion. Coming so close to understanding the nature of chaos, he was still like an old-guard rationalist working to use his knowledge to dominate and control.

Marat is important, but the real threat to Coulmier's world – and equally unacceptable to ours – is Sade's perspective, one of "general copulation" (reminiscent of the ranting Lear's "Let copulation thrive"), which appears to be in line with a standard absurdist's perspective. While it triumphs as a message of the play-within-a-play, and while it holds temporary dominion over the asylum during and immediately following the asylum's *Marat* performance, the absurdist sway is finally suppressed by the asylum keepers and Coulmier. Given the alternative of Sade's vision or Coulmier's vision, most "civilized" human beings would likely opt for Coulmier's aggressive, arbitrary order.

However, built into the whole production, into the play itself, is a suggestion of an option not yet attempted, but nonetheless suggested: a fusion of Brecht's alienation effect with Artaud's theatre of cruelty by coupling linear reason with its nonlinear alternative, culturally labeled insanity. Could Sade's chaotic/absurdist engagement in life benefit from Marat's intellectual detachment and manifest an orderly disorder paradigm? Or could Marat's chaos transform Coulmier's aggressive order also into an orderly disorder paradigm? Marat's perspective could be seen as a catalyst to temper Sade's perspective or to loosen Coulmier's, bringing both from extremes along a scale of order–disorder to a realm that permits fluctuation between what both represent. To loosely paraphrase Stoppard's Valentine, Marat may be the attraction both Coulmier and Sade have left out, a possibility the plaguelike asylum invites for consideration.

Two British playwrights who have also centrally utilized the plague – in their cases occasions of real plagues – as a liberating condition are John Whiting and Peter Barnes. What they essentially present is a landscape devastated by the plague in which society chooses to retrench and do battle with the scourge while only a few actually benefit from the visitation.

Whiting's 1961 play *The Devils,* based on Aldous Huxley's book *The Devils of Loudon,* offers the hysteria of the plague as the opportunity to convert the vain and self-important Grandier to a man of understanding among a fear-ridden community headed by a priesthood attempting to make sense of the chaos of their literally and metaphorically plagued existences. In the process Grandier is defeated by civilized institutions but comes to atone for his own past shortcomings as a civilized oppressor and to understand the fears of the masses, revealed by plague but cloaked by the clergy's artificial controls. The plague has forced civilization to create fictions – by way of forced confessions – and to impose even harsher laws and penalties than previously resorted to. In the midst of the disorder, Grandier gains insights into the world, becomes attached even more strongly to his God – who is a God of peace and of plague – and dies with an understanding incomprehensible to the "civilized" priesthood and "civilizing" masses.

Laubardemont, Grandier's prosecutor, utilizes logical procedure to outline Grandier's likely thought processes during his impending torture: "First: how can man do this to man? Then: how can God allow it? Then: there can be no God. Then: there is no God."[13] Jeanne, Grandier's accuser – and eventually his only convert – while listening to the torture, asks, "Is it only in the very depths that one finds God?" (*The Devils,* p. 106). The answer is yes. Fear of confronting reality, a fear cloaked by the delusions of a "superior" civilization united against chaos and plague, prevents direct contact with reality. Traditional causal reason is not the means to attain understanding. Grandier observes to Laubardemont, who asks that he confess to sins that have led to the town's chaos, "Don't persist. I can destroy you. At least in argument. Keep your illusions, Mister Commissioner. You'll need them all to deal with the men who will come after" (p. 109).

Grandier understands that the terrible plague has acted as an awakening, a disruption calling for personal evaluation. As a result of facing the plague, Grandier's understanding of the chaos in nature, that it provides means of attaining new order, leads him to understand the world in a new light. His understanding has led to a truth beyond that allowable by the orderly civilized world. Chaos has, paradoxically, given him the opportunity to atone for his previous "vain and disordered life" (p. 100), a life that he now knows was only superficially ordered by a rationalist sleight of hand. Ironically, the tortured disorder of his physical being at its end is also only a superficial fact; his spiritual life at that point is more ordered than at any time previous. Understanding has led to "control." It is, however, not a traditional control of his body or of nature but a new ordering control of his mind, predicated on the understanding that such control comes through submission to nature's forces. His consolation comes from redefining what he means by and wants from control.

Barnes's 1985 play *Red Noses* (written in 1979) presents a sect of comic artists during the time of the Black Death who, as their leader Marcel Flote says, bring to the world images of "peacocks not ravens, bright stars not sad comets, red noses not black death."[14] These "Floties" utilize laughter as the means by which to live, confidently facing death's unknown rather than being destroyed by a fear of its consequences. Embracing the incomprehensible as part of the overall rhythm of nature – moving through phases of decay/disorder and order/generation – is humanity's one hope. Moving away from individualization of understanding (and fear of death) to collective understanding of process (of which death is a natural part) provides a naturalized perspective of hope. That the Floties only succeed to a limited degree is a consequence of societal fear of universal mayhem negating any transformational potential of human nature. The final action in the play is the pronouncement made by Pope Clement VI, following the Floties' destruction:

> Let the Floties sleep forgotten, their light, ashes. They have never been. Sand out their names. Yet to be nameless and have lived, showing how men should live, is a true remembrance. . . . Father Flote thought he'd failed. No man fails completely who shows us glory. . . .
> Heaven is dark and the earth a secret. (*Red Noses*, p. 107)

Prophetic words for the keeper of the delusional, institutional faith, the pope's speech is a confession that his unnatural control – predicated on a collectively individualized fear of death – will ultimately fail if humanity begins to renature itself and accept an embracing Flotie philosophy. As "Flote's Voice" says in the Epilogue, "Every jest should be a small revolution" (p. 108).

Universal revolution, whether in the form of a disruptive jest or general copulation, will eventually lead to a return to sanity, an order rising out of the currently sighted chaos of existence heightened by the plague. The plague, literal or metaphorical, is a disruption critical to human awakening. Historically, however, it has led to reinvigorated efforts at reactionary entrenchment.

In "Lucretius: Science and Religion," Serres identifies the generative powers of chaos as "Venutian" and the ordered existence of civilization as "Martian": "The hymn to Venus is a song to voluptuousness, to the original power, victorious – without having fought – over Mars and over the death instinct, a song to the pleasure of life, to guilt-free knowledge."[15] Serres continues:

> [T]he time of the *clinamen* is not necessarily simultaneous with leaving the dead to bury the dead. Space and time are thrown here and there. There is no circle. But, stochastically, turbulences appear in space and time. And the whole text creates turbulence. Everywhere. Venus, *circumfusa,* is diffused all around the reclining body of Mars, who has been thrown down to the nadir he had searched for. She bothers him and disturbs his law. The creative science of change and of circumstance is substituted for the physics of the fall, of repetition, and of rigorous trains of events. Neither a straight line nor a circle: a spiral. ("Lucretius: Science and Religion," p. 99)

Trains of events are disrupted in the extreme by the plague but less markedly throughout daily existence, returning to patterns of a new order, perhaps less a spiral than a strange attractor. It is incumbent on humanity – first as individuals, then as societies – to recognize the need to shift perspectives on existence, from what Serres calls the Martian to the Venutian model, or from what science would call from the Newtonian to the chaotics model.

Nietzsche, too, makes similar chaotics claims through his Zarathustra: "Once blasphemy against God was the greatest blasphemy; but God died, and therewith also these blasphemers. To blaspheme the earth is now the dreadfullest sin, and to rate the heart of the unknowable higher than the meaning of the earth."[16] Zarathustra continues: "I tell you: one must still have chaos in one, to give birth to a dancing star. I tell you: ye have still chaos in you" (*Thus Spoke Zarathustra*, p. 12). Nietzsche's near-mystical philosophy now has a place in the scientific community, as do Lucretius's clinamen and Artaud's plague. It falls upon our culture to accept what we've moved ourselves toward. To one degree or another, all the above philosophers and artists have been moving toward chaotics.

Back to the Future: Tony Kushner's "Angels in America"

Tony Kushner's two-part work *Angels in America, A Gay Fantasy on National Themes* (1992), provides a recent example – complete with a contemporary setting – of how cultural resistance to plague results in rationalist linear retrenchment and an attendant cruelty and moral decay that rejects the vision of chaotics for delusional personal gain.

Though far more ambitious than Marsha Norman's *'night, Mother*, Kushner's work shares at least two points of significance with Norman's work: they both highlight the plights of two underrepresented groups of society, and they both advocate re-visionings of our modes of understanding our worlds. As has been the case with *'night, Mother, Angels in America* has been highly celebrated (as well as condemned) for the former point – representing the underrepresented – which has to a degree eclipsed the enormous significance of the latter – its broader conceptual challenge. At one level, *Angels in America* is a solid presentation of the difficulties of being gay and assaulted by the spectre of AIDS in a straight world hostile to homosexuality. It is, however, much more than that. What Kushner has created is a work that challenges linear order and its urge to dominate reality, positing in its place an acceptance of uncertainty and change. In essence, Kushner has produced a theatre of the clinamen, plague, and chaos in a way that strives to promote a fundamental shift in the theatre world away from traditional rationalism and toward the "magic" of unexpected chaotics.

Through his character Prior Walter, the last of a long line of Walters (traceable back to William the Conqueror), Kushner makes his universal intentions concrete. Visited by the ghosts of his former namesakes, Prior – and the audience – is asked to put the AIDS epidemic that has ensnared him into perspective. Says Prior 1: "The pestilence in my time was much worse than now. Whole villages of empty houses. You could look outdoors and see death walking in the morning, dew dampening the ragged hem of his black robe."[17] Prior 1 was a victim of an earlier plague unrelated to the AIDS epidemic. So was Prior 2, who comments that his "[c]ame from a water pump, half the city of London, can you imagine?" and that Prior 1's plague "came from fleas" (*Angels in America, Part One,* p. 87). The effect of this ghostly visitation recounting two of the various plagues of the past is that we move beyond placing a moral stigma upon the lifestyles of those afflicted with AIDS and come to realize the universal condition of human mortality and our perpetual vulnerability to plaguelike circumstances, despite frequent assurances from the scientific community (now growing less frequent and convincing) that science one day (never too soon) will have solutions to all ills. As with the above-noted plays concentrating on the plague, and as with Lucretius's and Artaud's analyses of the plague, Kushner uses the AIDS "plague" to highlight the intensified reality of existence as being unpredictably and often violently held hostage by death. This intensification by plague in turn exaggerates human behavior, shrinking bounds of tolerance and forcing evaluation of both self and society in ways less dramatic in prolonged, more naturally lifelong evaluations.

Death pressurizes life. Prior's lover Louis, for example, despite his liberal, leftist posturing, cannot face up to the task of comforting a fellow human being when comfort is most needed, even (or especially) when that human being is his own lover. His liberal posturing, his efforts to be humane, have broken down. Society's general claims of humaneness are likewise tested and fail. America is neither caring for its weak and vulnerable nor capable of controlling existence as it so strongly pretends to be. Fear, intolerance, and prejudice emerge from beneath surfaces requiring little real pressure to reveal hidden truths. Perhaps communal confession of these weaknesses may help to secure necessary adjustments.

Our efforts to control and dominate are likewise revealed for the delusions they are, revelations, too, that may help to secure necessary adjustments. Roy Cohn, the radical conservative who boasts of having the power of life and death, who claims to have all the power America can muster, is a study in delusional belief in such power of domination. His political and judicial manipulations are demonstrated and summarized, but Kushner goes even further. When Cohn is diagnosed with AIDS, he denies being homosexual in an assault that demonstrates the central fallacy of believing humanity can control reality. The point is made metaphorically here, but the connections are clear:

> I want you to understand. This is not sophistry. And this is not hypocrisy. This is reality. I have sex with men. But unlike nearly every other man of whom this is true, I bring the guy I'm screwing to the White House and President Reagan smiles at us and shakes his hand. Because *what* I am is defined entirely by *who* I am. Roy Cohn is not a homosexual. Roy Cohn is a heterosexual man . . . who fucks around with guys. (*Angels in America, Part One,* p. 46)

Roy Cohn, an American power broker, controls reality by sheer force of will. Linguistic and logical tools, however, fail him, as they do Rabe's and Shepard's characters.

As with the other AIDS victims in the play, as with other homosexuals and indeed with all of society, Cohn is forced to realize that nature/reality will eventually prevail and cannot be controlled by devices of logic or by devices of science. Nature reveals itself through the intensified force of plague, which urges a revision of our perceptions of reality, linguistic, logical, political, and scientific tools included. Either literally or metaphorically, the AIDS plague has infected the very fabric of society, catalyzing a radicalization of inhuman behavior – the negative result – but also triggering a growing realization that reassessment is critical – the positive result and virtually a life imperative for postmodern society.

Kushner's highly theatrical script, stage instructions, and alternately realistic and expressionistic scenes are valuable in themselves in that they explode any audience expectations of linear explanations. However, events occur that follow plausibly from previous events, amounting to a blending of determinate – though never predictable – and indeterminate plotting and suggesting a chaos mode of integrated dynamics. The play's structural fusion of the fantastic with traditional (even graphic) realism, I would suggest, reflects a chaos pattern – a chaos realism akin to Stoppard's *Arcadia* structure – though it is not clear that Kushner is aware of the chaos paradigm any more than Rabe, Shepard, or Norman. It is unquestionably clear, however, that Kushner has absorbed it at least as thoroughly as Rabe, Shepard, and Norman.

Prior notes in *Part Two: Perestroika*[18] that the actual "Angels in America," the moving forces in the current world order, are "basically incredibly powerful bureaucrats, they have no imagination, they can *do* anything but they can't invent, create" (p. 49). America's "guiding angels" are linear robots, beautifully attractive sirens hungry to ensnare creativity and thereby eliminate the feared "clinamenal" or chaotics prospects of change. Theirs (and ours) is a world of stasis, of forever sameness and tedious causal interconnectedness that permits no variety or diversity. The Angels encourage Prior to embrace the static security of their deathlike eternal existences, a sort of purchasing of Prior's human power to create change, which humanity apparently has grown to fear anyway, therefore an easy payment for most. As the Angel observes: "In creating You, Our Father-Lover unleashed / Sleeping Creation's Potential for Change. / In YOU the Virus of TIME began" (*Angels in America, Part Two*, p. 49). If only time could be controlled (or, as Newton presumed, even reversed) and along with it the feared quality of change, then humanity's longing for stability could be satisfied. This stability and stasis is what the Angels offer Prior, eternal security in exchange for life's guaranteed decay and death. But life introduces the potential for change, vitality, unpredictability, qualities that standardly make life worth living. The choices are placed before Prior: eternal security or vitality cased in mortality.

Partly correct in fact but not in evaluation, the Angel entreats Prior: "Seek Not to Fathom the World and its Delicate Particle Logic: / You cannot Understand, You can only Destroy, / You do not Advance, You only Trample" (p. 52). The Angel summarizes how humanity has used its creativity to try to secure control of its universe. The Angel observes that humanity has failed and will continue to fail, but for a simple price Prior can actually secure the very thing humanity has so long sought to secure: stability. However, being a creative product of unpredictability – unlike the Angels – Prior is not necessarily destined to follow the path the Angels anticipate. In fact, he rejects these Angels in America and all they represent, choosing to stay his own uncertain course as a mortal subject to orderly disorder and all the good (and bad) it entails.

Himself something of a clinamen personified — as all humans potentially are — Prior *will* in a way usher in a new order, one that redirects the purpose and goals of understanding, from an effort to control and dominate reality to an effort to understand and appreciate its changeable beauty and uncertain harmony. He thwarts the Angels' desire for domination by choosing not to side with them, and in the process he declares a new course of action, much as his various forefathers (Norman conquerors and Pilgrim New Englanders) did but on a frontier that has no geographic boundaries.

The goal of control versus appreciation is what science historian Stephen H. Kellert has distinguished as the difference between the quantitative goals of traditional science and the qualitative goals of chaos theory.[19] Traditional science aims at complete predictive power, which could lead to dominion. Chaos theory, however, describes the general nature of events, goals that provide an appreciation of natural phenomena but don't or can't provide information that can anticipate and control nature. That "imprecision," however, marks our window of freedom, freed as we are from a predictive, unalterable, unchanging "destiny."

What Prior, and Kushner, seem to realize is that the temporary, immediate gains of domination have been earned at incredible cost to the human spirit, imprisoned as it has been in the delusion of strict determinism. Prior rejects the Angels' siren call of order in favor of engaging the orderly disorder of a life actually lived rather than an existence merely experienced. Returning to an appreciation of natural patterns — ceasing to resist such forces — is the direction Prior takes. He announces, "I want more life" (*Angels in America, Part Two*, p. 136), and rejects immortality (a seemingly universal human desire) and its unchanging eternity, accepting that choosing life may mean only a few more months, but at very least there is inherent implicit vitality.

On his way out of the chambers of the Angels, Prior stops in Heaven (an even further break from strict realism) and meets his lover Louis's Jewish grandmother and her rabbi friend. He asks them why they play cards in Heaven, to which the Rabbi replies:

Cards is strategy but mostly a game of chance. In Heaven, everything is known. . . . So from what comes the pleasures of Paradise? *Indeterminacy*. . . . [S]till there is Accident, in this pack of playing cards, still is there the Unknown, the Future. You understand me? It ain't all so mechanical as they think. (p. 137)

As chance grimly defeats Kott's grotesque absolute, so indeterminacy for Kushner triumphantly inheres in life itself, making it all worthwhile. Life is determined but vitality remains in the form of that which appears indeterminate, that which appears to be (and from a linearist's perspective is) Accident. The Rabbi, now witness to a perspective predictively able to unfold the universe before him, praises the virtues of unpredictability. The Rabbi (and Kushner) speaks against the urge to know all and to dominate all that is known. Instead, vitality and diversity are for him the very definition of life. When Prior recovers his strength, his friends observe, "It's the dawn of man," and "Venus rising from the sea" (p. 139), an unintentional though accurate acknowledgment of what Serres would call the triumph of Venus (and Venutian thought) over Mars (and Martian thought). Chaos theory essentially mirrors the vision Kushner espouses. Life's patterns are to be understood, the details to be left to their own variety of possibilities. As chaos theory and Kushner's Rabbi suggest, demanding more will lead at best to disappointment and at worst to catastrophe. Somehow achieving our goals, as the Angels offer, leads to a tedious, Hell-like stasis at best.

Kushner, however, suggests that we are beginning to accept a modification of our goals. Through Louis in the Epilogue, Kushner proclaims, "Perestroika! The Thaw! . . . The whole world is changing! Overnight!" (p. 145). Not naive enough to suggest uninterrupted progress, Kushner does acknowledge the dangers of "making a leap into the unknown" (p. 146), but more significantly he argues to throw caution to the wind: "You can't wait around for a theory," adding, "It's all too much to be encompassed by a single theory now" (p. 146). Change is erupting, in vital orderly–disorderly fashion, in the most unexpected of places.

Of Kushner's assault on theory, I would both agree and disagree. We cannot wait for theories – perhaps some alternative, say, to Communism or Marxism – that would provide us quantitative and controllable understanding. But chaos theory, as noted earlier, is a web of interdisciplinary understanding that transcends even the science–art chasm. Given that chaotics is more a theory about theories than a theory itself, then perhaps it is exactly the "theory" – using this much-adjusted sense of the term – that would serve Kushner's vision, one that can, as Louis and Hannah alternately observe, embrace "the sprawl of life, the weird. . . . Interconnectedness. . . . the sheer size of the terrain" (p. 146). When Louis says,

"It's all too much to be encompassed by a single theory now" (p. 146), he is accurate only until we adjust what we mean by "theory."

Theatre of Chaos and the End of Humanism

In 1982, Richard Schechner observed in *The End of Humanism* that he is

> a person who wants to see preserved the "human values" of com-passion, individual expression, various and sundry freedoms (expression, opportunity, religion, etc.: those proclaimed by the American Declaration of Independence and Constitution; good 18th century rationalist values).[20]

He adds: "Yet humanism as an ideology is also very connected to the sense that human beings, male human beings especially ('man' to use another 18th century term), are the lords and masters of the world" (*The End of Humanism*, p. 9). The impossibility of main-taining that belief has become manifest to Schechner, and he pro-poses an alternative to such humanism: "Respect for the planet and all that dwells therein. Measure humans against planetary needs, not the other way around. And see the planet against the field of the cosmos. No one really knows what the needs of the cos-mos might be, if any" (p. 9). Perhaps with the qualitative assess-ments of nature found in chaos theory, rather than the eighteenth-century-inspired quantitative assessments, we can discover more respectfully what the cosmos needs. In fact, what Schechner pro-poses, originating out of a despair over humanity's solipsistic turn toward greater and greater self-absorption, may be best unlocked through the methodology, goals, and cosmology of chaos theory.

True to his own feelings – and reflective of the feelings of most humans – Schechner honestly reports that he is not entirely com-fortable with giving up his illusion of omnipotence: "[A]s I bid farewell to Faust and Satan I share with them their eternal rage against the end of omnipotence" (p. 106). But he – and we – must accept the necessary and inevitable repositioning of humanity not as gods but as participants in our surroundings, because this acceptance, according to Kushner and others, will pay dividends, a return on our investment that will ultimately outdistance our current returns. In this regard Schechner, Kushner, and the others in this study are of one mind.

In his "Afterword" to *Part Two: Perestroika*, Kushner observes:

> We pay high prices for the maintenance of the myth of the Individual: we have no system of universal health care, we can't pass sane gun control laws, we elect presidents like Reagan, we hate and fear inevitable processes like aging and death, and on and on. (p. 150)

Confessing, much as Schechner does, that the Individual is "a very popular myth" (p. 151), Kushner nonetheless hopes that "maybe in this spacious, under- and depopulated, as yet only lightly inscribed country, the Individual will finally expand to its unstable, insupportably swollen limits and pop" (p. 152). Conjuring an image of a plague-infected body as well as a system bifurcating to a chaos phase, Kushner sees instability as a hopeful sign of disruption leading to future awakening and progress. It appears he hopes the "plague," to use the AIDS epidemic as metaphor, will not need literally to infest America (and the world in general), but will remain only a metaphor, not needing to develop to a full-blown catastrophe. The risks are great, but change is necessarily inevitable: we must either brace for destruction by plague or work for accommodation with nature.

Kushner's apparent avenue for change appears distinctly Brechtian. As Louis points out in *Part Two: Perestroika*, "only in politics does the miraculous occur" (p. 146). More precisely, Kushner is likely suggesting that for politics to achieve the miraculous, humanity must be prepared to allow politics to run its "natural" course rather than to prop up our desire to maintain individual, humanistic control of our environs.

As such, perhaps the best answer to the current human dilemma is a combination of the numerous goals set down by the playwrights addressed above, an Artaudian invocation of a need for organic change in human desires and a Brechtian call to social action. All these avenues may best be paved by an appreciation and understanding of chaotics, manifest in both the science of chaotics and the art of the theatre of chaos.

The Lingering Question of First Cause

"To begin at the beginning: is God?" asks George in Stoppard's 1972 play *Jumpers*,[21] to which he adds, "I sometimes wonder whether the question ought not to be, 'Are God?'" (*Jumpers*, p. 10).

George splits the question to consider the existence of a God of Goodness and a God of Creation.

Like chaos theory in the sciences, this study of a theatre of chaotics has engaged in an empirical *description* of nature and existence, including the repercussions of that new description. In the process, the chaos paradigm has explained away the need for many supernatural invocations of material and existential origins, updating our uses of "theological" terms such as "providence" and "fate" and replacing trolls and extraterrestrials with scientifically viable alternatives. For many, however, chaotics leaves us only partially satisfied because as we perceive the rhythms of nature outlined by the chaos paradigm, we are left to wonder that if we "hear music," shouldn't we presume the existence of a composer?

At the natural level, at least, we have a more precise sense of a fundamental benignity in operation – not exactly a God of Goodness, but something akin to that incarnation, since chaotics has minimized the need to presume a hostile other, in the form of the grotesque or otherwise. Shepard offers an apt summary portrait of the chaotics position in his 1972 play, *Back Bog Beast Bait,* wherein an incarnation of the malignant grotesque – the Back Bog Beast – is rendered benign when the human characters accept their natural selves rather than strive to confront or challenge that essential nature. That play, in microcosm, summarizes the general point of this study, that humanity must renature itself, specifically benefiting from the liberating pronouncements of chaotics and the new sciences.

What we see is a vision advocating a re-engagement with nature espoused by the very thought processes – the scientific process – that formerly separated humanity from nature and that attacked invocations of the supernatural – or theological – as mere superstition. Ironically, the new sciences, discovering a rich dynamic complexity in nature previously denied, have emerged, full-circle, to create, as David Ray Griffin's edited work pronounces, *The Reenchantment of Science,*[22] a re-enchanted view of nature itself. Instead of wood sprites, trolls, or extraterrestrials, however, science has rediscovered marvel in the scientifically explicable.

Triggered by such re-enchantment stemming from a new vision of the chaotics complexity of nature, science has begun to move on to even larger, formerly exclusively theological, questions. Francis

Crick (the co-discoverer of the molecular structure of DNA), for example, published a 1994 work entitled *The Astonishing Hypothesis: The Scientific Search for the Soul.*[23] Though the book doesn't live up to the promise of the title, other scientists are also engaging such issues. Less sensationally but perhaps more substantially, Roger Penrose, in *Shadows of the Mind: A Search for the Missing Science of Consciousness,*[24] suggests that the sparks of consciousness – only one step from the matter of soul itself – may find their origins through the science of complexity (an umbrella term that includes chaotics as well as other theories of "emergence"), including the possibility of chaos science (though he is less than convinced himself), but more likely quantum physics.

That the playwrights in this study have likewise begun to reconstruct meaningful ways to re-engage a re-enchanted nature is impressive and may embolden them (and others) to assay new answers to George's questions, "Is God?" and "Are God?" Or perhaps we should be satisfied with refining where we now are, tapping into our descriptive comprehension of the rhythms of existence, since, as philosophers have urged for centuries, finding a "first cause" (a traditional definition of God) will always lead to the ensuing question of who/what was the cause of the first cause. This forever embedded matter should perhaps be pursued; but at the very least, through the chaos paradigm and through theatre of chaos we have come in contact with a complexity that for believers can be seen as the orchestrated traces of a higher being. For the rest of us, seeing a sort of consciousness in nature itself may be enough.

"Is God?" may never find an answer, but humanity's potential reunion with nature, after centuries of prodigal negligence, is at the very least a major fruitful step in the right direction. The playwrights in this study seem themselves convinced of the virtues of this new direction. A new sense of "godlike" goodness within nature is finally what may come from our use of the new paradigm.

CONCLUSION

Chaos and
Cultural Futures

He's inventing a new form of chaos theory
that works for him.

*White House aide describing President
Clinton*[1]

N 1993, the United States experienced devastation in its
heartland from the failure of one of its most extensive
attempts to control nature. Over a series of decades the
U.S. Corps of Engineers had trapped, controlled, and diverted the
forces of the Mississippi River and welcomed countless commu-
nities to build on the river's flood plain. In the summer of 1993, the
river, swollen by rain, destroyed large sections of the network of
dikes, quays, and levees, defeating the effort of humanity to control the forces of nature.

Such defeats are, of course, not uncommon, but what is uncommon about this encounter has been the way the government has
reacted. Instead of defiantly reorganizing against the Mississippi,
it has begun to evaluate the wisdom of its policy, suggesting that
there is a need to let the river run its course more or less as *it*
chooses. This willingness by the government to negotiate with
nature, to concede that nature needs to progress in its pattern of
orderly disorder, suggests a growing awareness of the need to compromise. It is a compromise nature is willing to accept, one
wherein it will likely accept reasonable confinement within certain parameters but will insist on periods of disorder within a gen-

erally orderly frame. With a new sense of the need for compromise, the U.S. government seems willing to operate in a manner so that chaos or disorder will no longer bring catastrophic loss or plaguelike results. The river's chaos phase will no longer be considered a foe but rather could be embraced for the benefits it would provide. As ecologists would argue, allowing the Mississippi to flood its banks would result in a sort of beneficial chaos, reducing the amount of silt carried to the Gulf of Mexico and rejuvenating the soil along the river's banks. Yet another sign of the U.S. government's growing awareness of nature's orderly disorder can be seen in a recent shift in wildfire management: total suppression of natural wildfires – a practice that leads to catastrophic, major blazes – is now being replaced by an acceptance of fire as an ecologically beneficial natural force, a disorder that assures ultimate order of a higher sort. Seeing the disorder of nature not as a Newtonian but as a chaotician could actually benefit humanity.

On the level of world politics, the dichotomous structure of the Cold War did indeed control much disorder around the globe. But the controls provided no solutions, only deferring inevitable disorder. The Balkan Peninsula is perhaps our most painful but by no means only example of the inevitable results of human-made, artificial controls. When controls imposed by Communist domination are lifted, as they must eventually be lifted – note that nature, even human nature, is incredibly patient – we discover that situations are rarely genuinely improved by human-imposed restraints and often require even more violent adjustment than if they had initially been left alone. As with the United States and its Mississippi River, the world community must consider the degree to which it should control disorder in the Balkans,[2] deciding whether to control the region as Communists (and the Austro-Hungarian Empire) once attempted or to allow the region to resolve its numerous conflicts unfettered by civilized restraints. Perhaps the solution is not to choose between the two extreme options but to develop a balance between total control and no control at all. Total control would result in numerous short-term benefits (minimizing the scale of human suffering) while no control at all would produce a brutal resolution but with numerous long-term benefits (quite likely a lasting peace). One must consider, too, that without Cold War politics (and imperialist politics before that), this region quite possibly would have long ago settled into a balanced condition. That point conceded, it now becomes a matter of determining the degree of intervention, hopefully more fully predicated on a desire for natural resolution and long-term results. When people are dying, the dilemma is, of course, much more dire. However, the abstract question remains the same here as with the Mississippi River. There is only so much that humanity can do to control the "natural" forces of collective hatred and revenge without that control becoming a counterproductive deferral of a chaos pattern that will be all the more explosive because of the deferral.

Policy makers and world leaders are caught between a sense of having lost an old world wherein chaos/disorder seemingly could be forcibly controlled and a new world where randomness reigns and where old means of control are too costly – at many levels – to maintain. I would suggest, however, that the radical controls of the old world order must accept responsibility for the plaguelike disorder we currently witness around the world. The desire to re-create order through former means is a foolhardy wish. Rather, the new order must accept some degree of disorder – even the immediate discomforts of radical adjustment – and accept the fact that out of disorder will come its inevitable consequence, order. Order is the consequent, not destruction or annihilation, which were the consequents perceived by the old world view.

Humanity has the responsibility to consider the "local," that is, the needs and suffering of living beings directly affected by disorder, but it must also look globally at the need to allow for the larger patterns of rising order following the disorder. *This,* to the artists and philosophers in this book, is the direction humanity must take. The way has in fact been paved by art – often an unlikely guide – and by an even more unlikely colleague, science.

To return again to Lucretius, the proto-chaotician, James H. Nichols, Jr., summarizes Lucretius's conclusions:

> To look to [current] politics for a solution to the problems of human happiness is necessarily, for Lucretius, to forget what is most important: a clear understanding of the nature of things and our place in it. . . . To seek an improvement in man's estate through the technological conquest of nature is self-forgetting, impossible, and undesirable: self-forgetting because it obscures our real insignificance in relation to an infinite and eternal natural universe; impossible because that infinite nature, far from being mastered, will eventually destroy our world and all our works; and undesirable because

it rests on a surrender to the unlimited desires of the imagination, which must be curbed for the sake of genuine happiness. To lead a better life requires a change in man himself.[3]

In order to improve human existence, we must understand our place in nature, which can only occur if we first understand nature itself. Chaos theory argues that nature is neither an absurd or grotesque automaton to be ignored, nor some rational, ordered entity vulnerable to human mastery. Neither "other-worldly" escapism – through either religion or nihilistic withdrawal – nor combative confrontation will succeed. Rather, we must work to understand the complexity of nature and how our happiness – and how much of it – may fit into its scheme. As Nichols observes,

> By analyzing the complexity and difficulty of attaining genuine happiness without false beliefs and empty hopes, Lucretius enables us to see the limits of what politics can achieve for us. . . . Reasonably lowered expectations might contribute not only to our private contentment but to the well-being of the political community as well. (*Epicurean Political Philosophy*, p. 210)

Prigogine and Stengers echo Nichols's thought on Lucretius but speak of chaos theory rather than Lucretius when they observe that much like nature itself,

> societies are immensely complex systems involving a potentially enormous number of bifurcations exemplified by the variety of cultures that have evolved in the relatively short span of human history. We know that such systems are highly sensitive to fluctuations. This leads both to hope and a threat: hope, since even small fluctuations may grow and change the overall structure. As a result, individual activity is not doomed to insignificance. On the other hand, this is also a threat, since in our universe the security of stable, permanent rules seems gone forever. We are living in a dangerous and uncertain world that inspires no blind confidence, but perhaps only [a] feeling of qualified hope. . . .[4]

Bohm and Peat express the same concerns when they observe:

> Indeed the ever-increasing torrent of change threatens to sweep humanity into a "black hole" singularity. What is inside that singularity is unknown. Will it be increasing misery and ultimate extinction or an unimaginably different and better way of life for all?[5]

The pre–Cold War delusional security of neo-Newtonianism can no longer be relied upon, nor can the impotent absurdist despair of existentialism. Our destinies lie somewhere in between.

That President Clinton's governing style can be described, as noted at the beginning of this chapter, as a "new form of chaos theory" is both heartening and disturbing. If Clinton is successful at implementing some version of the form and if the political world acknowledges and applauds his efforts, then we should truly be heartened. If and when chaotics in politics receives both proper application and recognition, then humanity can truly be said to have moved into a new epoch. Whether or not that change is in sight is still very much a matter of debate.

That many of the playwrights discussed here as part of a theatre of chaos have been described as, at best, apolitical, goes without saying. And that scientists themselves are typically apolitical is also something less than a surprising observation. Yet the above discussion of these men and women creates the obvious nexus between their apparent apoliticism and a generally unrecognized heightened politicism. They are in ways, as Stoppard suggests in *Arcadia,* heirs to a Romantic tradition advocating a change in human perception and behavior that could usher in a new epoch of human activity. But while they overtly argue for a change on the individual level, their pleas extend to a raising of the communal consciousness as well. Understanding the possibilities of the individual functioning within natural bounds extends to understanding how society and its political arm can likewise function. Limitations are perhaps difficult to accept for a proud and vain race, but we simply have reached a critical juncture in our existence where denying our limitations could prove catastrophic. These playwrights, and this science, offer the warning, hoping it hasn't come too late. Bohm and Peat observe that people

> generally tend to be rigidly attached to the tacit infrastructure of their cultural milieu so that they resist all social change in a blind and often destructive way. Others, however, are rigidly attached to the call for revolutionary change and pursue their ends in a similarly blind fashion. (*Science, Order, and Creativity,* p. 111)

Neither timidly reactionary nor foolishly revolutionary, the playwrights discussed in this study have created art that insightfully bridges both worlds, engaging audiences on familiar ground but urging them to move to necessary new grounds. Their success or failure may indicate for society whether or not the inevitable change that society must undergo will be transitionally instituted or catastrophically imposed.

Notes

Introduction. The New Science Metaphor and Modern Drama

1. Hesiod, *Theogony*, in *The Poems of Hesiod*, tr. R. M. Frazer (Norman: University of Oklahoma Press, 1983), lines 116, 123–5, p. 30.
2. Lucretius, *On the Nature of the Universe*, R. E. Latham (Harmondsworth, England: Penguin, 1951), Book II, p. 67.
3. Michel Serres, "Lucretius: Science and Religion," in *Hermes: Literature, Science, Philosophy*, ed. Josué V. Harari and David F. Bell (Baltimore: Johns Hopkins University Press, 1982), p. 99.
4. N. Katherine Hayles, *Chaos Bound: Orderly Disorder in Contemporary Literature and Science* (Ithaca: Cornell University Press, 1990), p. 202.
5. Ilya Prigogine and Isabelle Stengers, *Order Out of Chaos: Man's New Dialogue with Nature* (New York: Bantam Books, 1984), p. 27.
6. Note that I use the term "Newtonianism" in the sense of the ideas and world view that have come to be associated with Newton's discoveries in celestial and terrestrial mechanics. Frequently, these ideas have been liberal interpolations that bear little resemblance to Newton's actual ideas. Interestingly, there is evidence that Newton turned to alchemical studies later in his life, apparently dissatisfied with the incompleteness of "Newtonianism." Likewise, I do not discuss Aristotle so much as Aristotelianism, that philosophy derived from the works of Aristotle rather than the works themselves.
7. John Briggs and F. David Peat, *Turbulent Mirror: An Illustrated Guide to Chaos Theory and the Science of Wholeness* (New York: Harper and Row, 1989), p. 22.
8. James Gleick, *Chaos: Making a New Science* (New York: Penguin, 1987).
9. See Gleick, *Chaos*, for an intriguing account of how chaos theory

172

surfaced in the 1970s. Seemingly, it was a cultural endorsement of counterculturalism that resulted in this paradigm shift.

10. See David Bohm, *Wholeness and the Implicate Order* (London: Routledge & Kegan Paul, 1980).

11. Renée Weber, "The Search for Unity," in Renée Weber, ed., *Dialogues with Scientists and Sages: The Search for Unity* (London: Routledge & Kegan Paul, 1986), p. 13.

12. Stephen H. Kellert, *In the Wake of Chaos* (Chicago: University of Chicago Press, 1993).

13. Robert Shaw, "Modeling Chaotic Systems," in H. Haken, ed., *Chaos and Order in Nature* (New York: Springer-Verlag, 1981), p. 218.

14. Karen Warren, "The Power and the Promise of Ecological Feminism," *Environmental Ethics* 12 (1990), p. 128.

15. A. S. Wrightman, "Introduction to the Problems," in A. S. Wrightman and G. Velo, eds., *Regular and Chaotic Motions in Dynamic Systems* (New York: Plenum, 1985), p. 22.

16. Robert Shaw, quoted in Gleick, *Chaos*, p. 262.

17. David Bohm and F. David Peat, in *Science, Order, and Creativity* (New York: Bantam, 1987), draw the compelling parallel between scientific resistance to new ideas, such as relativity, and similar cultural resistance to new artistic expression, such as Impressionism, noting that neither "revolution" was truly new but rather was merely an extension of previous ideas, though perhaps a radical extension. Only when an audience/culture accepts these radical extensions (often perceived as revolutionary) can either the scientist or the artist finally be said to have succeeded.

18. Ralph Abraham, *Chaos, Gaia, Eros* (San Francisco: HarperCollins, 1994), p. 209. Abraham identifies a process whereby models from the physical world have with increasing success been used in large social and smaller interpersonal relationships to identify processes as patterned and to identify possible paths of resolution based on an understanding of the dynamics involved. He identifies this "new" branch of chaos theory as Erodynamics.

19. Martin Esslin, "Naturalism in Context," *The Drama Review* 13.2 (Winter 1968), p. 70.

Chapter 1. Quantum Physics as Metaphor

1. Quoted in J. C. Polkinghorne, *The Quantum World* (Princeton: Princeton University Press, 1984), p. 60.

2. Robert Brustein, *The Theatre of Revolt* (Boston: Little, Brown, 1962), p. 8.

3. The paradigmatic examples that follow are borrowed from J. C. Polkinghorne's introduction to quantum physics, *The Quantum World*, which draws from well-known material in the field of quantum mechanics.

4. Martin Esslin, "Naturalism in Context," *The Drama Review* 13.2 (Winter 1968), p. 72.

5. David E. R. George, "Quantum Theatre – Potential Theatre: A New Paradigm?" *New Theatre Quarterly* 5.18 (1989), p. 172.

6. Natalie Crohn Schmitt, *Actors and Onlookers: Theatre and Twentieth-Century Scientific Views of Nature* (Evanston, IL: Northwestern University Press, 1990), p. 3.

7. Herbert Blau, *The Audience* (Baltimore: Johns Hopkins University Press, 1990).

8. Natalie Crohn Schmitt, "Theorizing About Performance: Why Now?" *New Theatre Quarterly* 6.23 (1990), pp. 231–4.

9. Clive James, "Count Zero Split the Infinite," *Encounter* 45 (Nov. 1975), pp. 68–76; reprinted in Anthony Jenkins, ed., *Critical Essays on Tom Stoppard* (Boston: G. K. Hall, 1990), pp. 27–34, quotation on p. 29.

10. James D. Watson, *The Double Helix: A Personal Account of the Discovery of DNA* (New York: Atheneum, 1968).

11. See Katherine E. Kelly and William W. Demastes, "The Playwright and the Professors: An Interview with Tom Stoppard," *South Central Review* 11.4 (Winter 1994), pp. 1–14 (especially p. 4), for Stoppard's insights concerning the writing process.

12. Katherine E. Kelly, *Tom Stoppard and the Craft of Comedy* (Ann Arbor: University of Michigan Press, 1991), p. 152; referring to Richard Feynman, Robert B. Leighton, and Matthew Sands, *The Feynman Lectures on Physics,* vols. 1–3 (Reading, MA: Addison-Wesley, 1963).

13. James Gleick, *Chaos: Making a New Science* (New York: Viking, 1987). For a reference to Stoppard's acknowledged debt, see Kelly and Demastes, "The Playwright and the Professors," p. 5.

14. See Kelly and Demastes, "The Playwright and the Professors," p. 5.

15. Tom Stoppard, *Hapgood* (London: Faber and Faber, 1988), p. 45.

16. Richard Feynman, in *Lectures on Physics,* as cited in *Hapgood,* p. vii, prior to the text of the play.

17. Hersh Zeifman, "A Trick of the Light: Tom Stoppard's *Hapgood* and Postabsurdist Theater," in Enoch Brater and Ruby Cohn, eds., *Around the Absurd: Essays on Modern and Postmodern Drama* (Ann Arbor: University of Michigan Press, 1990), pp. 175–201.

18. Enoch Brater, "After the Absurd: Rethinking Realism and a Few Other Isms," in Brater and Cohn, eds., *Around the Absurd,* p. 300.

19. Arthur Miller, *Death of a Salesman* (Harmondsworth, England: Penguin, 1949), p. 81.

20. Una Chaudhuri, *Staging Place: The Geography of Modern Drama* (Ann Arbor: University of Michigan Press, 1995).

Chapter 2. Chaos and Theatre

1. Martin Esslin, *The Theatre of the Absurd* (Harmondsworth, England: Penguin, 1961), p. 17.

2. Ruby Cohn, "Introduction: Around the Absurd," in Enoch Brater and Ruby Cohn, eds., *Around the Absurd: Essays on Modern and Postmodern Drama* (Ann Arbor: University of Michigan Press, 1990), p. 2.
3. Jan Kott, *Shakespeare Our Contemporary,* tr. Boleslaw Taborski (London: Methuen, 1964).
4. Arnold P. Hinchliffe, *The Absurd* (New York: Methuen, 1969), p. 81.
5. Enoch Brater, "After the Absurd: Rethinking Realism and a Few Other Isms," in Brater and Cohn, eds., *Around the Absurd,* p. 300.
6. Martin Esslin, ed., *Absurd Drama* (Harmondsworth, England: Penguin, 1965), pp. 7–9.
7. Vivian Mercier, *Beckett/Beckett* (New York: Oxford University Press, 1977), pp. 73–87.
8. David Bohm and F. David Peat, *Science, Order, and Creativity* (New York: Bantam, 1987), p. 127.
9. Una Chaudhuri, *Staging Place: The Geography of Modern Drama* (Ann Arbor: University of Michigan Press, 1995), p. 81.
10. David Hesla, *The Shape of Chaos: An Interpretation of the Art of Samuel Beckett* (Minneapolis: University of Minnesota Press, 1971).
11. Martin Esslin, "Samuel Beckett-Infinity, Eternity," in Enoch Brater, ed., *Beckett at 80/Beckett in Context* (New York: Oxford University Press, 1986), pp. 120–1.
12. Hersh Zeifman, "A Trick of the Light: Tom Stoppard's *Hapgood* and Postabsurdist Theater," in Brater and Cohn, eds., *Around the Absurd,* p. 198.
13. James P. Crutchfield, J. Doyne Farmer, Norman H. Packard, and Robert S. Shaw, "Chaos," *Scientific American* (Dec. 1986), pp. 56, 57.
14. John Briggs and F. David Peat, *Turbulent Mirror* (New York: Harper & Row, 1989), p. 74. The original source of this idea is Crutchfield, Farmer, Packard, and Shaw, "Chaos," p. 49.
15. The following explanation of turbulence is largely indebted to Stephen H. Kellert, *In the Wake of Chaos* (Chicago: University of Chicago Press, 1993).
16. See Kellert, *In the Wake of Chaos,* pp. 9–10.
17. See Edward Lorenz, "Deterministic Nonperiodic Flow," *Journal of the Atmospheric Sciences* 20 (1963), pp. 130–41.
18. Robert Brustein, "The Crack in the Chimney: Reflections on Contemporary American Playwriting," *Theatre* 9 (Spring 1978), pp. 21–9; reprinted in Arthur Edelstein, ed., *Images and Ideas in American Culture* (Hanover, NH: Brandeis 1979), pp. 141–57.
19. Henrik Ibsen, *The Master Builder,* in *The Complete Major Prose Plays,* tr. Rolfe Fjelde (New York: Farrar, Straus, & Giroux, 1978), p. 854.
20. Tom Stoppard, *Arcadia* (London: Faber and Faber, 1993), p. 48.
21. Michel Serres, "Turner Translates Carnot," in *Hermes: Literature, Science, Philosophy,* Josué V. Harrari and David F. Bell, trs. (Baltimore: Johns Hopkins University Press, 1982), pp. 54–62.

22. Serres also, incidentally, connects Turner to Lucretius in this essay: "Read Lucretius and see how the shipwreck, the alpustria scattered in the surf, and the convulsive waves are the obsessive metaphors of dissolution, of mingling, of exhaustion. The image, perhaps of the second principle of thermodynamics" ("Turner Translates Carnot" p. 59).

23. Bohm and Peat, *Science, Order, and Creativity*, p. 168.

24. Kellert, *In the Wake of Chaos*, pp. 15–16.

25. See Benoit B. Mandelbrot, *The Fractal Geometry of Nature* (New York: W. H. Freeman, 1977).

26. See Manfred Schroeder, *Fractals, Chaos, Power Laws: Minutes from an Infinite Paradise* (New York: W.H. Freeman 1991), for a good explanation of the notion of scaled symmetry.

27. See Ronald H. Brady, "Form and Cause in Goethe's Morphology," in Frederick Amrine, Francis J. Tucker, and Harvey Wheeler, eds., *Goethe and the Sciences: A Reappraisal* (Dordrecht, Holland: D. Reidel, 1987), pp. 257–300.

28. Bohm and Peat, *Science, Order, and Creativity*, p. 183.

29. N. Katherine Hayles, *Chaos Bound: Orderly Disorder in Contemporary Literature and Science* (Ithaca: Cornell University Press, 1990), p. 285.

30. This resistance seems in part, however, to be diminishing, though not as rapidly as perhaps one would like. In fact, Ralph Abraham, in *Chaos, Gaia, Eros* (San Francisco: Harper, 1994), records the birth of a new field of study: "Erodynamics, named in 1989, applies dynamical systems theory to human social phenomena" (p. 3). It is a fast-growing discipline, according to Abraham.

31. Chaudhuri, *Staging Place*, p. 81.

Chapter 3. Intuitive Intersections

1. Robert Brustein, "The Crack in the Chimney: Reflections on Contemporary American Playwriting," *Theatre* 9 (Spring 1978), pp. 21–29; reprinted in Arthur Edelstein, ed., *Images and Ideas in American Culture* (Hanover, NH: Brandeis University Press, 1979), pp. 141–57.

2. Martin Esslin, *The Theatre of the Absurd* (Harmondsworth, England: Penguin, 1961), p. 230.

3. Samuel J. Bernstein, *The Strands Entwined: A New Direction in American Drama* (Boston: Northeastern University Press, 1980). See also Michael Vanden Heuvel, *Performing Drama/Dramatizing Performance* (Ann Arbor: University of Michigan Press, 1991).

4. Enoch Brater, "After the Absurd: Rethinking Realism and a Few Other Isms," in Enoch Brater and Ruby Cohn, eds., *Around the Absurd: Essays on Modern and Postmodern Drama* (Ann Arbor: University of Michigan Press, 1990), p. 300.

5. Walter Kerr, "When Does Gore Get Gratuitous?" *New York Times* (22 Feb. 1976), sec. 2, p. 7.

6. In *Beyond Naturalism: A New Realism in American Theatre* (Westport, CT: Greenwood Press, 1988), I have documented numerous examples of such resistance, especially in the cases of Rabe, Mamet, Shepard, Henley, Norman, and Fuller.

7. David Bohm and F. David Peat, *Science, Order, and Creativity* (New York: Bantam, 1987), p. 136.

8. See Thomas S. Kuhn, *The Structure of Scientific Revolutions,* 2d ed. (Chicago: University of Chicago Press, 1970).

9. David Rabe, *Hurlyburly* (New York: Grove, 1985), p. 162.

10. David Rabe, *Goose and Tomtom* (New York: Grove, 1986), unpaginated frontmatter.

11. William Worthen, *Modern Drama and the Rhetoric of Theatre* (Berkeley: University of California Press, 1992), p. 17.

12. Quoted in David Savran, *In Their Own Words: Contemporary American Playwrights* (New York: Theatre Communications Group, 1988), pp. 200–1.

13. Sam Shepard, quoted in Carol Rosen, "'Emotional Territory': An Interview with Sam Shepard," *Modern Drama* 36.1 (March 1993), p. 6.

14. Sam Shepard, *A Lie of the Mind* (New York: Plume, 1986), p. 2.

15. Sam Shepard, quoted in Rosen, "Emotional Territory," p. 4.

16. Sam Shepard, *States of Shock, Far North, Silent Tongue: A Play and Two Screenplays* (New York: Vintage, 1993), p. 6.

17. Gary Grant, "Shifting the Paradigm: Shepard, Myth, and the Transformation of Consciousness," *Modern Drama* 36.1 (March 1993), p. 126.

18. N. Katherine Hayles, *Chaos Bound: Orderly Disorder in Contemporary Literature and Science* (Ithaca: Cornell University Press, 1990), p. 173.

19. Stanley Kauffmann, "More Trick than Tragedy," *Saturday Review* (Sept./Oct. 1983), p. 47.

20. All quotes by Jill Dolan are from her work *The Feminist Spectator as Critic* (Ann Arbor: University of Michigan Press, 1988).

21. All quotes by Jeanie Forte are from her work "Realism, Narrative, and the Feminist Playwright," *Modern Drama* 32.1 (1989), pp. 115–27.

22. See Elizabeth Stone, "Playwright Marsha Norman: An Optimist Writes About Suicide, Confinement and Despair," *Ms.* (July 1983), p. 58.

Chapter 4. Theatre of Chaos, Past and Future

1. Enoch Brater, "After the Absurd: Rethinking Realism and a Few Other Isms," in Enoch Brater and Ruby Cohn, eds., *Around the Absurd:*

Essays on Modern and Postmodern Drama (Ann Arbor: University of Michigan Press, 1990), p. 300.

2. Jan Kott, "Hamlet of the Mid-Century," in *Shakespeare Our Contemporary,* tr. Boleslaw Taborski (London: Methuen, 1964), p. 49.

3. Ruby Cohn, "Introduction: Around the Absurd," in Brater and Cohn, eds., *Around the Absurd,* p. 3.

4. Kott, "Hamlet of the Mid-Century," pp. 48–61.

5. Ilya Prigogine and Isabella Stengers, *Order Out of Chaos: Man's New Dialogue with Nature* (New York: Bantam, 1984), p. 6.

6. Jan Kott, "'KING LEAR,' or ENDGAME," in *Shakespeare Our Contemporary,* pp. 101–37.

7. Charles Segal, *Lucretius on Death and Anxiety: Poetry and Philosophy in* De Rerum Natura (Princeton: Princeton University Press, 1990), p. 231.

8. Laurie Garrett, *The Coming Plague: Newly Emerging Diseases in a World Out of Balance* (New York: Farrar, Straus, & Giroux, 1994).

9. Antonin Artaud, "The Theatre and the Plague," *The Theatre and Its Double* (1938), tr. Mary Caroline Richards (New York: Grove, 1958), p. 15.

10. Ronald Hayman, *Artaud and After* (Oxford: Oxford University Press, 1972), p. 147.

11. Marvin Carlson, *Theories of the Theatre. A Historical and Critical Survey, from the Greeks to the Present* (Ithaca: Cornell University Press, 1984), p. 393.

12. Peter Weiss, *The Persecution and Assassination of Jean-Paul Marat As Performed by the Inmates of the Asylum of Charenton Under the Direction of The Marquis de Sade* [*Marat/Sade*] (1964), tr. Geoffrey Skelton (New York: Atheneum, 1972), p. 54.

13. John Whiting, *The Devils* (New York: Hill and Wang, 1961), p. 101.

14. Peter Barnes, *Red Noses* (London: Faber and Faber, 1985), p. 13.

15. Michel Serres, "Lucretius: Science and Religion," in Josué V. Harrari and David F. Bell, eds, *Hermes: Literature, Science, Philosophy* (Baltimore: Johns Hopkins University Press, 1982), p. 98.

16. Friedrich Nietzsche, *Thus Spake Zarathustra,* in *The Complete Works of Friedrich Nietzsche* (vol. 11), tr. Thomas Common (New York: Gordon Press, 1974), p. 7.

17. Tony Kushner, *Angels in America. A Gay Fantasia on National Themes. Part One: Millennium Approaches* (New York: Theatre Communications Group, 1992), p. 86.

18. Tony Kushner, *Angels in America. A Gay Fantasia on National Themes. Part Two: Perestroika* (New York: Theatre Communications Group, 1992).

19. See Stephen H. Kellert, *In the Wake of Chaos* (Chicago: University of Chicago Press, 1993), p. 154.

20. Richard Schechner, *The End of Humanism: Writings on Performance* (New York: Performing Arts Journal Publications, 1982), p. 9.

21. Tom Stoppard, *Jumpers* (New York: Grove, 1972), p. 8.

22. David Ray Griffin, ed., *The Reenchantment of Science: Postmodern Proposals* (Albany: State University of New York Press, 1988).

23. Francis Crick, *The Astonishing Hypothesis: The Scientific Search for the Soul* (New York: Scribner's, 1994).

24. Roger Penrose, *Shadows of the Mind: A Search for the Missing Science of Consciousness* (Oxford: Oxford University Press, 1994).

Conclusion: Chaos and Cultural Futures

1. Michael Duffy, "The State of Bill Clinton," *Time* (7 Feb. 1994), p. 26.

2. Chaos theory may one day help us to identify such hot spots as well as possibly help to determine ways to avoid such flash points. See Alvin M. Saperstein, "War and Chaos: Complexity theory may be useful in modeling how real-world situations get out of control," *American Scientist* (Nov.–Dec. 1995), pp. 548–57.

3. James H. Nichols, Jr., *Epicurean Political Philosophy: The De rerum natura of Lucretius* (Ithaca: Cornell University Press, 1972), p. 207.

4. Ilya Prigogine and Isabelle Stengers, *Order Out of Chaos: Man's New Dialogue with Nature* (New York: Bantam, 1984), pp. 312–13.

5. David Bohm and F. David Peat, *Science, Order, and Creativity* (New York: Bantam, 1987), p. 110.

Bibliography

Plays

Barnes, Peter. *Red Noses*. London: Faber and Faber, 1985.

Ibsen, Henrik. *The Master Builder. The Complete Major Prose Plays*. Rolfe Fjelde, tr. New York: Farrar, Straus, & Giroux, 1978.

Kushner, Tony. *Angels in America. A Gay Fantasia on National Themes. Part One: Millennium Approaches*. New York: Theatre Communications Group, 1992.

   Angels in America. A Gay Fantasia on National Themes. Part Two: Perestroika. New York: Theatre Communications Group, 1992.

Miller, Arthur. *Death of a Salesman*. Harmondsworth, England: Penguin, 1949.

Norman, Marsha. *'night, Mother*. New York: Hill and Wang, 1983.

Rabe, David. *Goose and Tomtom*. New York: Grove, 1986.

   Hurlyburly. New York: Grove, 1985.

Shepard, Sam. *A Lie of the Mind*. New York: Plume, 1986.

   States of Shock, Far North, Silent Tongue: A Play and Two Screenplays. New York: Vintage, 1993.

Stoppard, Tom. *Arcadia*. London: Faber and Faber, 1993.

   Hapgood. London: Faber and Faber, 1988.

   Jumpers. New York: Grove, 1972.

Weiss, Peter. *The Persecution and Assassination of Jean-Paul Marat As Performed by the Inmates of the Asylum of Charenton Under the Direction of The Marquis de Sade [Marat/Sade]*. Geoffrey Skelton, tr. New York: Atheneum, 1972.

Whiting, John. *The Devils*. New York: Hill and Wang, 1961.

Texts on Drama, Literature, Politics, and Philosophy

Artaud, Antonin. *The Theatre and Its Double*. 1938. Mary Caroline Richards, tr. New York: Grove, 1958.

Bernstein, Samuel J. *The Strand Entwined: A New Direction in American Drama.* Boston: Northeastern University Press, 1980.

Blau, Herbert. *The Audience.* Baltimore: Johns Hopkins University Press, 1990.

Brady, Ronald H. "Form and Cause in Goethe's Morphology." In *Goethe and the Sciences: A Reappraisal,* pp. 257–300. Frederick Amrine, Francis J. Tucker, and Harvey Wheeler, eds. Dordrecht, Holland: D. Reidel, 1987.

Brater, Enoch, and Ruby Cohn, eds. *Around the Absurd: Essays on Modern and Postmodern Drama.* Ann Arbor: University of Michigan Press, 1990.

Brustein, Robert. "The Crack in the Chimney: Reflections on Contemporary American Playwriting." *Theatre* 9 (Spring 1978), pp. 21–9. Reprinted in Arthur Edelstein, ed., *Images and Ideas in American Culture,* pp. 141–57. Hanover, NH: Brandeis University Press, 1979.

The Theatre of Revolt. Boston: Little, Brown, 1962.

Carlson, Marvin. *Theories of the Theatre: A Historical and Critical Survey, from the Greeks to the Present.* Ithaca: Cornell University Press, 1984.

Chaudhuri, Una. *Staging Place: The Geography of Modern Drama.* Ann Arbor: University of Michigan Press, 1995.

Demastes, William. *Beyond Naturalism: A New Realism in American Theatre.* Westport, CT: Greenwood Press, 1988.

Dolan, Jill. *The Feminist Spectator as Critic.* Ann Arbor: University of Michigan Press, 1988.

Duffy, Michael. "The state of Bill Clinton." *Time* (7 Feb. 1994), pp. 24–9.

Esslin, Martin. "Naturalism in Context." *The Drama Review* 3. 2 (Winter 1968), pp. 67–76.

"Samuel Beckett–Infinity, Eternity." In *Beckett at 80/Beckett in Context,* pp. 110–23. Enoch Brater, ed. New York: Oxford University Press, 1986.

The Theatre of the Absurd. Harmondsworth, England: Penguin, 1961.

Esslin, Martin, ed. *Absurd Drama.* Harmondsworth, England: Penguin, 1965.

Forte, Jeanie. "Realism, Narrative, and the Feminist Playwright." *Modern Drama* 32.1 (March 1989), pp. 115–27.

George, David E. R. "Quantum Theatre–Potential Theatre: a New Paradigm?" *New Theatre Quarterly* 5. 18(1969) pp. 171–9.

Grant, Gary. "Shifting the Paradigm: Shepard, Myth, and the Transformation of Consciousness." *Modern Drama* 36.1 (March 1993), pp. 120–30.

Griffin, David Ray, ed. *The Reenchantment of Science: Postmodern Proposals.* Albany: State University of New York Press, 1988.

Hayles, N. Katherine. *Chaos Bound: Orderly Disorder in Contemporary Literature and Science.* Ithaca: Cornell University Press, 1990.

Hayman, Ronald. *Artaud and After.* Oxford: Oxford University Press, 1972.

Hesiod. *The Poems of Hesiod.* R. M. Frazer, tr. Norman: University of Oklahoma Press, 1983.

Hesla, David. *The Shape of Chaos: An Interpretation of the Art of Samuel Beckett.* Minneapolis: University of Minnesota Press, 1971.

Hinchcliffe, Arnold P. *The Absurd.* London: Methuen, 1969.

Jenkins, Anthony, ed. *Critical Essays on Tom Stoppard.* Boston: G. K. Hall, 1990.

Kauffmann, Stanley. "More Trick than Tragedy." *Saturday Review* (Sept./Oct. 1983), p. 47.

Kelly, Katherine E. *Tom Stoppard and the Craft of Comedy.* Ann Arbor: University of Michigan Press, 1991.

Kelly, Katherine E., and William W. Demastes. "The Playwright and the Professors: An Interview with Tom Stoppard." *South Central Review* 11.4 (Winter 1994), pp. 1–14.

Kerr, Walter. "When Does Gore Get Gratuitous?" *New York Times* (22 Feb. 1976), sec. 2, p. 7.

Kott, Jan. *Shakespeare Our Contemporary.* Boleslaw Taborski, tr. London: Methuen, 1964.

Lamberton, Robert. *Hesiod.* New Haven: Yale University Press, 1988.

Lucretius. *On the Nature of the Universe.* Harmondsworth, England: Penguin, 1951.

Mercier, Vivian. *Beckett/Beckett.* New York: Oxford University Press, 1977.

Nichols, James H., Jr. *Epicurean Political Philosophy: The De rerum natura of Lucretius.* Ithaca: Cornell University Press, 1972.

Nietzsche, Friedrich. *Thus Spake Zarathustra. The Complete Works of Friedrich Nietzsche,* vol. 11. Thomas Common, tr. New York: Gordon Press, 1974.

Rosen, Carol. "'Emotional Territory': An Interview with Sam Shepard." *Modern Drama* 36.1 (March 1993), pp. 1–11.

Savran, David. *In Their Own Words: Contemporary American Playwrights.* New York: Theatre Communications Group, 1988.

Schechner, Richard. *The End of Humanism: Writings on Performance.* New York: Performing Arts Journal Publications, 1982.

Schmitt, Natalie Crohn. *Actors and Onlookers: Theater and Twentieth-Century Scientific Views of Nature.* Evanston: Northwestern University Press, 1990.

"Theorizing About Performance: Why Now?" *New Theatre Quarterly* 6.23 (1990), pp. 231–4.

Segal, Charles. *Lucretius on Death and Anxiety: Poetry and Philosophy in De Rerum Natura.* Princeton: Princeton University Press, 1990.

Serres, Michel. *Hermes: Literature, Science, Philosophy.* Josué V. Harrari and David F. Bell, tr. Baltimore: Johns Hopkins University Press, 1982.

The Parasite. Lawrence Schehr, tr. Baltimore: Johns Hopkins University Press, 1982.

Stone, Elizabeth. "Playwright Marsha Norman: An Optimist Writes About Suicide, Confinement and Despair." *Ms.* (July 1983), pp. 56–9.

Vanden Heuvel, Michael. *Perfoming Drama/Dramatizing Performance.* Ann Arbor: University of Michigan Press, 1991.

Worthen, William. *Modern Drama and the Rhetoric of Theatre.* Berkeley: University of California Press, 1992.

Texts on Science

Abraham, Ralph. *Chaos, Gaia, Eros.* San Francisco: HarperCollins, 1994.

Bergé, Pierre, Yves Pomeau, and Christian Vidal. *Order Within Chaos: Towards a Deterministic Approach to Chaos.* Laurette Tuckerman, tr. New York: John Wiley and Sons, 1984.

Bohm, David. *Wholeness and the Implicate Order.* London: Routledge & Kegan Paul, 1980.

Bohm, David, and F. David Peat. *Science, Order, and Creativity: A Dramatic New Look at the Creative Roots of Science and Life.* New York: Bantam, 1987.

Bohr, Niels. *Atomic Energy and the Description of Nature.* Cambridge: Cambridge University Press, 1961.

Briggs, John, and F. David Peat. *Turbulent Mirror: An Illustrated Guide to Chaos Theory and the Science of Wholeness.* New York: Harper and Row, 1989.

Crick, Francis. *The Astonishing Hypothesis: The Scientific Search for the Soul.* New York: Scribner's, 1994.

Crutchfield, James P., J. Doyne Farmer, Norman H. Packard, and Robert Shaw. "Chaos." *Scientific American* (Dec. 1986), pp. 46–57.

Feynman, Richard, Robert B. Leighton, and Matthew Sands. *The Feynman Lectures on Physics.* Vols. 1–3. Reading, MA: Addison-Wesley, 1963.

Garrett, Laurie. *The Coming Plague: Newly Emerging Diseases in a World Out of Balance.* New York: Farrar, Straus & Giroux, 1994.

Gleick, James. *Chaos: Making a New Science.* New York: Penguin, 1987.

James, Clive. "Count Zero Split the Infinite." *Encounter* 45 (Nov. 1975), pp. 68–76.

Kellert, Stephen H. *In the Wake of Chaos.* Chicago: University of Chicago Press, 1993.

Kuhn, Thomas S. *The Structure of Scientific Revolutions.* 2d ed. Chicago: University of Chicago Press, 1970.

Lorenz, Edward. "Deterministic Nonperiodic Flow." *Journal of the Atmospheric Sciences* 20 (1963), pp. 130–41.

Mandelbrot, Benoit B. *The Fractal Geometry of Nature.* New York: W. H. Freeman, 1977.

Penrose, Roger. *Shadows of the Mind: A Search for the Missing Science of Consciousness.* Oxford: Oxford University Press, 1994.

Polkinghorne, J. C. *The Quantum World.* Princeton: Princeton University Press, 1984.

Prigogine, Ilya, and Isabelle Stengers. *Order Out of Chaos: Man's New Dialogue with Nature.* New York: Bantam, 1984.

Saperstein, Alvin M. "Chaos – a model for the outbreak of war." *Nature* 309 (24 May 1984), pp. 303–5.

"War and Chaos: Complexity theory may be useful in modeling how real-world situations get out of control." *American Scientist* (Nov.–Dec. 1995), pp. 548–57.

Schroeder, Manfred. *Fractals, Chaos, Power Laws: Minutes From an Infinite Paradise.* New York: W.H. Freeman, 1991.

Shaw, Robert. "Modeling Chaotic Systems." In *Chaos and Order in Nature*, pp. 218–31. H. Haken, ed. New York: Springer-Verlag, 1981.

Thom, René. *Structural Stability and Morphogenesis.* 1972. D. H. Fowler, tr. Reading, MA: W.A. Benjamin, 1975.

Warren, Karen. "The Power and the Promise of Ecological Feminism." *Environmental Ethics* 12 (1990), pp. 125–46.

Watson, James D. *The Double Helix: A Personal Account of the Discovery of DNA.* New York: Atheneum, 1968.

Weber, Renée, ed. *Dialogues with Scientists and Sages: The Search for Unity.* London: Routledge & Kegan Paul, 1986.

Wrightman, A. S. "Introduction to the Problems." In *Regular and Chaotic Motions in Dynamic Systems*, pp. 1–26. A. S. Wrightman and G. Velo, eds. New York: Plenum, 1985.

Index

Printed in the United States
36778LVS00003B/112-114

9 780521 619868